Acting: Onstage and Off

Acting: Onstage and Off

SECOND EDITION

Robert Barton
University of Oregon

HARCOURT BRACE COLLEGE PUBLISHERS
Fort Worth   Philadelphia   San Diego   New York   Orlando   Austin   San Antonio
Toronto   Montreal   London   Sydney   Tokyo

Publisher	Ted Buchholz
Executive Editor	Bill McLane
Acquisitions Editor	Janet Wilhite
Developmental Editor	Barbara J.C. Rosenberg
Project Editor	Cliff Crouch
Production Manager	Erin Gregg
Book Designer	Brian Salisbury
Cover Photo	Cliff Coles

Library of Congress Cataloging-in-Publication Data

Barton, Robert, 1945–
    Acting : onstage and off / Robert Barton.— 2nd ed.
      p. cm.
    Includes bibliographical references and index.
    ISBN 0-03-072192-X
    1. Acting.   2. Method (Acting)   I. Title.
    PN2061.B294   1992
    792′.028—dc20   91-45183
                                            CIP

ISBN: 0-03-072192-X

Requests for permission to make copies of any part of the work should be mailed to: Permissions Department, Harcourt Brace & Company, Orlando, Florida 32887.

Address editorial correspondence to: 301 Commerce Street, Suite 3700
Fort Worth, Texas 76102
Address orders to: 6277 Sea Harbor Drive
Orlando, Florida 32887
1-800-782-4479, or 1-800-433-0001 (in Florida)

Printed in the United States of America
0 1 2 3 4 5 6 7 8 9   039   18 17 16 15 14 13 12

To my son Andrew,
whose sense of wonder
renews my own

CONTENTS

2 RELAXED READINESS   29

Getting Calm Enough, Yet Energized Enough,
to Perform Fully

4 STANISLAVSKI'S SYSTEM   105

*Understanding the Only Complete Process By
Which Actors Build Characters*

5   TRUTH/TECHNIQUE   155

Balancing Open, Honest Spontaneity With
Steady, Polished Consistency

6 SCENE STUDY   188
Discovering Character Through Script

7 PERFORMANCE PROCESS   223

*Recognizing Standard Procedure and
Appropriate Behavior From First Audition
Through Closing Night*

Contents

PREFACE

Acting to Understand

Acting is one of the best ways to learn about being alive. Because we actors get to become other people, we have stronger opportunities than most to understand more and co-exist better. We stop making instant judgments of others, given the chance to play those others. Only the shallowest of satirists can portray fellow humans, however strange or villainous, without gaining some lasting empathy for their pain and feeling for their perspective. A worthwhile performance class does more than impart knowledge; it humanizes. An acting class can help each participant become less narrow and provincial, more a citizen of the world. Each actor can end up knowing more about herself, about others, and about how the self and others connect. Each actor can learn the arts of compromise and collaboration. Throughout these heady, high-sounding lessons, there can also be a lot of laughs.

This book is designed for the beginning acting student, for whom the life-enhancing aspects of actor training are a higher priority than technical skills. Its basic assumptions are: (1) offstage performance can be effectively adapted for the theatre; (2) onstage training can be applied toward leading a full life outside the theatre; and (3) the two can feed each other in ways that both illuminate and amuse, which is a pretty good combination. The study of acting can encourage dealing with important issues in a way that is neither smug nor pompous, but playful.

Acting: Onstage and Off is divided into eight chapters that address those areas of greatest concern to novice actors. The book begins by exploring each student's past and present offstage life, to help him find confidence, experience, and texture, all of which can be used in class. Once the actor no longer thinks of himself as inexperienced and inept, the text moves on in chapter 2 into learning to warm up (body, voice, and mind; individually and collectively), then to understanding the actor's own equipment, and the ways in which adjustments can be made by mastering that equipment (chapter 3). The assumption is that *self*-awareness is crucial before *other*-awareness can be accomplished, whether those others are living or fictional persons.

Warmed up and self-aware, the actor pursues in chapter 4 the basic means for putting together a character, as devised by Stanislavski and extended by the behavioral sciences. Once these fundamental principles of performing as someone else are established, chapter 5 explores the need to balance honesty with precision, and considers methods for blending the two. At this stage, the actor is ready to tackle the unique traditions and history of this art. Chapter 6 addresses the actor's relationship with the script and with basic textual and character analysis. Chapter 7 sets forth rehearsal and performance etiquette and unwritten standards of behavior and support in the theatre. This chapter allows the new actor to quickly settle nagging procedural questions, so that he gets the help he needs, and avoids, as one of my students put it, "blowing it without knowing it." It is also geared toward quickly picking up the survival information needed when entering *any* new world. The book's final chapter helps the student decide among various options for more involvement, and teaches some ways of applying all that has been learned, even if this course is the student's last direct contact with the art form.

Each chapter leads to successively more complex levels of understanding. If in completing a chapter, the reader were likely to say, "Okay, this is fine, but what if . . . ," an attempt has been made to answer that impending question. Above all, this book aims to help each actor find some joy and wonder in herself as a performer. An actor needs many skills *eventually,* but joy and wonder should come first.

Using This Text

Acting classes vary from three hours a week for a single term to six hours (plus lab sessions) for a full year. It would be useless for an introductory text to try to serve everyone equally. There are, however, three ways to adapt this text to varying time strictures and changing class enrollments. It is possible to work through the book in sequence for a full year of activity. It is also possible to move by targeting a particular subject or skill (such as voice, which is dealt with in separate sections of each chapter)—or by sampling every chapter, and doing only the earlier exercises of each. This last alternative is suggested for short-term (e.g., summer) classes, so that students get at least a taste of each area that concerns them.

Most acting students enroll with a desire to do scene study work—that is, for the chance to work with scripts. I sympathize with those students who find themselves in a one-term class that accomplishes nothing but warm-ups and improvisations before, suddenly, the term is over. These students didn't get what they came for. They have not really acted. In our program at the University of Oregon, we read the entire book in the first quarter, then go back and review for greater depth during the subsequent two terms of the school year.

This book has far more exercises, and more questions within those exercises, than most readers will wish to attempt. An excess of choice is offered deliberately, so that teacher and/or reader may pick, choose, reject, and modify. These exercises may be cut back in scope easily, and written assignments adapted into thought–discussion questions and improvisations, in those instances where a minimum of academic work is deemed appropriate.

An unusually focused group of actos may be able to move quickly over the background examination and warm-up activities of the first two chapters. Most students, however, will need the training in relaxation and channeling of energy provided in chapter 2 before undertaking the relatively sophisticated demands of chapter 3. The activities in chapter 1 are largely passive and undemanding. By chapter 3, each student is asked to accomplish acute, systematic analysis of not only himself but others in the class.

An extensive list of scene suggestions is given in chapter 5, and a sample scene, called *The Rehearsal,* appears in Appendix K. This scene may be used to apply all the concepts discussed here. However, the book's basic approach focuses on life experience, rather than dramatic literature, for instances and background material. All other examples and exercises in the book are therefore drawn entirely from the actor's own life rather than plays. Some instructors may thus wish to supplement this book with a scene anthology.

This text aims for a sound and traditional, rather than revolutionary, approach to the principles of acting. Five elements treated here, are, however, uncommon to other basic texts:

1. The constant connection between life in the theatre and life removed from it.
2. The personal examination of one's self and one's classmates as an initial pathway to characterization.
3. An extended treatment of the actor's responsibility for in-rehearsal active contribution and out-of-rehearsal exploration.
4. Auditions as a basic, rather than advanced, concern.
5. An emphasis on the actor's need to become self-sufficient.

Auditions are considered by many to be a subject for only advanced or pre-professional programs, and outside the appropriate scope of a beginning acting class. I strongly disagree. Auditioning is what you do to get into another class, to apply what you've just learned in a show, to get a job, to win a scholarship, to make any temporary and tentative condition permanent and definite. Far too often, beginning classes whet the appetite of novice actors without showing them how to get more chances to pursue this art. I believe it is this very postponing of auditioning that makes it so terrifying to the actor.

Acknowledgments

I thank Wandalee Henshaw for permission to use Open Scene materials, and Kathleen George for Open Scene concepts. Reviewers of this edition included Wil Denson of the University of Wisconsin, Eau Claire; Rozsa Horvath of Los Angeles Pierce College, Woodland Hills; and Porter S. Woods of Colorado State University, Fort Collins. I am also grateful to the following graduate teaching fellows in the acting program at the University of Oregon: John Schmor, Amy Sarno, Marion Rossi, Jay Pyette, David Mason, Jim Queens, Karen Bain, Don Naggiar, and Andrew Langoria. Their experiences in the classroom helped to shape this new edition. Finally, my thanks to Carrol Barton, for her assistance in locating sources, and for her abiding support.

Acting: Onstage and Off

ACTING ACKNOWLEDGED

Recognizing That You're Already an Experienced Actor and Are Almost Always Acting

---

As we act our lives, we have to make up our dialogue and create ourselves as we go along.[1]
—MICHAEL CAINE

People are incredible actors. We're masters at hiding what's really going on most of the time.[2]
—GLENN CLOSE

I was born to act. I was a showoff. That's all acting is—showing off.[3]
—MORGAN FREEMAN

Everyone acts almost all the time. You are a highly experienced actor even if you've never taken a class or been in a show. You may not be a *skilled* actor, but you are experienced. Acting is what we do to cope with groups: to survive in an old group, to gain membership in a new group, or even to be left alone by a group we do not wish to join. We're learning to act all our lives. We're always trying to figure out how *they* (current group members) want us to behave, what qualities to punch up or play down, what feelings to show or hide, what behavior will be rewarded or punished. We try to give our audience what it wants and still stay as much ourselves as possible, to avoid feeling cheap and compromised. This is called acting. This is what we do to survive.

1

ALL THE WORLD'S A STAGE

People are always trying to tell you how to act. Consider these familiar lines:

"That's no way to act."

"Stay in your room until you learn to act like a young lady."

"He's been acting so strange lately."

"You don't need to act as if you own the place."

"I can't go there. I'm afraid I just wouldn't know how to act."

"Stop acting as if the whole thing were my fault."

"Oh, yeah, she acts innocent, but I know better."

"O.K., so how would you have acted if you'd been there?"

"Do you think maybe this is all some kind of act?"

"He acts like he hasn't got a care in the world."

"When are you going to start acting like yourself again?"

"Don't worry about it. Just act natural."

And, of course, this all-time favorite we may hear at any time between birth and death:

"Act your age."

The world is full of actors. No one has said it better than William Shakespeare:

> All the world's a stage,
> And all the men and women merely players:
> They have their exits and their entrances;
> And one man in his time plays many parts,
> His acts being seven ages. At first the infant,
> Mewling and puking in the nurse's arms.
> And then the whining school-boy, with his satchel,
> And shining morning face, creeping like snail
> Unwillingly to school. And then the lover,
> Sighing like furnace, with a woful ballad

Made to his mistress' eyebrow. Then a soldier,
Full of strange oaths, and bearded like the pard,
Jealous in honour, sudden and quick in quarrel,
Seeking the bubble reputation
Even in the cannon's mouth. And then the justice,
In fair round belly with good capon lin'd,
With eyes severe and beard of formal cut,
Full of wise saws and modern instances;
And so he plays his part. The sixth age shifts
Into the lean and slipper'd pantaloon,
With spectacles on nose and pouch on side,
His youthful hose, well sav'd, a world too wide
For his shrunk shank; and his big manly voice,
Turning again toward childish treble, pipes
And whistles in his sound. Last scene of all,
That ends this strange eventful history,
Is second childishness and mere oblivion,
Sans teeth, sans eyes, sans taste, sans everything.[4]

We players recognize ourselves and others in each phase. In contemporary, nonpoetic terms this speech might read:

The whole world is just a stage and everyone is just an actor, entering and exiting. Everyone plays roles during his life. Seven major ones:

1. Baby crying and throwing up while being held.

2. Whining boy, dragging your backpack slowly to school, complaining about having to go.

3. Lover, groaning as loud as any furnace and writing sad songs to any part of your girlfriend's body.

4. Tough guy—swearing, growing a beard that makes you look like a leopard, wanting to win all the time, ready to fight over anything, trying to get famous. Not noticing that fame lasts no longer than a bubble, you're even willing to stick your head inside of a cannon to get it.

5. Statesman—fat from eating so much fried chicken—looking serious, trimming the beard to look respectable, always dropping words of wisdom, even when nobody asked, acting all the time.

6. Skinny old man, glasses sliding down your nose, your old trousers in perfect condition but miles too big for you. What used to be a strong voice now cracks and breaks just like a child's.

7. Second childhood and senile emptiness—no more teeth, no more taste, no more anything.

Seven Ages

1 Mewling Infant

Every baby learns to cry in order to get picked up, loved, changed, or fed, later learning to enhance the feeling of need and even to create the impression of it whether it exists or not. My infant son sat blissfully with me while I wrote the first edition of this book. But whenever my wife passed through the room, he would suddenly focus on her breasts and break into a fairly convincing imitation of all the starving children of three, maybe four African countries. Since we both knew he had eaten within the hour, she would continue on her way, as he sighed and gurgled happily again, as if to say there was no harm in trying. This phase is never left entirely behind. Any of us may resort to mewling when we aren't getting enough (or the right kind of) attention.

2 Whining Schoolboy

No longer an infant, my son now sometimes pretends to be sick (or sicker than for real) to avoid school. Haven't we all? And then later pretended to be well (or better than for real) to go to some function we *wanted* to attend? Is there anyone who hasn't whined and pouted through some responsibility that has been forced on them? We let everyone around know how much we're suffering, what a great sacrifice this is, how noble we are for plugging on, how much they owe us for being such a brick. "Poor me" routines are favorites of those who enjoy themselves as martyrs.

School is also where one learns that some acting is required even to *avoid* a group. If you are a bookish, artistic wimp who does not want to join the jock bullies at recess, you still need to figure out how to act so they will not make your jocklessness the focus of their bullying.

3 Sighing Lover

When we are smitten by somebody, many of our actions are guided by what we feel a lover *should* act like, by our observations of other, presumably more experienced lovers in movies and books. In the performances you give for the object of your affection, you try to act in such a way that the adored one is never disappointed, always pleasantly surprised. ("Maybe if I write her an eyebrow poem; I'll bet nobody else has done that.") You try to be wittier, smoother, better read, stronger, and/or wilder than you've ever been in your life—whatever qualities your beloved seems to admire. If the relationship is worth it, the forced acting eventually fades, to your mutual relief, into the sunset.

4 Reputation-Seeking Soldier

Everyone goes through a soldier stage, in which the main objective and primary performance is to appear unafraid, in control, tough, and possibly threatening—even when what you really want to do is cry and run home for a hug. During adolescence, a time when we can be easily hurt, it seems important to pretend that *nothing* can hurt. Acting tough seems to be a crucial rite of passage into adulthood, but not everyone makes it through the passage. Some get caught in this phase forever. A huge percentage of the population, largely male, linger long in the land of swagger.

5 Saw-Spouting Justice

Some well-fed people are always speaking as if what they say will be carved in granite somewhere. Everything has quotation marks around it. I now find *myself* in danger of flirting with this phase, while trying to skip it. Because I am in charge of an acting program, people listen to me and often even hover expectantly, pencil in hand. It's very easy to believe, when someone gives you such authority, that Moses wasn't the only one to climb the mountain and chat with God. People who are used to being listened to, without fighting for an audience, can pontificate to the point of self-parody. As with the other stages, age is not the determining factor here; a student returning home as a member of the winning debate team or queen of a local beauty pageant may suddenly assume an exalted manner as he or she passes on advice to mere mortals aspiring to the same glory.

6 Lean and Slipper'd Pantaloon

Some seniors shrivel, and are surprised at how small their impact has suddenly become. In this confused moment, some cling desperately to old casting and past power, exploding with rage when everything is no longer in place. Others begin to enjoy the freedom from responsibility, the lightness that comes with no longer being at the center of everything.

7 Second Childishness and Mere Oblivion

Shakespeare's final image is sad and desolate. Some old people die long before their last breath. Others have a great final season. The universal image is "second childishness." Some older people return to childlike wonder and discovery, with no more complicated issues to deal with than getting caught being naughty, or the boredom of not discovering enough things to do to have fun. Memory brings forth a way of acting that is like their early days of discovery. Small children and old people sometimes find themselves to be kindred spirits, capable of complete sharing as they casually reach across all the generations between them.

Shakespeare wrote powerfully of these seven common roles in the play of life. Yet there are countless chances to vary each stage and defy the established pattern. We never leave an age entirely behind, but instead store it in our repertoire. Some aged people remain lucid and mature, even brilliant and inspiring, to the end. Without warning, dignified statesmen may mewl and puke, tired old men become brave soldiers again, and cynics sigh like furnaces and begin writing love poems. As you review your own ages, have you already found yourself returning to some for a visit?

> *In America, the seven ages of man have become*
> *preschooler, Pepsi generation, baby boomer, mid-*
> *lifer, empty-nester, senior citizen, and organ donor.*[5]
> —BILL COSBY

AGES EXPERIENCED, AGES OBSERVED

For each of the first five ages recounted by Shakespeare (infant, schoolboy, lover, soldier, justice) write a sentence describing your most vivid performance in that role. (You may want to check your memory against your parents' for at least the first three.) For the last two (pantaloon, second childishness) write sentences describing the most vivid performance you have observed.

ANSWERING AGES

Choose your most vivid memory of an age you have experienced or observed. Working with a partner, act out the event, with your partner feeding the lines, such as a simple request (''What time is it?''), and respond as you might in each of the seven ages. Note how easy it is to slip into Shakespeare's attitudes.

Seven Acts

In addition to passing through ages, we all perform "acts," or specialized performances, in our lives outside the theatre. Most have their roots in the simple childhood game of Let's Pretend. Here are seven varieties.

Pageants

> Toto in a grade-school *Oz*? Third "Wise Person" carrying myrrh in a church nativity play? Part of a living totem pole in a Scout jamboree? Ring-bearer at a wedding? Toastmaster at an anniversary gathering? Member of the Homecoming Queen's court?

You're dressed up, it's a very big occasion, and the place is packed; in fact, many of the essential ingredients of theatre are present. You may be cast in a defined role (even though it might be as an inanimate object, like a rock). Or, in public rituals, you may be cast as You, without any convenient camouflage. But this is a *transformed* You, amazingly cleaned up, polished, and sanitized. The stakes here are very high, and the price for failure beyond your means to pay, but usually you feel very proud.

> *I made my stage debut as an altar boy, or, more*
> *aptly, a falter boy. I used to trip over my cassock or*
> *light myself on fire.*[6]
> —MEL GIBSON

Disguises

> A ghost or monster at Halloween? A Disney or *Star Wars* character for a costume party? A sophisticated world traveller, headed for some bistro where you hope not to get carded?

Disguised performances are looser and more improvisational. Your intent is to *avoid* recognition. You experiment endlessly with your costume, you work on your walk and your gestures, and you practice certain lines to get the voice, the timing, the inflection just right. Then you enter the world. Sometimes you only make it downstairs before returning to your room for a few adjustments based on early family reviews. But you get better and better as the evening progresses.

> *Acting is just a matter of farting about in disguises.*[7]
> —PETER O'TOOLE

Alter Egos

The Muscle-Bound You who enters the playing field? The Oxford Scholar You who stands up to debate First Affirmative? The *Vogue* Cover-Girl You who glides onto the prom dance floor?

Alter egos are second selves, often with improvements: You with Cheekbones and a Ph.D. Some of us click into the alter ego as a way of bolstering courage. Seeing yourself slightly enhanced often has a startling effect on observers, who may see you that way, too. Some people go so far as to name their other selves, which tend to be more assertive and colorful than the main you. They are used by many as a means of rising to the occasion. Sometimes alter egos compete for your attention. Sometimes they even take on a life of their own.

> *My first successful characterization is what I devised for myself in high school. I played the blond homecoming queen for several years. I laid out my clothes for the [coming] week every Sunday so that I wouldn't repeat.*[8]
>
> —MERYL STREEP

> *So eventually the big brassy broad beat the crap out of the little torch singer and took over.*[9]
>
> —BETTE MIDLER (discussing two of her alter egos)

Role Models

You decide to: Lower your voice when angry, just like your father? Walk like a certain rock star? Emulate the unshakable dignity of your favorite teacher?

Other human beings and literary figures serve as sources for the basic characterization you would like to present to the world. You may want just to shake your hair to the side like a certain actress, not to *be* her. You try on qualities like items of clothing, discarding one if it doesn't seem to fit. Borrowing may involve anything from a small mannerism to an entire outlook. Much borrowing may happen before you're satisfied with the whole package.

*I gradually created someone I wanted to be and
finally I became that person.[10]*
—CARY GRANT

Understudying

Your folks aren't home and someone tries to deliver a gross of electric can openers—what do you do? Your boss is gone and a customer is getting unruly—what do you do? You're left entertaining your great-aunt Helga who speaks only Swedish—what do you do?

Standing in for someone who usually handles a problem situation and attempting to troubleshoot involves more than just trying to figure out how the other person would handle it. It may also involve trying to get their actions down pat—their manner of authority, their way of ending a sentence firmly. It's harder than with role models, where you willingly pick whom you want to emulate. In this situation, you may not even like or understand the person for whom you're substituting, and you have no time to practice. Even if lines of dialogue come to you, you may find yourself struggling for the right word emphasis. You know the other (missing) person should be starring in this scene, and that you're merely an understudy. Like most understudies, you try to give a pretty good imitation of the star.

*At the age of eight or nine, I'd create scenes for
myself and I'd act out all the parts—usually
as people I knew.[11]*
—JESSICA LANGE

Suppression

Mortified beyond human endurance, but determined to appear unruffled? Flattered, but striving to appear as if compliments come hourly? Ecstatic over winning, but afraid the other competitors will respond badly to your leaping and shrieking?

Cooling down your first response to something more manageable, less foolish or overbearing is an acting challenge which may go on for hours before you can finally let it rip. If you win, you want to appear happy, even thrilled, but not obnoxious. If you lose, you want to appear transcendent, not devastated. Immense acting energy is invested in stifling emotional display and avoiding humiliation.

> *I have such a fear of embarrassing myself that I will*
> *do anything not to embarrass myself. That's it.*
> *That's the key to my success.*[12]
> —MICHELLE PFEIFFER

Deception

> "It wasn't you who emptied the cookie jar, was it?"
> "And the reason your jeans are torn and muddy is that you were attacked
>   by a band of pygmies?"
> "You've never tried smoking that awful stuff, have you?"

We all act, to some degree, less guilty than we are. It can run from a few harmless fibs to profoundly immoral lies. Feigning innocence is a universally acknowledged form of offstage acting. If the deception helped bring off a surprise party or visit, we feel triumphant and skillful when the amazed recipient gets the joyous news. Even the most honest of us look back on a few occasions and still cringe at not 'fessing up to our deeds, but also feel some measure of pride in pulling it off.

> *When we got bored Jules could be real creative.*
> *She could muster up tears in a second to get*
> *out of homeroom and I'd have to follow her*
> *out to help her.*[13]
> —JULIA ROBERTS' best friend
> (describing her in high school)

While serving jury duty during the writing of this book, I was stunned to hear the judge instruct us that it would be our duty to figure out who was acting and who wasn't. He later said to me, "If there weren't so many actors in the world, I'd be out of a job."

> *Having to confront policemen and judges*
> *is an excellent way to train your imagination.*
> *In a few seconds, you have to improvise a role*
> *with talent and emotion.*[14]
> —GERARD DEPARDIEU (on his adolescence
> as a runaway and street punk)

Some cases and some careers are based on lies. But the vast majority of our performances, particularly in the categories of suppression and deception, are humane, caring, even loving. Imagine getting up on any given day and following only gut impulses, without any effort to please others. The damage done to furniture and egos could be enormous in the first hour alone. Daily acting involves sparing other people's feelings. You perform so as to appear not quite so bored, so offended, so amazed at their lack of sensitivity or tact, so appalled that they missed the point or the appointment. If a friend is hurting, you and I try to figure out how to act so that she will feel supported and nurtured. We figure out not just what to *do*, but also how to *act*. For many of us, even those of us who make our living in the theatre, the finest performances of our lives are given offstage.

EXERCISE 1.3

STRIKING/SUCCESSFUL ACTING

Keeping your description to one sentence, select your two most striking/successful performances you can recall in each of the preceding seven areas, listed again below. It may have been striking but a total flop, or it may have been extremely successful but very low-key.

1. pageants
2. disguises
3. alter egos
4. role models
5. understudying
6. suppression
7. deception

EXERCISE 1.4

MY MOST MEMORABLE ACT

Again work with a partner. Pick the event from the above exercise that lingers most powerfully in your memory. Present a condensed version in which your partner may serve as narrator, interviewer, or respondent. Give the class a brief glimpse of your acting history. You decide whether to pick triumph, tragedy, or something in-between.

DUELING PERFORMANCES

The toughest moments in life can be when you are cast in two roles that you cannot play simultaneously with equal grace and believability. Your role as Loyal, Respectful Daughter comes straight up against your role as Militant Feminist if your father makes recurring sexist remarks. It is especially difficult if both roles are essential to your concept of yourself, way up near the top of those parts you fully intended to run for many seasons.

1. Try to identify five times in your life when you wanted to play two roles at odds with each other.
2. Which roles won?
3. Were you ever able to successfully blend the two? Is there a way the two women's roles in the above paragraph could possibly be combined without hurting either?
4. Work with a partner. Set up the conflict. Force yourself to choose. Make the choice you made in real life. If the one you would make now is different, repeat the scene as you would play it now.

SCRIPTING AND IMPROVISING

A basic difference exists between offstage acting, which has no script, and onstage acting, which does. Right? Not entirely. People who require risk as a constant in their lives will work a lot of improvisation into each day. Others, craving constancy, will nearly script themselves, with only the slightest variation in day-to-day dialogue. *Everyone* scripts and rehearses certain crucial encounters (a seduction scene, a telling-off-the-boss scene, a finally-persuading-the-folks scene) carefully, hoping others will pick up the right cues. Recall two of your

1. most carefully scripted or planned encounters;
2. least planned, most challenging, freewheeling improvisations.

Write four single-sentence descriptions, beginning with "The time I . . ."
Keep these four memories in mind as you begin to explore other dimensions of your acting outside the theatre. (See Appendix A, "My Acting History," at the end of the book, for an optional format for summarizing the acting you have experienced so far.)

EXERCISE 1.7

SHARED PASTS

Sit in a circle and each share this information with others in your class as a way of breaking the ice and getting to know each other.

1. **Your Acting History**
   As much onstage, as much off, as you want to share. Only a summary, to give others a feel for what you've done. A paragraph tops. Don't *dare* say you don't have any. Reread chapter 1.

2. **Your First Role, Your Favorite Role**
   Two highlights out of the general pattern above. If you've not yet done a play, you must have done a pageant. No one totally escapes these things. We're talking about your debut: the occasion you choose to think of as launching you as a potential ham. Your favorite may not be the same as your first. It may be one you've actually never played but dream of playing. It may be on or off. Try to identify, in no more than a sentence, why it's your favorite, what delights or thrills you when you think about it even now.

3. **Why You're Here**
   The truth. If this was the only time slot open in your schedule, 'fess up, so others will know you do not worship daily at the altar of Dionysus. If you have already decided to pursue a professional acting career, have the courage to say so. The real reason you happened to end up in this class, at this school, at this time. The more straightforward you are, the more you'll get from all this.

OBSERVING YOURSELF ACT

What happens at the exact moment that an actor acts? There are ten ingredients present in any real-life encounter. Take a look at your life. Any moment involving you and someone else will involve:

1. Some way of defining what you and this other person mean to each other (*relationship*).

2. Something you want *(objective)*.

3. Something in the way *(obstacle)*.

4. Your plan to get what you want *(strategy)*.

5. Specific maneuvers within your overall plan *(tactics)*.

6. Things said by you and the other person *(text)*.

7. Things implied but not really said *(subtext)*.

8. Times when you do not speak at all but are actively thinking *(interior monologue)*.

9. Moments when the other person says or does something that makes you pause, consider, and reject several different answers before choosing a reply *(evaluation)*.

10. Changes within the scene, signaling that some kind of transaction has been completed and a new one is starting—for example, a topic of conversation is changing; another attack is being tried; a new person is changing the direction of the conversation; or a new objective is being pursued *(beats)*.

Terms in parentheses above are actor language for scene ingredients. There is no simpler or more difficult lesson in acting than learning these ten items. They provide the basis of the Stanislavski System (which will be covered later), but they are really the basis of all human interaction. Almost all actors who perform well identify these ten elements in every scene they play. Almost all actors who fail have forgotten this basic homework.

Imagine that you want to finish reading this chapter (only a few more pages to go!), but your roommate's CD player is blaring away. You decide to neutralize her. First you ask if she shares your hunger for a pizza. Then you mention her promise to call her parents tonight. But she's not interested. She only wants to sing along with the music and tell you how this album changed her life. Finally, you level with her: You can't concentrate, and you must have 15 minutes of silence. She agrees. CURTAIN.

Active Ingredients

1. *Relationship*
   Newly assigned roommates who don't know each other but seem to have differing tastes and lifestyles.

2. *Objective*
   To finish your homework.

3. *Obstacle*
Your roommate's throbbing CD player.

4. *Strategy*
To somehow get rid of roommate.

5. *Tactics*
Offering bait (pizza), inducing guilt (over parents' waiting for phone call), speaking frankly (asking for quiet).

6. *Text*, and

7. *Subtext*
Here's a sample script, with the *text* in regular type, and the italicized *subtext* in parentheses.

You: Say, didn't you, uh, *(God, I hope this isn't too pushy)* promise your folks you'd call tonight? *(Good. That sounded pretty casual)*

Her: *(What do your care?)* Uh . . . yeah. So? *(Let's change the subject)* I love this song. "Shake your body, your body, your body, your BAH-DEEEEEE!" *(Can I shake it, or what?)*

You: *(I hope THIS doesn't sound too pushy)* Well, shouldn't you call them, then? *(It did. I'm such a jerk)*

Her: *(One mother is enough, thanks)* I already tried. They aren't home. *(Buzz off . . . Oh, I guess she means well)* I left a message on their machine. *(Satisfied?)* Ooh, I REALLY love this NEXT song! *(So buzz off, why don't you?)*

8. Your *Interior Monologue*
This precedes the dialogue above:

That music of hers is driving me crazy. All right, now, what is this . . . Observing myself acting? What is this guy talking about? How many more pages? "I wanna BANG, I wanna CLANG" . . . I can't get that stupid lyric out of my head. Please, God, make the power go out. I have to write out all this private stuff? I wonder who's gonna see this. "Clanga banga uh-HUH! Clanga banga you-WOO!" You-woo? What does that mean? Damn, I need some quiet. I gotta get her out of here. What could I . . . Hey, what about that phone call she's supposed to make?

Was some of this hard to follow? Reread it. Almost everyone's interior monologue will confuse someone else.

9. *Evaluation*
Here's one possible continuation of the above scene, in which you

evaluate potential responses to her attitude. Again, the *text* is in regular type, and the italicized *subtext* is in parentheses.

> Her: . . . Ooh, I REALLY love this NEXT song!
> You: *(Considering the alternatives:*
> > *1. SHUT THAT THING OFF NOW OR I'LL KILL YOU. No, that's a little confrontational . . .*
> > *2. WELL, I GUESS I'LL GO TO THE LIBRARY AND STUDY NOW. Hey! Why should I give up my living space? What if this becomes a habit?*
> > *3. LOOK, HALF OF THIS LIVING SPACE IS MINE, AND I DO HAVE A RIGHT TO SOME PEACE AND QUIET, YOU KNOW . . . No, that's too whiny.*
> > *4. THIS BOOK IS AWFULLY HARD TO READ OVER ALL THAT MUSIC. Well, that's the right idea. How about . . .*
> > *5. You finally decide to say:)*
> > Listen, I like that album so much that it's distracting me, and I have GOT to get this reading done, so could you do me a favor and let me have 15 minutes of quiet? I'll owe you. *(Much better. Now shut that thing off or I'll kill you.)*
> Her: Okay.

10. Titles of *Beats*
    (1) Fuming over Book until Breaking Point; (2) Making Pizza Pitch, which Falls Flat; (3) Making Phone-Home Pitch, which also Fails; (4) Ode to Music, and Ensuing Pause; (5) Request for Silence, and Agreement.

The wonderful thing about this simple list of ten elements is this: If you concentrate on each one in turn, you will become so involved that there will be no room in your mind for nervousness, awkward self-consciousness, or distractions. People who fail to get what they want often do so because they don't state their *objectives* strongly enough, they fail to switch *tactics* (to one that succeeds), or they don't consider enough alternatives during *evaluation* to pick the best possible response.

EXERCISE 1.8

PLAYING OBJECTIVES

Improvise another version of the above scene, with a different objective, and a different conflict provided by the roommate character. Identify the ten ingredients.

Go back and repeat the exercise trying to persuade

1. your parent to let you take one of the family cars back to school for a few weeks;
2. a policeman not to give you a speeding ticket;
3. a salesperson to take an out-of-town personal check;
4. a professor to accept a late paper;
5. someone working in course registration to let you into an overcrowded acting class.

EXERCISE 1.9

REAL LIFE

The scenes above are merely conjecture.

1. Find some real ones and jot down the ingredients before the encounter has passed from memory. Pick two scenes with different partners and quite different objectives.
2. Write down what happened in such a way that the outline of the experience emerges. (See Appendix B, "Acting Observed," for an optional format for this observation and others to follow.)
3. Identify: relationship, setting, other character, basic situation, objective, obstacle, strategy, tactics, text and subtext (at least four lines of dialogue), interior monologue (one or two paragraphs at a crucial moment), evaluation (at least four rejected alternatives plus the one chosen), and beats.
4. Repeat the process for a different encounter, using the fewest possible words to describe the event. Don't let yourself get bogged down in description or detail. The result should scan easily. It should be clean and virtually free of verbiage.
5. During the next week, stop and notice when you shift beats, what range of tactics you employ, and when you regret your choice during an evaluation and wish you'd gone with one rejected. You want to let the ten-item vocabulary become second nature to you, and to heighten your awareness of the theatre present in each life.

Actor Guidelines

To keep choices active, clear, and strong, use the following reminders:

1. Objectives should be stated with the preposition *to*, followed by an active verb. Never use the word *be*—it has no dynamics unless it is all by itself (as in ''to be or not to be''). Objectives such as ''to be happy''

or "to be loved" are so passive that they cannot be actively acted. As stated, they give you nothing to pursue. "To find joy" and "to get a lover" are somewhat more actable. "To win the trip to Maui" and "to boff Lois" are even more actable. To goad, defy, needle, force, or tease are more actable objectives than to tell, get angry, suggest, inform, or wonder, because the former demand results.

2. Keep language simple. Keep words to a minimum. Use down-to-earth, unambiguous words that click quickly into consciousness. Your analysis of a scene should read like traffic signals, guiding you through the part.

3. Subtext may support the text, modify it, or qualify it. It may add dimensions that the text did not seem to imply by itself. It may actually contradict or work against the text, as in the old vaudeville routine.

Straight Man: Nervous?
   Comic: NOOOPE! *(spoken with so much terror and anxiety that it*
       wipes out the word itself)

Subtext is an actor's food and air. Finding, changing, and shading subtext is what actors most love to do and what audiences most love to watch. Stanislavski says that subtext is what the audience comes to the theatre to see—if all they wanted was the *text*, they could have stayed home and read the script. A hard remark is modified with a gentle, warm tone, and the most polite, civil response (in words) can be filled with dangerous warning (in delivery) not to tread further. Subtext is a phenomenal source of power. It may totally alter the text.

> *I like the challenge of conveying an emotion or*
> *idea that isn't right there in the dialogue. I like to be*
> *able to say, "I think I'll have a drink," and let the*
> *audience know that what I mean is "I love you."* [15]
> —MEL GIBSON

EXERCISE 1.10

TEXT VS. SUBTEXT

Two actors are given an activity, a circumstance, and a topic of conversation. They must stick solely to the topic of conversation. Example: A couple is packing suitcases. He is going off to war. They discuss only the weather. Try this with additional suggestions from the audience. What do you find out about the relationship between text and subtext?

---

4. Don't write out interior monologues as you would term papers, with formal word choices and perfect sentences. Interior monologues are jagged, incomplete, often interrupted thoughts with illogical twists and turns. The language (because it goes on in your head and doesn't need censoring) may be rough, crude, irrational, profane, even silly. Your interior monologue is like a tape that runs continuously, day and night, in your head, and when you are scattered or disorganized, it is doubly so. It is a "stream of consciousness," but this stream holds a lot of debris, driftwood, algae, and a few dead fish. No one's interior monologue is tidy.

5. The relationship between strategy and tactics is like that in sports between a game plan and the individual plays. There is always a general plan of attack, but then there is a wide range of maneuvers within the plan. The plan may not change, but the maneuvers may shift constantly.

Alternatives

What you consider but reject will vary from person to person and according to mood. If you're feeling ill and surly, your evaluation may include some insults and at least one obscene howl. Most evaluations, however, include the following:

Response	Sample Line
Complete rejection	*"No way. Not in your lifetime. Not in this century. Eat garbage and die."*
Complete acceptance	*"Whatever you say."*
Stalling	*"I don't get it. Could you run that by me again?"*
Guarded, ambiguous response	*"Thanks for your frankness. I hear what you're saying."*
Logical, reasonable answer	*"Let's go over each one of your points."*
Emotional, passionate answer	*"Oh, God! I love it!"* or *"X#@!!! You piece of *#∧!!!"*

Something menacing	*"Go ahead. Make my day."*
Something endearing	*"You sure have a way with words."*
Any combination of the above	

Actors often leave out the evaluations people use in life. The result is bad acting. It's easy to omit evaluating because the lines are already there and the actor doesn't *have* to search for responses. It is this search, however, that is compelling to watch. Great actors fill evaluations with original, powerful alternatives. Whenever they are handed a difficult cue, we watch, intrigued by what they consider but choose not to unveil, enthralled as they prepare to respond.

Tactics can be characterized as charm ("I win, you win, we all win") or threat ("I win, you lose, so give up"). During an evaluation, we may hover and then move in one direction or the other. Here are some tactics most often chosen.

Charm Tactics

1. *Validate*

   Make them feel important. Nod, smile, laugh appreciatively, flatter, pay tribute, bow, shrug, bend, appear powerless and impressed, give them an identity to live up to.

2. *Soothe*

   Calm them, lull, hum, hush, use a bedside manner, salve, quell, relax, caress, croon, offer reassuring sounds and comforting words.

3. *Open up*

   Use candor. Claim to be open and frank because we honor their intelligence and character. Speak plain, shoot from the hip, be direct, be vulnerable, go for the bottom line. (The idea is that some people might be hoodwinked, but not the listener.)

4. *Play*

   Amuse them, flirt, beguile, delight, find shared jokes, wink, whisper, captivate, convulse, get them to be silly with you and to drop their guard.

5. *Stir*

   Inspire them, call them to wonder, challenge their ideals, turn them on to ideas (or to you), get them hot, overwhelm them with fire (of thought, deed, or action), whip them into a frenzy, whip up their patriotism, their idealism, or their gonads.

Threat Tactics

1. *Command*
   Jump in and take charge, dominate, bulldoze, interrupt, seize the moment, grab leadership and authority. Take over.

2. *Intimidate*
   Overwhelm with your height, size, physical strength, projection/volume, any ingredient of yours that's bigger than theirs. Flex, clench, menace, bluff, appear dangerous. Overpower.

3. *Outspeak*
   Speak with greater crispness, clarity, and assertiveness, find more vivid words than theirs, dart with consonants, twist endings of phrases, finish statements like curtain lines or by demanding a response. Use words as weapons.

4. *Scrutinize*
   Stare as if you have the goods on them and know all their secrets. Study, undress, glare, look through them. Answer questions with questions. Imagine you have a hidden weapon, dossier, evidence, photos (the shots with the donkey in Tijuana), a surprise witness, or a secret arsenal.

5. *Yell*
   Throw a tantrum; scream; appear irrational, nonnegotiable, at the edge of violence, and past reason. (Use this one selectively.)

Tactics raise ethical questions. For now, stay clear of what is right and simply note what people *do*.

EXERCISE 1.11

GET THE DOLLAR

Have someone offer a dollar to the classmate who can come up with the best tactic. Let everyone who wants to have a try. Either the person with the dollar chooses the recipient, or everyone votes on a winner. Discuss the range of tactics employed. Did any somehow combine both charm and threat maneuvers?

CHANGING TACTICS

Write out the tactic categories above on slips of paper. Give two actors a basic situation to improvise, and periodically signal them to draw a different tactic to pursue until it is time to draw another. Variation: Side coach the scene by calling out the name of the actor and the tactic to be tried next.

OBSERVING ALTERNATIVES

Take turns challenging others in the class with difficult questions (like pretending you hate the color of someone's sweater and how dare she wear it to class?), and listening carefully to the answers. Have the class identify alternatives they saw considered, but left unchosen, before the actual answer.

OBSERVING AND IDENTIFYING

Designate someone, at the beginning of the hour, to stop class at any given moment during the first half hour of the session. Then review the period so far in terms of the ten basics. What were the shared objectives? What was the first noted obstacle? What was the most noteworthy evaluation? What general strategies and specific tactics were employed? How was this class period divided into beats?

OBSERVING OFFSTAGE ACTING

1. Observe and record an offstage encounter exactly as you did one in which you starred in the last section.

2. Do the same thing, but secretly pick one of the people to support, so that you have a much stronger sense of one participant's subtext than the other.

OBSERVING ONSTAGE ACTING

1. Attend a production and observe a character with whom you feel some identification. Compare responses with your classmates.

2. Do the same with a character for whom you feel no identification or sympathy, and use the exercise to allow some understanding and compassion for the perspective of this character who is so different from yourself.

WHY STUDY ACTING?

If all the world is acting, why study it? First of all, because acting *often* does not necessarily mean acting *well*. We can all get better at something so important to living fully.

One strong motive for acting is *l'esprit de l'escalier*, an evocative French term which translates literally as the spirit of the stairs (or, more loosely, as staircase wit). Imagine attending a party at which someone says something so astonishingly rude to you that you are struck speechless. The evening goes on. You are leaving the party, descending the stairs, and suddenly the *spirit* comes to you. You think of the most devastating, witty comeback line in the world—a perfect retort, very civilized, but sure to end all such rudeness forever. Unfortunately, the party is over, you are outside, your rude assailant is nowhere to be seen, and too much time has gone by for an effective retort anyway. You would love to rewind the tape of your life. No such luck. But the line was *perfect*.

You arrive home and are sorely tempted to tell the story as if you did execute your key line at the key moment. Once enough time has gone by, you might start telling the story that way. You might even start *believing* it happened that way. It would have, if there were justice in the world.

There *is* justice in the theatre. Characters often *do* think of the perfect comeback. Life is more the way it ought to be. And sometimes it rubs off. The more time you spend speaking the great lines of others, the better chance you have to think of them yourself. There is a bumper sticker that reads: "If all the world's a stage, I need better lines." Proximity to better lines can help. You may develop into someone who gets the spirit long before descending the stairs.

A Richer Life

Acting is life-enhancing. Even if you never enter the doorway of a theatre after the last day of class, you can gain vivid personal awareness, higher communication skills, and a strong sense of compassion for your fellow humans. There are many ways of studying human behavior, but most disciplines do it from a distance, looking at large groups and leaving the student with more theory than experience. There may be no better, more involving way to learn about yourself, and about the phenomenon of being alive, than acting.

You learn how to relax and focus. You find out how your body, voice, and personality affect other people. You get tools for change if you dislike what you find. You develop a stronger sense of the kind of figure you cut in the world. You get to free dormant creative impulses, unchanneled emotional expression, and suppressed playfulness.

You also gain insight regarding others, both as individuals and groups. You learn to observe more carefully and interact with greater sensitivity. You may start out as an atheist, a pacifist, and a political liberal. Before your study of acting is over, you may get to play a fundamentalist, a gung-ho soldier, and a John Birch Society member. You may even be in class with such people and bond with them. You will never again be able to casually judge or thoughtlessly generalize about them. You will never be able to think of them as nothing more than members of their groups.

You come to understand connections between you and others: how to make them, avoid them, solidify them, and break them. You learn to sense hidden agendas, nuances, layers of interaction. There is a good chance you will be able to "play" your own life better.

The study of acting allows you to return to the game of Let's Pretend. You may replace playing Peter Pan with pretending to be French while you're in a restaurant, being stinking rich as you peruse the sapphires in a jewelry store, or giving yourself a made-up background to share with the stranger seated next to you on the plane. Most of us were much better at Let's Pretend in days of yore than we are now. An acting class can get you back in touch with the child in yourself. Acting can unlock the You who existed before the locks were put on your imagination—your capacity for delight, your sense of wonder. It can unlock your dormant ability to transform yourself and the world around you.

*Actors are people who were good at playing
"Let's Pretend" as kids and now we're getting
money to play house.*[16]
—MICHAEL J. FOX

*I come from a tightknit, conservative Catholic
family. What kind of girl would go for that? They
were looking for exotic, hot-blooded Cuban boys
with skintight pants and forbidden, dark-eyed lust.
I presented myself as the wrong kind of guy.
I was acting, even at that age.*[17]
—ANDY GARCIA

Actors vs. Others

All human beings act, but what about the actor as a recognized artist, a professional, someone *known* as an actor? What makes some of us get up and perform, even show off, where others fear to tread? The story of Og, the Caveman, freely adapted here,[18] is one possible explanation.

Imagine a society of prehistoric types where strength and courage are admired above all. Imagine a small Caveman named Og living in this group and not quite fitting in. Most males like to hunt and all take their turns killing dinosaurs [I told you this was freely adapted]. Og likes to carve on walls, eat, talk, and mate. He is scared of hunting. But his day comes along like everyone else's.

Og spends the whole day observing dinosaurs and other powerful creatures, having neither the heart nor the courage to kill anything. He drags his club home at sundown, only to encounter all the powerful brutes standing around the cave entrance. "Hey, Og, where's dinner?" one asks menacingly. Og pauses nervously and considers trying to run away.

Suddenly he is inspired. "Wait 'til I tell you about it," he says. "There I was on the plain, the sun beating mercilessly down on my neck when suddenly this enormous green creature roars (he stops and roars) and rolls his head (he rolls) so fiercely that I got chills (his listeners get chills) and then . . . " (The details of his story can be omitted since, with some embellishment, he takes them through his day so vividly, that they almost feel as if they were there in his place.) Og has his audience mesmerized. He imitates the dinosaur to perfection, he gets the sound of dinofeet on the sandy plain, all the details. Cheers follow the end of his story.

All is forgiven. There is ample leftover dinosaur around anyway. The group quickly agrees that Og should be excused from hunting from now on. Instead, he should follow the hunters and observe the hunt, recreating it for everyone at supper each evening, acting out all the parts. Well, most of the parts. Already others are volunteering to help out. He is happy to be excused and glad to have a function. As Og and his mate head off to their corner of the cave, she says to him, "Og, you've got it all over those dumb brutes. You're a real artist."

As another couple moves to their corner, she says "That Og. Isn't he amazing? The way he got just how the dinosaur's head swings back and forth. It was perfect." Her mate replies, "Well, it was pretty good. Personally I wouldn't have swung my head so far. It's more of circle than a swing, actually."

And so the first actor was born. And minutes later, the first critic.

In every culture, someone finds he is better at showing society how it lives than in living at its center. His gifts are for recreating human experience. He can give life back to an event from the past or give form to something in the mind. One of the questions you are probably exploring by taking an acting class is whether that sort of person is you.

> *I didn't get the role, but suddenly I knew that what*
> *was going on in that room was where I wanted to be.*
> *I began to go to acting classes four or five nights*
> *a week. I just couldn't get enough.*[19]
> —KEVIN COSTNER (describing his first audition)

Nearly everyone fantasizes about an acting career, and acting teachers are plagued by first-term students wanting to know if they have what it takes. The question is premature. No decent teacher will answer until a student has studied the art for a few years. A teacher will tell you what your strengths appear to be, where you've made progress, what kinds of goals you should set, and what training you should pursue next. But no one should give you thumbs up or down but you. If, ultimately, you decide to pursue the profession, it will be because you know you must. It will be because the art has chosen and possessed you and you have no choice. You may or may not be Og.

> *Everything else in my life receded,*
> *once I discovered theatre.*[20]
> —BETTE MIDLER

Already an Actor

A profile of you as a performer emerges out of real-life situations you thrive in, fantasies and visions that inspire you, your areas of vulnerability and strength (in calm and in crises), areas of childlike wonder (those still very much alive and those that need resuscitation), the events in your life that you script and those where you choose to wing it.

Many of these offstage experiences can give you confidence and texture onstage. Your acting experience can be brought into the theatre and used there. You already boast a lengthy resumé of performances. Some were Oscar-caliber triumphs. Others were such disasters you still don't care to think about them—unless enough time has passed to make them funny. All were sources of learning, so don't start any acting class convinced that you're an acting virgin. Your life is a fascinating fund that you can draw upon to help you become a better actor and a more complete human being. You have an acting past and present. Learning more about this art can give you a future that includes

a fascinating lifelong endeavor,

a chance to utter great words and thoughts,

more insight and compassion,

stronger self-awareness,

more successful human interaction, and

a reawakening of the child in you.

Not bad for a single area of study. It's ironic that some people regard acting as a frivolous pursuit, far from the fundamentals. What could be more fundamental than feeling full of possibility?

> *The actor is Camus's ideal existential hero, because*
> *if life is absurd and the idea is to live a more vital*
> *life, the man who lives more lives is in a better*
> *position than the guy who lives just one.[21]*
> **—JACK NICHOLSON**

Notes

1. Public Broadcasting System, "A Tribute to Cary Grant," original television broadcast November 1990.

2. Michael Bandler, "A Star Who Learned to Be Happy," *Parade*, March 26, 1989.

3. Wallace Terry, "Want to Be a Force for Healing?" *Parade*, November 25, 1990.

4. William Shakespeare, *As You Like It*, act II, sc. vii, lines 139–166.

5. Laurence Zuckerman, "Cosby, Inc.," *Time*, September 28, 1987.

6. Nancy Griffin, "Lethal Charm," *US*, December 12, 1989.

7. John Cottrell, *Laurence Olivier* (Englewood Cliffs, N.J.: Prentice Hall, 1975).

8. Bob Greene, "Streep," *Esquire*, December 1984.

9. Richard Corliss, "Bette Steals Hollywood," *Time*, March 3, 1987.

10. See Note 1 above.

11. Bob Greene, "Jessica Lange Speaks for Herself," *Esquire*, December 1985.

12. David Ansen, "Fabulous Pfeiffer," *Newsweek*, November 6, 1989.

13. "The Jewel Who is Julia," *People*, November 12, 1990.

14. "Gerard Depardieu—Filmography," *Premiere*, February 1991.

15. Tim Cahill, "Mel Gibson—Back from the Edge," *Premiere*, December 1988.

16. Dan Yakir, "The Future Is Now," *Cabletime*, April 1987.

17. Stephanie Mansfield, "Andy Garcia Keeps His Shirt On," *Gentlemen's Quarterly*, December 1990.

18. Adapted from Robert Edmund Jones, *The Dramatic Imagination* (New York: Theatre Arts Books, 1941).

19. "Kevin Costner," *People*, November 19, 1991.

20. See Note 9 above.

21. Ron Rosenbaum, "Acting: The Creative Mind of Jack Nicholson," *New York Times Magazine*, July 13, 1986.

RELAXED READINESS

*Getting Calm Enough, Yet Energized
Enough, To Perform Fully*

*Even in the beginning, when I was doing junk
television, I still had one thing—focus.*[1]
—MICHELLE PFEIFFER

I'm not a talented man . . . I'm a focused man.[2]
—WILLIAM HURT

*A lot of it is awareness. I've learned to use my eyes
to focus attention. I'm real good at concentrating.*[3]
—KATHLEEN TURNER

Warming Up

Actors who are focused are fascinating. You are focused when you have a point of concentration, a center of attention, when your consciousness is controlled and directed where you want it. Your energies are so united that you cannot be distracted. Your powers are brought to bear upon one clear course. All irrelevancies and digressions fade away.

The best way to achieve focus is to learn how to warm up. Because acting challenges the body, the voice, and the mind, all three deserve some attention. All three can be eased into a higher state of alertness, responsiveness, and sharper focus. In the great offstage performances of your life so far, focus came suddenly, perhaps accidentally. But this state can be achieved deliberately.

*The eye of a focused actor attracts the spectator . . .
a blank-eyed actor lets the attention
of the spectator wander.*[4]
—CONSTANTIN STANISLAVSKI

An acting class, like a cast, is a group needing instant trust and mutual acceptance. Everyone depends on everyone else. They have no choice. Time cannot be wasted while each individual frets over when and how to open up to the others. Each person needs to warm up his own instrument and to warm up *to* those around him. This chapter will deal with preparing you to act, both as an individual and as a member of the group.

Balancing Opposing States

If you are too relaxed, you fall asleep. If you are too ready, you can explode. The actor seeks a balance between ease and eagerness, between indifference and anxiety. Someone heavily anesthetized is relaxed, but then so is a corpse. A guru of the 1970s used to admonish his Quaalude-besotted disciples that they should aim to become "laid back, not laid out." Concentrate on relaxation only, and your performance is likely to come up short on energy, vitality, clarity, and power. At the other extreme is the player who works himself into a locker-room frenzy, overflowing with energy and anticipation, ready to explode. This works for sprinting and high decibel rock, but leads to acting that burns out quickly, and to performances that lack nuance, shading, and variety.

Images of cats permeate acting literature because no other creature seems quite so loose, yet alert. Acting warm-ups aim for relaxed readiness because actors are not automatically blessed with a cat's perfect energy state. As you learn the following sequences (or any other used by your class), keep yourself open and responsive. Avoid prejudging any exercise. Don't pick favorites, don't decide early which you don't like—don't decide at all yet. Just let go. It may seem for a while as if nothing is happening. When you finally master each exercise, and are free enough to allow it to work on you, you will begin to benefit.

MENTAL WARM-UPS

The body and voice are worth little if the mind fails to respond to the call for adventure. The mind can free your acting spirit, which is an elusive combination of imagination, energy, and openness to experience. Your acting spirit is strongly connected to the child in you. You start by tapping your inner willingness and then turning with trust to those around you, letting them give you courage, and conquering your own fear of unmasking.

You don't act alone. Everything covered in this book so far could be done without coming to class. The old post-performance cliché goes: "I don't know what happened. It was great when I did it at home in front of the mirror." I often joke with casts, as we approach opening night, that the audience will soon come and interfere with everything we've done, rudely interrupting us with their laughter and applause. But communion with other actors and the audience is the whole point. It just takes adjustment. The others often don't respond the way they did at home in your head (or your mirror). You need to allow others to become your mirrors and your guides.

Demons

The first step is to exorcise yourself of the demons that torment all actors. These are some of the things they whisper in your ear, so that it sounds like you speaking:

"These people are all much more talented than I am."

"They've all acted a lot already. I'm the only baby here."

"I'm the only one who looks bad in tights [substitute any worrisome item of clothing]."

"They're all so colorful. They'll think I'm too straight."

"They're all so normal-looking. They'll think I'm too weird."

"Everybody remembers the warm-ups [substitute any topic covered so far] but me."

"They all know each other already. I'll bet they all signed up as a group."

"Maybe I should have taken art history [substitute any other course offered in the world] instead."

This list and this paranoia are boring, and a waste of time. All of the things on the list are false, and you know it. And most of the fears are shared fears. Yet nearly everyone gives in to some demons. Promise yourself you won't.

EXERCISE 2.1

DUMPING THE DEMONS

1. Write out the list of fears above.

2. Cross out those items to which you haven't succumbed yet.

3. Add your own fears. The possibilities (for example, "The teacher already hates me" or "They'll never cast me here") are endless.

4. Scrawl something colorful over each item ("B.S.," "hogwash," your own favorite retaliation).

5. Perform a private exorcism in which you dramatically shred the paper, toss it out to sea, burn it, or all of the above. If you do the exercise the Journey, included in this chapter, symbolically slay your own demons at the end.

6. Get on with your acting.

Class Commitment

If you will decide today that you have an emotional investment in your acting-course classmates, you will receive dividends of which few stock-brokers have ever dreamed. The dividends are intangible, inspirational, and impossible to exchange on any market. When you have invested in someone, you want that person to do well and you project your hope onto her; you bend a little when she disappoints you; you always look ahead to what she might become with a little support. Instead of seeing this person as competition, you equate your own progress with hers. You want to be a part of a group of actors who are, without exception, exceptional. You want your teacher to find the task of making qualitative distinctions among you impossible.

> *The actors must understand each other,*
> *help each other, absolutely love each other.*
> *They absolutely* must.[5]
> —LAURENCE OLIVIER

If you are late for some classes, it doesn't matter that much. If you are absent for one day from your psychology class of 300 students, it matters to no one but you; and your grades are usually stacked up against your classmates'. Acting classes, however, are rarely graded on any kind of curve, so everyone in the class could get an A (or, of course, an F). But with this fellowship comes mutual responsibility. In your acting class, you may be partnered with different people each time to lead warm-ups, perform someone's offstage adventure, imitate, explore subtext, or perform a scene. If class time is devoted to these activities, you could leave a virtual platoon of partners in the lurch by not being there on any given day. If you're late for Acting I, someone may end up in a corner by himself because you, his partner, weren't there to start off the day's activities.

Even if you've been a flake all your life, now is the time to feel responsible—and to *take responsibility*—for the others in your group, to move beyond your own habitual self-indulgence to a sense of community. Once you do, it will feel so good.

Stage Fright Substitutes

The term *stage fright* has largely dropped out of use, because we now know that dwelling on something this malevolent gives it power. If I tell you not to be afraid, you may dwell on your fear. If I say, do not think of fast-food burgers under any circumstances, a line of them will parade through your mind. The key to most fears is *substitution*. On the simplest level, you replace the ogre with something less menacing, to fill your consciousness.

A great actor is like a great host, whose concern is for the comfort and well-being of both his family (his acting partners) and his guests (the audience). Great hosts ease you into a feeling that everything will be fine. They soothe you and make you feel effortlessly open to the next course of your meal. They never force you with overwhelming offers of "More dip?" while brandishing the green stuff millimeters from your mouth. Once they have welcomed guests into their home, there is no room in their consciousness to fret about whether the baseboards were dusted or if the stain on the rug shows. There's no room in the head for such monsters. If you will instead project your concern to your listeners, thinking more about their comfort than their verdicts, everything will fall into place.

The best advice I ever received from a veteran actor was, "Step out of the center of the universe." Once you do that, your perspective and your humanity are both back in place.

Accepting the Audience

An audience is an audience, whether it's one friend, a handful of classmates, or thousands of paying customers.

> *I don't think of the audience as someone separate*
> *from me. You have to seduce an audience. You can't*
> *beat 'em and you can't kiss their asses.*[6]
> —HARRISON FORD

Here are some other hints for allowing those *out there* to be with you, instead of assuming they're against you:

1. No matter who is out in the audience, place a familiar, nurturing, warm somebody out there. Place the spirit of someone who supports you.

2. Make friends with a piece of furniture, a window, a radiator, a blackboard, any object that seems comfortable and familiar, perhaps reminiscent of some place you like. Connect back with it occasionally for assurance.

3. Remind yourself that at the same moment you are walking up front to tell your little joke in acting class, millions are being born and dying, someone is performing heart surgery, a couple is making love on some secluded Bahamas beach, someone toils in some lab trying to discover a cure for AIDS or heart disease, a pilot has just landed a damaged plane with all on board grateful that only a *few* have been killed or injured. What you are doing is not the beginning, and not the end, of life. You are a grain of sand (albeit a great grain), and this moment is not even a semifinalist among the big triumphs and traumas going on right now in this world.

4. Tell yourself those people out there could be your best friends. In acting class, this is definitely true. In a performance hall, it is potentially true. You go out in front of a crowd. It is not merely a crowd. It is 1200 of your best friends, or at least *potential* best friends. What you want in dealing with your audience (especially if you address them directly) is a sense of confiding in someone you trust. If you will project that trust out into the house, the audience will receive it lovingly.

5. No one sits in the audience hoping to be bored and disappointed. In fact, empirical studies have shown that when mistakes (line-drops, fumbling pieces of business) have been deliberately inserted into performances to test audience response, almost no one could recall these errors later because they had cheerfully edited them out at the time. That's how much every person watching is on your side.*

> *The camera is just like this adoring dog; it just looks at you all the time. It's so flattering, it's ridiculous.*[7]
> —KATHLEEN TURNER

---

*If the audience happens to be a camera lens instead of people, you still can give it a friendly, unthreatening identity.

GROUP WARM-UPS

Although trust can be projected onto strangers, it helps a lot if you can stop being strangers to one another. It's worth taking time, during the first weeks of acting class, for people to get to know each other. I believe it's worth a *lot* of time. Here are some of the things others usually want to know. Sharing this information will help you skip steps and drop barriers.

Sharing Now

Some sharing of your past was suggested in chapter 1. Now is a good time to share what you think and feel, not just what you've done. Think about what you would like to say or show in each category below, 1–7. Have an answer even if it is only a conjecture, your best guess at the moment.

EXERCISE 2.2

SHARED OPINIONS

1. **How You Would Be Typecast**

Whether you choose to accept your type, fight it, change it, or expand it, is something to determine later. Now is the time to *acknowledge* it. You need to know how others perceive you, even if you elect to alter that perception. How would a casting director place you? What sorts of parts would she be likely to send you out for? How do most strangers perceive you? This question requires some self-awareness.

Remember, type has little to do with the person you are deep down. It is the impression you leave. It may also have little to do with your chronological age. Audrey Hepburn was the screen's reigning ingenue for many years, playing innocent young girls well into middle age, because her essential quality was ''young love.'' Margot Fonteyn and Roberta Peters were her counterparts in ballet and opera, respectively.

It may also not relate to the parts you've played so far. You may have done certain roles in your hometown because you were the only one around with the size or the voice to pull it off. In a larger casting pool, this may not be your perceived type at all. Offstage, you may have been cast as a leader, heading student governments, managing fund-raisers, you name it. But you may not look and sound like a leader at all.

Are you cringing at the whole idea of having to be any type when you
want to be a great, versatile, limitless actor? Of course you are. But you
must know how you are viewed *now* in order to do that. If you are uncertain, your friends will be glad to help you. Your best information will come
from new friends who do not have unfair information. Ask others:

What sorts of roles on TV they feel you could fit into (if the current actor disappeared)?

What celebrities you remind them of (if even just slightly)?

Which people in the dorm or in this class are you most like (and least like)?

This information can be eye-opening.

2. Your Favorite Actor

"Oh, I don't really have a favorite. There are so many wonderful ones."
Come on. Pick one. This isn't engraved in stone. You may change your
mind next week. But right now, who is someone you admire greatly? And
why?

Pick an actor, not just a star. *Just* a star, you say? There are actors who
are stars, but there are stars who are not actors. If you're serious enough
about the art to study it, you're ready to make that distinction. Pick people
whose artistry, skill, or versatility you admire at least as much as their
charisma, build, or sex appeal. When you think of an actor, you should
think of quality work, not just a great set of eyes or biceps. Not that there's
anything wrong with those.

> *I picture my epitaph:* Here lies Paul Newman, who
> died a failure because his eyes turned brown.[8]
> —PAUL NEWMAN

Pick someone whose art you admire at least as much as anything else about
him or her.

3. The Performance That Impressed You Most

Sometimes, watching an actor at work fills you with awe. You are vividly
aware that this is art of the highest order. You get chills, glassy eyes, a dry
mouth—the works. What is the closest you have come to feeling that way?

SHARED PERFORMANCES

4. The Offstage Performance You'd Most Like to Share

You reviewed these as you went through chapter 1 exercises. Which, out of your repertoire, would you enjoy telling about? Or demonstrating? Which would be most likely to help these classmates feel they know you? To get a sense of you, acting in the world?

5. Your Offstage Performance of the Week

If a vivid one has not recently been thrust upon you (by an unexpected visit, Rush Week, or new living arrangements), you may want to stage one, armed with all the information you now have. If you had to recreate this moment for the class, how would you cast it from among your classmates?

6. Your Favorite Story Joke

A story joke takes a minute or two to tell. You need to establish characters and circumstances that involve change, so that there is quite a bit more than a setup and punch line. Again, imagine it two ways: one with you just telling it, the other with the story staged and featuring you and some of the other actors in class. If you don't have one you like, this is a great time to ask everyone you know to tell you theirs, until you find one you'd like to tell.

7. A Character Identification Monologue

You've probably noticed that this list moves gradually from simple information sharing, to opinions and thought questions, to recreated events or small performances. This last item is the closest to traditional theatre, since it is a written speech which you memorize and present. Something one to two minutes in length is best. It does not have to be from a play. It could be from an interview, magazine article, essay, someone's advice column, your favorite novel, or even some john wall, as long as the character speaking is not you, but someone with whom you identify.

You may identify with the material because the humor clearly matches your own, the political or moral position is one you hold strongly, the pain of the speaker deeply moves you, or this is the kind of situation you could see yourself getting caught in. Try to share, in a sentence, why you identify with this speech.

"But I don't read plays and have nothing in mind. I don't even know where to start." Not so. You cannot possibly be that unformed. Somewhere on this earth, and probably on your bookshelf at home, there must be some speech that speaks to you and for you. Give yourself credit. This is a chance to share something you love.

Too Much, Too Soon?

How will you ever share all this? You probably won't. Your teacher might elect to go through the whole sequence but will more likely pick and choose and skip some items as the sense of the group becomes evident. Whether it gets done in or out of class, this gives you good stuff to talk about with your classmates as you get to know each other outside of class. These questions, incidentally, are fairly standard at an audition or actor interview, so many actors spend their lives refining and changing their answers as *they* change.

I suggest the following ground rules:

1. As others share, stop and ask them for clarification of anything said. Question each other if curious. But try to stay with curiosity that is likely to be universal. If you wonder whether someone had the same homeroom teacher you did, find out outside of class.

2. Everybody learn the line "Just the high points." Chant it to the occasional motormouth who goes through everything he's ever done, recites a book of reasons for taking the class, or needs to pick *ten* favorite actors, with an ode to each. This can be done good-naturedly. Anyone can forget and rattle on.

3. If someone is genuinely drawing a blank, others might offer their impressions. If others in the group disagree with the actor's own self-perception (this happens often with typecasting), everyone should feel free to speak up. All are in the process of defining the self and can use help.

4. This is nonjudgmental sharing. There are no wrong answers. There are no preferred responses. The whole idea is just to get to know others, so the work that follows will be grounded on awareness.

5. You shouldn't ask to have your answers, offstage performance, and monologues critiqued by teacher or others. Critical response is not the point here. The whole experience should be completely free of evaluation. You want to share who you are, without others telling you, in any way, if that meets with their approval. Not every theatrical act needs reviews. The sharing is enough.

EXERCISE 2.4

SHARED VIEWING

As a group, decide on one or more audience experiences that everyone will share this term. If a play is being performed by your theatre, everyone should try to read the script, attend a performance, agree on what acting elements will be observed, and use this show as the basis of discussions for the rest of the term. If everyone agrees to watch several episodes of the same TV series, a different kind of basis for discussion and improvisation is possible. Acting concepts are much easier to understand if you've all witnessed the same performances. Also, the act of shared viewing itself eases informal, offstage discussions among members of the group.

Names

Try to get everyone's name down the first week. Keep pencil and paper nearby as these exercises progress. If you are terrible at names, draw cartoons of people, associate them with animals or old acquaintances they remind you of, find words that rhyme with their names, note particularly memorable things they have said about themselves, whatever it takes. Just as it is important to get past a stiff formality early in acting class, it's vital to know who your peers are. When people start to speak, say their names to yourself beforehand, then check to see if you are right. During lulls in class, look around the room and try to identify everyone. Remember, you are investing in these people, and the first step is knowing who they are.

NAME TRUNK

1. Imagine an enormous, empty trunk in the middle of the room, waiting to be packed with something belonging to each person in class.

2. Everyone in turn pantomimes putting in an imaginary possession that begins with the first letter of his first name (Terry's trapeze, Gloria's guitar, Sandy's skateboard). Pick an object that expresses your personality, or at least your sense of humor—not just anything alliterative.

3. Each person repeats both the pantomiming and the naming of every item that went before. By the time the trunk is packed with objects, their owners' names should be firmly in place.

Group Contact Exercises

The following activities work well for establishing contact and rapport with others around you:

PARTNER GREETINGS

1. Wander around the room until your teacher or a group leader signals you to stop. Within a few minutes, find a distinctive way of making physical contact with the person nearest you. This will become your way of greeting each other.

2. Work your way through the whole group, finding a different way of making contact with every person. Each time, look at each other for a moment and try to let an impulse guide you. No words should be exchanged. Remember, if you shake hands with one person, that's fine, but that's it for that form of greeting. Thereafter you'll need to explore less conventional forms.

3. If time runs out and the teacher signals everyone to move on, just pick something quickly and go with it.

4. Stop halfway through the exercise and write down your greetings, so you won't forget them.

5. Greet your classmates this way whenever you run into them on campus or in the hall.

6. At a later session, add a distinctive sound. Whenever the two of you are partnered in future exercises, repeat your greeting.

GROUP GREETINGS

1. At some point in the term, every couple should demonstrate their greetings for the entire class.

2. Some similarities of moves and sounds will emerge, so a group greeting can be developed out of all the partner ones. Exploring this can be silly and enjoyable for quite some time. It's a good feeling to have a group greeting established by at least the term's end, but the exploration is the main idea.

CIRCLE JUMPS

1. Let the group pick a word or sound of the day. It might be something fun to say, like "raspberries," or a noise like a Bronx cheer. Or it might be a name—that of someone in the group who's having a birthday, or of some world figure everyone would like to cheer or hiss.

2. Gather into a tight circle, arms locked together, and begin dipping and breathing as a unit, repeating the word, name, or noise lightly.

3. Let the sound build in volume, and the dips grow into leaps, so that there is a final group leap quite high in the air, and the word explodes one last time.

GROUP BREATH AND SOUND

Sit in a tight circle, with your legs crossed and knees touching one another's (and, if you wish, your arms entwined), or stand in the same configuration. Proceed to find a common group-breathing pattern, an agreed-upon sound shared by everyone, a hum shared by all. Let the hum develop naturally into a group chord.

EVERYBODY'S *ESPRIT*

Remember our old friend *l'esprit de l'escalier*—the spirit of the stairs?

1. Pick out a great lost opportunity from your own past, and let the class help you act it out the way it should have been.
2. Cast your antagonist, and any other characters needed, from among your classmates.
3. At your cue, take a deep breath and make the Killer Retort that the Fates should have allowed before; the class should cheer, and go berserk with admiration, once you finally get the line out.

Everybody deserves a chance at this little taste of psychodrama.

PHYSICAL WARM-UPS

Although actors vary widely in their rituals of preparation, the following sequence of physical warm-up activities is widely used:

Meditation

Tensing/Releasing

Alignment

Shaking

Stretching

Breathing

Aerobics

Meditation (optional)

One or two exercises follow from each of these categories. Choose between the options to devise the physical warm-up that works best for you. You may wish, at the end of the sequence, to return to the meditation exercise by way of conclusion.

Following the given sequence is important, however, no matter which exercise you choose in each step, because each step prepares you for the next one. Skipping steps in the exercise sequence may mean strain or even pain; you may not be loose enough yet for the step to which you've jumped.

To perform these, you will need clothing that lets you roll around on the floor, and either very soft-soled shoes or no shoes at all.

Narrowing Your Circle

When it comes time to do the exercises in class, find a space for yourself and narrow your focus, so that you don't make eye contact with anyone. Treat the instructions as side-coaching (listen to the words but don't look at the speaker), so you are alone even though surrounded by others. Imagine that you have a circle surrounding your immediate territory, with no need to move outside it. Work in a state of public solitude, developing the capacity to be comfortably alone even in the midst of a large group. This is a state the actor often needs to enter in performance.

Modify any exercise if it gives you strain today. Feel free to drop out of the activity if you don't feel well. No need to explain your decision. Instead, just fade out subtly until you feel you can rejoin. Because all of these exercises are standard and tested, however, consistent problems with any of them means you should see a physician.

Breathe fully throughout each exercise, alternating a complete inhalation in one position with a generous exhalation as you move to the next. Don't concentrate so hard on getting the moves right that you forget to breathe. Let the air-flow move you along and help you to loosen up.

Meditation

Even a few minutes spent silent and still, eyes closed, focus narrow, can be calming. Meditation involves repeating a sound silently to yourself, usually while you're sitting or lying on the floor. Breathing tends to get more and more shallow as concentration turns inward. For example:

EXERCISE 2.11

HERE AND NOW, PART ONE

1. Let go of responsibilities carried from the past and expected in the future. Past and future are like heavy, cumbersome layers of clothing you let drop so you can breathe. Give yourself permission to

be in no time or place but this moment, in this room, surrounded by these other actors. Feel the earlier part of the day and the later part ahead drift away, so you feel completely here in this moment.

2. Help yourself focus here and now by picking out small physical sensations: feelings of jewelry against your skin, places where clothes feel loose and draped, a radiator humming, your own shallow breathing, the places your body makes contact with the floor. Nothing is too tiny or trivial to notice if it is immediate.

3. Choose a word or sound that pleases you: a suggestive verb like *soothe, ease, release, complete, renew,* or something purely sensual and abstract like *velvet, music, embrace,* or *dawn,* the name of a favorite object, place, or a nonsense syllable that makes you feel good. Repeat the word silently to yourself, continuously, without any effort, letting the qualities of the word wash over you and allowing your mind to wander where it will.

The time devoted will vary with the need of the group. If everyone seems high-strung on a given day, this exercise may be extended. If there is a sense of calm unity already in the room, even two minutes may be enough.

Tensing/Releasing

The practice of adding some tension to an area of the body just prior to letting that area relax or fall free is widely accepted as a means of producing greater release. A muscle relaxes more after being moderately tensed than it does from a neutral state, and the immediate contrast produces a pleasurable, easy feeling for most people. For example:

EXERCISE 2.12

THE PRUNE

Lie on your back with your arms and legs uncrossed and loose. As each area of the body is named below, tense it up, while keeping everything lower on your body loose and relaxed. The tension will accumulate, moving from head to toes, before you finally let everything go and float from the release. Each tensing is more effective if you imagine you are tightening that area of the body to protect yourself against some shock.

1. First tense all your *facial muscles* inward toward the center of the face, as if it were rapidly withering and drying up into a prune.

2. Tighten the surrounding *skull* as if it were suddenly locked in a vise.

3. Shoot the tension into the *neck* as if it were in a brace and frozen in place.

4. Shoot it across the *shoulders*, locking at the shoulder joints. (Remember, everything below the shoulders is still loose.)

5. Tighten the *upper arms*—both sets of biceps and triceps.

6. Tense at the *elbows*, locking the elbow joints,

7. into the *lower arms*,

8. locking the *wrists* as if they were tightly bound,

9. tightening the *palms* of the hands as if catching a ball,

10. drawing the fingers halfway into a *fist* that will not complete itself but remains suspended and partly closed.

11. Tighten *upper chest and back*, then the

12. *stomach and lower back*, as if protecting against a blow.

13. Tense the *hip joints*, which are then locked.

14. Tense the *groin* and *buttocks*,

15. stiffen the *upper legs*,

16. lock the *knee joints*,

17. draw the *lower legs* taut,

18. lock the *ankles*,

19. stiffen the *feet*, extending the *toes*.

20. Point your toes at the wall opposite you.

21. Final position: pull up with the center of your body toward the ceiling, so that your torso lifts off the ground and your body is supported only by the back of your head, your shoulder blades, and your heels, as if your whole body were drying up like a prune; hold; then

22. release, letting it all go, as if you're sinking into the floor or floating in the air, but in no way confined anymore by gravity. Relax and savor the sensation of easy, released floating.

23. Repeat the entire exercise more quickly, remembering to keep everything loose until its turn: tighten face, head, neck, shoulders, upper arms, elbows, lower arms, wrists, hands, fingers halfway into fist, upper chest and back, stomach and lower back, hip joints, groin and buttocks, upper legs, knee joints, lower legs, ankles, feet; point toes; pull body up toward ceiling; release. And savor.

Figure 2–1 The Prune
Full tension just before final release. Body supported in just three places.

Alignment

The spinal column has become universally recognized as a center of the body's energy and, unfortunately, tension. The vertebrae tend literally to close off in a way that shortens the spine and blocks physical and emotional responsiveness. Fortunately, the column can be returned to a relatively open state by exercises, beginning with lying flat on the floor and allowing the space between each vertebra to return as the back stretches toward alignment and the rest of the body follows.

EXERCISE 2.13

THE ACCORDION

1. While still on your back from the previous exercise, and without pushing to achieve it, allow your spine to stretch out along the floor. Imagine your body is thick syrup that has splashed on the floor and is now spreading slowly and easily in every direction.

2. Your back should be absolutely flat against the floor. For many people, this is most easily achieved by raising the knees slowly and/or extending the elbows slightly to the side. Shift around until you find your own flattest, easiest position.

3. Imagine the spine as a hand accordion stretching to its full length, but still undulating gently and under no pressure.

4. Imagine air whirling gently around each vertebra as they all ease apart. Imagine your head is several miles away from your tailbone as the two ease gently in opposite directions.

5. Roll over on your side into a curled position, and, getting to your feet in this curled stance, slowly uncoil to a standing position, with your head the very last part to reach the top and your spinal column returning to the same aligned, stretched sensation that it had when pressed against the floor.

6. Think of your head now as a balloon floating high above the rest of your body, which hangs comfortably from the balloon. Plant your feet firmly and imagine them many, many miles away from the balloon. You should feel as if your posture is terrific, but that it was achieved without effort and can be maintained without strain.

7. Sense your accordion spine moving imperceptibly, stretching comfortably.

EXERCISE 2.14

THE PUPPET (ALTERNATIVE ALIGNMENT EXERCISE)

1. Drop your entire upper body forward like a puppet's, breaking at the waist so that your hands almost brush the floor.

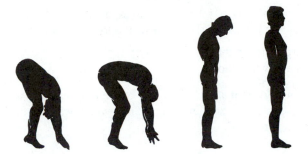

Figure 2–2 The Puppet
Note that the head is the very last part to rise, even after the entire torso is erect.

2. Let your knees bend slightly and use your lower body only for balance and support, ignoring it otherwise and letting your entire upper body hang loose and limp.

3. Test your looseness by swinging your arms and head, apelike, back and forth, until you are quite limp.

4. Imagine a string connected to your tailbone, which begins to tug you up as if a puppeteer were pulling you into life. Imagine similar strings connected to each of the thirty-plus vertebrae, all the way up into the back of your skull.

5. Allow yourself to rise very slowly, string by string, relaxing slightly with each tug. Avoid any temptation to pull your upper back, neck, and head up too soon. They're the very last strings. You'll reach a completely erect position before your neck even begins to rise.

6. Collapse again and repeat.

Shaking Out

At any of the joints (wrists, elbows, shoulders, and so forth), stiffness or the false sensation of cramp in a nearby muscle may be relieved by spinning the appendage in a circle or just shaking it out. The rush of activity tends to awaken that area of the body so that it rejoins the rest of you and takes part again.

EXERCISE 2.15

RAG DOLL

1. Imagine yourself as loose as a rag doll or scarecrow and simply shake out, standing in place, wherever you feel a little tight.

2. Spend some time shaking out just your wrists, then your elbows, then both arms from the shoulder joint down, then your legs (one at a time), finally all of these at random.

Return to shaking out whenever you feel like it during the exercise sequence. Don't isolate it at this point, but return to it regularly as a constant way of loosening up, and of filling time while waiting for others to complete an exercise.

Stretching

In physical conditioning, stretching is an effective counterbalance to muscle-building activity. As they build, the muscles narrow and contract, restricting flexibility (giving rise to the term *muscle-bound*). Stretching restores pliability and helps add grace to strength. More than any other single activity, stretching serves to prevent injury, by keeping muscles supple and the body flexible. It can be profoundly healing. Oddly enough, although animals seem to know instinctively how to stretch, humans have largely forgotten how. The upper back and neck tend to gather tension, and they particularly benefit from stretching. The following exercise may be the one most widely used by actors.

EXERCISE 2.16

HEAD ROLLS

1. Standing tall, with feet firmly planted, let your head drop forward onto your chest, chin landing gently on your clavicle.

2. Begin rolling your head slowly in either direction in a moderate circle which grows in size with each repetition.

3. Change directions after you work your way to a wide circle.

4. Keep the rest of your body upright, and limit the action to your head and neck; the shoulders and chest are in no way active. Make no effort to keep your mouth closed or eyes shut, but let them drop if you feel the impulse. Make no effort for any sort of regularity of rhythm; if, for example, you feel like lingering briefly as your head is over your right shoulder to relish the stretch there, go ahead. Let yourself sense where you need to linger. If you feel like it, increase the speed of the circles, but only if that feels good today.

5. It may help to think of the neck as a ball-bearing at the connection between torso and head, a ball-bearing firmly placed, but capable of a large range of safe motion.

A stretched body can reach farther without strain than one unstretched. *Physical* stretching can make you feel more capable of *emotional* and *creative* stretching as well. The following exercise may be difficult for those with lower-back problems. With this and all warm-ups, trust your body when it tells you to step out. You don't need to prove anything.

EXERCISE 2.17

THE SUN

This, one of many variations of a popular yoga-based exercise, not only stretches the whole body, but can be infused with spiritual connotations, as you praise the sun, salute it, or, if the day is overcast, try to will it to appear. There are eleven stages, of which numbers 1 and 11 are the same, as are 2 and 10, and numbers 5 and 7. This exercise is more complicated than any given so far, but the stretch is worth it.

1. **Hands**
   Stand tall, hands clasped, palms together, as in prayer or traditional Oriental greeting.

2. **Salute**
   Explode into a giant X figure, arms and legs wide apart, leaning back slightly to face the sun.

3. **Ankles**
   With your legs together and straight, bend your upper body over (as in toe touches) and grasp your ankles, getting a full stretch along the back of your legs.

4. **Side Stretch**
   Support your body with hands out on the floor, as at the beginning of a push-up, but with only one leg extended behind. Bend the other leg beneath your chest, so that it stretches the extended side of your body. Your overall position will be similar to that of a sprinter about to take off. (In each of these full-body stretches, your head should be tilted slightly back, so the line from head to foot is a very moderate C curve.)

5. **V**
   Straighten the bent leg, extending it back to join the other leg behind you. Move your body into an upside-down V, resting on only your hands and feet, with your buttocks high in the air, forming the point of the V.

Figure 2–3 The Sun

6. **Cobra**

   Lower your upper body as if to do a push-up, but, as your face nears the floor, curve your torso back into a cobra-like position, providing a gentle stretch along your lower back and upper legs.

7. **V**

   Repeat the upside-down V of step 5.

8. **Side Stretch**

   Repeat the stretch of step 4, but changing the extended and bent legs so that the stretch is on the other side of your body.

9. **Fetus**

   Feet together and supporting your weight, curl your body into the smallest possible position, approximately fetal—head against knees, arms wrapped around your lower legs. Squeeze yourself inward in preparation to explode out.

10. **Salute**

    Repeat the full X salute of step 2.

11. **Hands**

    Repeat the clasped-hands stillness of step 1.

Eventually, when each step is second nature, aim to perform the Sun as one continuous, flowing action. Pulse slightly in each location, but imagine the exercise as a floating, unbroken, and easy dance, always moving with the fluid, undulating quality of the cobra, for which position 6 is named.

If time and space make it difficult to perform the Sun, just take a few minutes to stretch anywhere you feel tight, working your way gradually through the body, as a simple substitute exercise.

Breathing

The term *breath support* means more than having enough air to speak with. The manner and depth of breathing you choose can produce differing energy states. Changing breathing patterns can change the way you feel. The act supports you in various ways—from the calm stillness of shallow meditation breathing, to the highly energized sensation of full diaphragmatic breathing, to the stamina of lower back breathing. The actor needs to call on a whole range of support for different moments. The following exercise touches on the deepest breathing, because most of us need to be reminded of our reserves of breath storage. Also, it's time for something energizing in this warm-up sequence.

LUNG VACUUM

This exercise literally forces out stale air and replaces it with fresh. Some dizziness is natural at the very beginning, particularly for smokers.

1. Collapse exactly as in the Puppet, simultaneously blowing out air vigorously (and audibly) through the mouth.

2. In the collapsed position, continue to blow out air in short, powerful spurts until you feel completely emptied of air. Imagine that you need to get rid of harmful fumes and replace them with clean air, but that it will only work if you are totally empty. (At this point all should proceed at their own rate with no need for group coordination.)

3. Rise slowly, keeping air out, making sure your footing is secure and solid. Keep air out as long as you can manage it. Note: Do not try to do this in sync with others in the group. This is not a competition, and lung capacity varies even among people who are identically fit.

4. When you feel you must breathe, allow air to sweep in, feeling it pour almost to the end of your fingertips and toes. You should feel much like Woody Allen looked in his balloon suit in *Sleeper*. Notice the rush of air to the small of the back. You should feel an intense rush as the new air sucks in with a vacuum force.

5. Repeat this sequence at your own rate.

Good actors always work to inhale faster (so they don't waste valuable time) and to exhale slower (so they can speak longer and more confidently). This exercise is an intensification of that sensation, with exhalation extended for quite a while, and inhalation compressed to an instant.

NOTE: The following two activities, aerobics and a return to meditation, are optional, depending on the needs of the group. If they are not performed, and the vocal warm-up is included, it should be performed at this point.

Aerobics

The value of a regularly raised, sustained heartbeat has been established for cardiovascular fitness and other health benefits. Some kind of aerobic activity is standard for anyone pursuing fitness, and the pay-off is especially strong for actors, who need endurance and controlled breathing.

Long-term benefits are not the reason for aerobic exercise in this warm-

up, however. A minimum of 15 minutes three times a week is needed for
that. The following activity is designed to get the heart pumping and the
blood flowing after the earlier, calmer exercises.

EXERCISE 2.19

THE BLENDER

This sequence is performed as fast as the group can manage it, and, unlike
earlier activities, it is usually done watching someone lead the movement.
The leader calls out the moves, setting the pace with a definite, clear beat.
Everyone bounces lightly on the balls of their feet throughout.

1. **Two jumping jacks**
2. **Two elbows to knees**
   One elbow touches opposite knee as the other arm swings high in the air, then other elbow touches
   other knee.

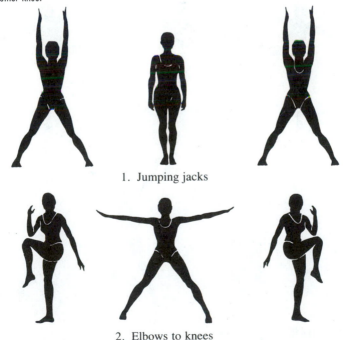

1. Jumping jacks

2. Elbows to knees

Figure 2–4 The Blender

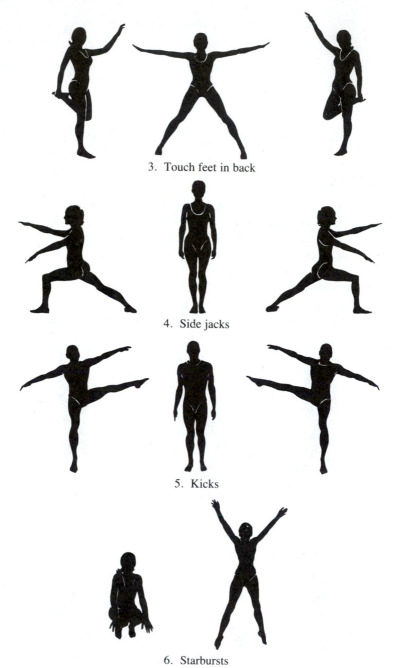

3. Touch feet in back

4. Side jacks

5. Kicks

6. Starbursts

Figure 2–4 The Blender (continued)

3. **Two touch feet in backs**
   One hand slaps the sole of the opposing foot (left hand to right foot, right hand to left foot) as foot is raised in back. Again, the unused arm swings high in air.

4. **Two side jacks**
   Same as jumping jacks, except the body is turned sideways each time, with one arm to the front and other to the back; one leg bent to one side, and the other leg straight and extended to other side.

5. **Two kicks**
   First one leg, then the other, up and forward, with arms extended out to the sides.

6. **Two starbursts**
   Similar to positions 2 and 10 in the Sun. Dip, with hands just above knees, then leap off the ground into a big open X in the air.

EXERCISE 2.20

THE JOURNEY (ALTERNATIVE AEROBIC EXERCISE)

Imagine that you are on a journey through various wild terrains, fleeing some monster or demon. Go through the following maneuvers in a stationary position. Explore as a group how best to represent the activity while remaining in one spot:

1. Swimming
2. Climbing a ladder
3. Skating
4. Climbing a rope
6. Riding a horse
7. Slalom skiing
8. Rowing a canoe
9. Trying to fly
10. Finally, you decide to stand up and confront the demon (as David did Goliath). Wind up your sling and fire your stone at the demon, jumping for joy as the monster crashes to the ground.

EXERCISE 2.21

ANYTHING AEROBIC (ALTERNATIVE EXERCISE)

Find a theme to keep everyone active and engaged for at least a minute and a half. Act out as many sports as possible with quick changes. Become as many different animals as you can in the time. Run outside and around the building and back into the classroom—anything that gets the pulse up and charged.

EXERCISE 2.22

HERE AND NOW, PART TWO (OPTIONAL RETURN TO MEDITATION)

Return to a sitting or lying position, close your eyes, and renew your sense of here and now with the added stimuli of the preceding exercises. Drop any lingering past or future distractions, touch on some immediate physical sensations, repeat a word or sound that makes you feel good. Allow yourself to feel a part of the group around you, with whom you've just shared the warm-up activity. Let yourself be the same as those around you—still you, but even and comfortable with others.

Changing Images

Countless exercises could be substituted for any of those above. Don't give in to the temptation, however, to want new exercises every day. If you're bored with a warm-up, it's because you're not giving yourself up to it yet. Acting warm-ups won't work until you can do them mindlessly, without struggling to remember what's next. The variety and enhancement can come with the images you change in your head.

Here are some possibilities:

1. *Prune*

    You age radically with each tensing. You're a hideous crone (as in Oscar Wilde's *Picture of Dorian Gray*) by the last "pruning." Youth and vigor all return as you release.

2. *Accordion*

   As your spine lengthens, so do you. You are Gulliver, being tugged at gently by the Lilliputians, or Paul Bunyan, napping luxuriously over acres of timberland. When you stand you can see across continents.

3. *Head Rolls*

   You are Samson or Rapunzel. You have an amazing mane of hair that whirls around you in slow motion like a cloud. Each roll of the head increases your own power, beauty, pride in your mane.

4. *Puppet*

   When you collapse, you turn into an ape. At each tug along the spine, you move through an evolutionary stage, from primitive to a fully formed human of the future (passing through the Og stage about one-third of the way up)—bright, complete and ready to conquer new worlds.

5. *Sun*

   You are a much revered pagan priestess-dancer or medicine man. Your people have pinned all their hopes for survival on you. Each move is a supplication to nature for spring to arrive and save your people from the cold. You literally *will* the sun to come out and warm those under your care.

6. *Lung vacuum*

   You are saving the world. At great peril to yourself you have breathed in toxic fumes, which you now blow out of your body and off the planet. You are successful, and when you inhale, you are cleansed and safe.

7. *The Blender*

   It is an Olympics far in the future, and you have been chosen as the healthiest and most beautiful human in the world. You are dancing for a throng of people who wish to emulate you. Each move makes them gasp with wonder. Each move fills you with power, which they share in because your energy is contagious.

It helps to warm up the mind if the physical maneuvers are accompanied by a rigorous workout of the imagination. You might pick a theme for a given session (the examples above are all about power and heroism) based on your interests or needs that day. If you are warming up for a character, you might direct images to the character's background/perspective, so you enter her world through each exercise.

VOCAL WARM-UPS

The vocal warm-up sequence, once mastered, should take about five minutes. It is more effective if it follows a complete physical warm-up (see suggested point of insertion in preceding sequence). When the body has been relaxed, aligned, and stretched, and when deep breathing has been tapped, then the voice can be freed. A vocal warm-up that isn't preceded by a physical one is like a building without a foundation. A standard sequence involves the following stages:

Releasing

Breathing

Rooting Sound

Shaping Sound

Precision Drills

Releasing

The muscles of the face and throat need to relax so breath and sound aren't constricted. A free, open passage needs to be created before the voice can pass untroubled. Some moderate tensing will be introduced again so that the relaxation, when it follows, is fuller.

EXERCISE 2.23

LETTING GO

1. **Lion**

   Stretch your face open and out in all directions, bug-eyed, like a Kabuki lion or like the Edvard Munch painting *The Scream*. It's as if you are executing a silent scream. Your mouth is wide open, tongue extended downward. Imagine a silent scream with full desperation but no sound.

2. **Skin Slide**

   Let the scream disappear. Allow all the facial muscles to collapse slowly, including the jaw, which drops open. Imagine the skin almost sliding off the skeletal structure of your face, because it is that relaxed. Your eyelids may drop half-shut. Let them.

3. **Jaw Drop**
   Open and close your mouth several times, effortlessly allowing the opening to increase slightly each time. Test to see if you can easily get two fingers into the opening without strain. From now on, let your jaw drop open or remain closed, expending no effort to control it unless an exercise calls for it.

4. **Full Body Yawn**
   Let your whole self participate, the body doing a big stretch, forming a loose X, and releasing a full, audible, lengthy sigh as your arms drop to your sides again.

5. **Shoulder Drops**
   Raise your shoulders very high, then let them drop. Repeat twice more, raising the shoulders slightly less each time.

6. **Inclines**
   Incline your head to right and left, back and forth, in a gently rocking motion; you should feel a light, soothing sensation in the throat with each move.

7. **Nods**
   Do the same inclining movement to the front and back as if you are agreeing with someone. Allow head to fall back as far as it falls forward. Remember to let the jaw hang loose.

Breathing

Now that the path is clear, breath is needed to help reach for sound and carry it forth. This exercise also pushes breath storage to the small of the back, more gradually than in the Lung Vacuum. Consciously observe the air passing through each of the following areas:

EXERCISE 2.24

RESPIRATING

1. **Nose and Throat**
   Inhale deeply.

2. **Upper Chest**
   Let air pass through without any expansion in this area.

3. **Floating Ribs**
   Three sets of lower ribs are unattached at the front, so when they part, air flows fully. Feel them open like a double door of welcome for the air.

4. **Diaphragm**

   Normally in an arched and raised position, it both lowers and flattens as deep breathing occurs. Feel the area in the lower torso expand to its fullest as the diaphragm descends. (See Figure 2–5.)

5. **Lower Back**

   Finally the air reaches deeply into this most efficient, often unused, storage room.

   Now sigh out in exhalation, observing the reversal of the process as the air moves out and past the:

6. **Lower Back**

7. **Diaphragm**

8. **Floating Ribs**

9. **Upper Chest**

10. **Mouth**

Repeat the process a few times, then follow with another *full body yawn.*

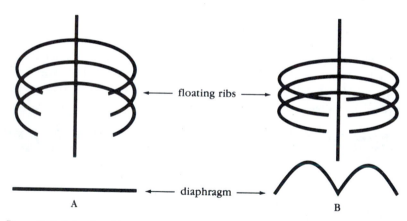

Figure 2–5 Active Breathing

Whereas much of the breathing process is passive, two distinct and striking activities occur within the torso when deep, full respiration takes place. First visualize air causing the three sets of floating ribs to expand and the diaphragm to lower and flatten as you inhale (A). Then visualize the diaphragm returning to its double-arched, humped position and the floating ribs returning to a more closed position as you exhale (B).

Rooting Sound

With air to ride, sound can be strongly summoned from deep in the torso, where your fullest, most resonant music lives. The specific physiological location is less important than what it feels like. Sound that feels rooted, like a firm, proud tree, will fill a space and vary itself with little deliberate effort.

EXERCISE 2.25

SOUNDING

1. **Planting**
   Plant feet firmly and imagine your voice planted way down in your tailbone, with roots passing down through your torso, through your legs, and into the ground beneath you.

2. **Humming**
   Reach down for sound on inhalation and hum on exhalation. Explore the tones and colors available. Let sounds resonate in the facial mask.

3. **Roller Coaster**
   Work the hum up and down your register from lower to higher pitches and back, like a roller coaster, rooting deeper each time sound descends. Note the sensation of vibrating sound along the front of your torso as you resonate. Note all the places the sound can vibrate.

4. **String**
   Imagine a string pulling sound out of you, louder as it tugs away, then softer as it returns to your mouth. Hum, then let the hum evolve into an AAAHHHH sound. Let the volume increase and decrease without raising the pitch, increasing tension in the throat, or allowing stridency in the sound, by confidently rooting the sound. As it gets louder, confidently extend the string to some great distance. As it gets softer, the sound is no more comfortable, but capable of greater subtlety.

Shaping Sound

Parts of the body may be exercised separately for particular benefits. Organs for shaping sound into words can benefit from individual exercises. Just as some parts of your body, if not worked, tend to add fat or lose flexibility more easily than others, your organs of articulation may need varying degrees of attention to keep them in shape. The consonants and vowels used in the drill sections below are those that give most people difficulty. These exercises can all be performed quite rapidly (not tensely, but quickly, for dexterity) once they are mastered. Most of these consonants (except *f*, *v*, *s*, and the dipthong *th*) can be struck more cleanly, quickly, and simply than is often done. They need to be tapped, not bludgeoned.

While the animal images below are evocative, the consonant and vowel drills are helped by making up specific occasions, messages, languages, or attitudes as you practice them (''PAY, PAY, PAY,'' cries the cossack to the Czar; ''KAY, KAY, KAY,'' orders the galactic ship captain to his staff; and so forth), filling the exercises with both imagination and purpose.

EXERCISE 2.26

ISOLATIONS

The Lips

1. *Fish*   Isolate and expand lips as if moving through water, stretching them like a guppy's, as if you have fish lips.

2. *Horse*   Make an unvoiced PPPPP sound which explodes, like the sound a horse makes when it shakes its head. Work for maximum vibration of the lips.

3. *Motor Boat*   A VVVVV sound, slowly starting the motor, taking off, changing gears, choking the engine, dying out.

4. *Lip Drill*
PAYPAYPAY	PAYPAYPAY	PAYPAYPAY	PAH
BAYBAYBAY	BAYBAYBAY	BAYBAYBAY	BAH
MAYMAYMAY	MAYMAYMAY	MAYMAYMAY	MAH

The Hard Palate

5. *Fly*   ZZZZZZZ sound, varying in pitch and volume.

6. *Snake*   SSSSS sound, threatening prey, varying in intensity.

7. *Palate Drill*
ZAYZAYZAY	ZAYZAYZAY	ZAYZAYZAY	ZAH
SAYSAYSAY	SAYSAYSAY	SAYSAYSAY	SAH

The Tongue Tip

8. *Cat Lap*   Lap at imaginary milk from all different directions and distances as rapidly as possible.

9. *Tongue Tip Drill*	LAYLAYLAY	LAYLAYLAY	LAYLAYLAY	LAH
	TAYTAYTAY	TAYTAYTAY	TAYTAYTAY	TAH
	DAYDAYDAY	DAYDAYDAY	DAYDAYDAY	DAH
	NAYNAYNAY	NAYNAYNAY	NAYNAYNAY	NAH

The Back Tongue

10. *Jungle Heartbeat*   Repeat the NG sound several times through an extended sigh.

11. *Tongue Back Drill*	KAYKAYKAY	KAYKAYKAY	KAYKAYKAY	KAH
	GAYGAYGAY	GAYGAYGAY	GAYGAYGAY	GAH

Precision Drills

Articulation drills can increase the crispness and clarity of sound, but should be preceded by full warming and releasing so that they don't add unneeded tension. Because of the challenge, some actors, even when warmed up, drop the benefits they have just acquired. They get tense in anticipation. It is important to keep a sense of looseness and enjoyment, which is why this last exercise is designed to play off a partner.

EXERCISE 2.27

LIP READING

1. Pick a partner and lock eyes with him.

2. Repeat together very slowly and precisely the following simple list of articulatory organs:
   THE TIP OF THE TONGUE
   THE ROOF OF THE MOUTH
   THE LIPS AND THE TEETH

3. Gradually speed up your synchronized delivery of these lines until delivery is rapid and highly crisp, but with no increase in tension, tightness in the throat, greater volume or rise in pitch.

4. When your eyes tell your partners' that you have gone as fast as possible, slow down gradually again, step by step, to a very measured, leisurely pace, and then stop.

5. Mirror each other on one last *full body yawn*.

This exercise doesn't *have* to be done with a partner. It's just more fun that way.

TWISTERS (ALTERNATIVE PRECISION DRILL)

Add the following tongue twisters to, or substitute them for, the corresponding consonant drills above.

P — "Pulchritudinous Paula provided poor, parched Paul passionate passage through puberty."

B — "Bitter bitch Bette bested Blake by buying back Boston for big bucks."

M — "My mogul mother might make many more major monster movies, Marilyn."

Z — "Zany zealot Zelda's zenith was Xeroxing zinc zodiac zippers."

S — "Sarcastic Sheila slowly sashayed south, Sunday, spouting several sharp, sick satires."

L — "Loathsome leech Louie lazed listlessly around Loretta's, lapping liquor like a lounge lizard."

T — "Due to too much testosterone, Todd tended to tirelessly tackle two-ton tyrants."

D — "Divinely decadent Dorothy delightedly destroyed downtown Dallas daily."

N — "No newly naked nervous nerd knows near enough novelties, Norm."

K — "Carpingly critical Carrol called Carl's Caliban a crude caricature."

G — "Go grab Grant's grandma's grotesque green garters, Gloria."

Vocal Progression

Because there are so many short exercises in a vocal warm-up, take time now to review all those just covered. If you can't recall any single one, go back until you can float through the sequence quickly.

Letting Go	Respirating	
Lion		*Exhaling*
Skin Slide	*Inhaling*	Lower Back
Jaw Drop	Nose and Throat	Diaphragm
Full Body Yawn	Upper Chest	Floating Ribs
Shoulder Drops	Floating Ribs	Upper Chest
Inclines	Diaphragm	Nose and Throat
Nods	Lower Back	Full Body Yawn

Sounding	**Isolations**	Hard Palate Drill
Planting	Fish	Cat Lap
Humming	Horse	Tongue Tip Drill
Roller Coaster	Motor Boat	Jungle Heartbeat
String	Lip Drill	Tongue Back Drill
	Fly	Lip Reading
	Snake	Twisters

WHEN AND WHERE TO WARM UP

Should you do these standard physical and vocal warm-up sequences in every single performance situation? No. That won't be possible. But all these exercises have been tested repeatedly. There is nothing kinky here. These are classics used in many acting programs, so you'll start with a sound, basic pattern and sense of progression. If you will persevere, warming up can free your own instrument to respond fully.

> *I know that when I feel strong and my back is*
> *the source of strength, I feel the earth beneath my*
> *feet, I feel something going right up through me,*
> *very strong, clean and washed all the way through.*
> *It is of the utmost importance for one's body*
> *to be so obedient to the impulses that come,*
> *that they obey you.*[9]
>
> **—Vanessa Redgrave**

Members of class should take turns leading the warm-ups here, working in pairs if possible. You don't indisputably know the exercises until you can speak them and guide others through them. The ability to lead this activity is also a skill that every performer wants. Any director should be able to turn to you and say, "Could you lead us in a warm-up?" without your dissolving into jelly. Work briefly from this book, then from note cards with exercise names, and then from memory. When you most need to get a group warmed up, you will probably not have your books or notes with you.

   Edit, vary, or expand an exercise according to the occasion and your own needs. If you're in a crowded room, a quick Prune (Exercise 2.12) isn't possible, physically or emotionally. If you've got two minutes, a complete Here and Now (Exercise 2.11) can't be done. But you can tense and release along the spine and both sides of the torso, even while sitting in a chair, if you work with modifications. And you can think of soothing images, or focus on something in this strange room that isn't strange, but comforting. You can repeat a sound that settles you, even for just a few moments. The secret of warm-ups is in adapting them but not neglecting them.

OFFSTAGE ADAPTATIONS

Just as every situation you encounter in the theatre has some parallel outside, every activity in this chapter has potential offstage use. The Prune is a great muscle relaxer, if you are having trouble sleeping (and if we didn't move on immediately in class, many actors *would* doze off). Sounding may be just the exercise you need prior to a difficult conversation with your parents, especially if your objective is to be viewed as an adult. If you still suffer from a baby voice, it's hard for anyone to listen to you seriously as a grown-up no matter what the other facts of your life may say about you. A Here and Now may help you enjoy the family reunion at hand, and stop dwelling on the fight you had with your girlfriend before vacation, and the paper that will be due (but you know you won't write until) the week after next. It may help you be with your family, so you don't miss the moment. Actors are hardly the only people inclined to become so caught up in their pasts and futures that they tend to overlook the present altogether.

EXERCISE 2.29

WARM-UPS IN REAL LIFE

1. Identify at least three major encounters within the past year when being able to warm up beforehand would have helped you to perform more effectively.

2. Identify three or more average situations—ones that are regular, predictable parts of your life—where warming up could help you to function better.

3. Imagine future major occasions, like those you cited in item 1 above, for which you could plan now to give yourself a sense of control by warming up in preparation.

The body, the voice, and the spirit can all be helped so that they readily respond with warmth to all the potential goodwill waiting for you when you perform, whether as an actor or as yourself.

> *All of us seem to be playing roles in real-life dramas*
> *that we are not only starring in but have been*
> *scripting, too. We are each the author and leading*
> *player in the entertainment called "My Life."* [10]
>
> —SHIRLEY MacLAINE

Notes

1. Ben Bradlee, Jr., "The Enigma Next Door," *Vanity Fair*, February 1989.
2. Jack Kroll, "William Hurt and the Curse of the Spider Man," *Esquire*, October 1986.
3. Liz Smith, "The New Queen of the Screen," *People*, November 3, 1986.
4. Constantin Stanislavski, *An Actor Prepares* (New York: Theatre Arts Books, 1948).
5. John Cottrell, *Laurence Olivier* (Englewood Cliffs, N.J.: Prentice Hall, 1975).
6. Guy Martin, "Harrison Ford and the Jungle of Gloom," *Esquire*, October 1986.
7. "Two Summer Shoot-outs," *Life*, June 1985.
8. Maureen Dowd, "Testing Himself," *New York Times Magazine*, September 28, 1986.
9. Interview by Clive Goodwin, in Hal Burton, *Acting in the Sixties* (London: BBC, 1970).
10. Shirley MacLaine, "Shirley MacLaine Goes Out on a Limb," *TV Guide*, January 17, 1987.

INDIVIDUAL INVENTORY

*Knowing Enough About Yourself
and Your Equipment to
Use Everything You Have*

*If you don't lead a real life and use it,
you lose truth in your work.[1]*
—MEL GIBSON

*The actor's instrument is only himself, and
the more interesting your instrument is, not only
are you going to be remembered, but the
more use you can be put to.[2]*
—RICHARD DREYFUSS

Taking Stock

Actors need to take inventory just like stores do. They need to know their merchandise. And no matter how similar an actor may be to others in small ways, the sum total of that merchandise is individual. No other creature has been put together quite like you. So your Hamlet, your Blanche Du Bois, your Tinker Bell, won't be quite like any other actor's. As comforting as that is, it helps if you have some idea of just *how* yours will be different. This chapter is about checking and counting you.

You won't like all the information you uncover. You may be carrying a self-image that you need to adjust, maybe even transform. But you'll get to know yourself better and feel more as if you live inside your own body. If you have an inflexible vision of what you should be, you'll miss wonderful revelations. If you've picked some god or goddess as the only model you can accept, you'll be devastated. But if you want to act well, you can kid yourself for only so long anyway. There's no point in doing inventory if you don't want to know what's on the shelves.

Knowing Your Instrument

Taking your individual inventory is a challenge because, unlike the merchant, you can't stand back and look objectively at the merchandise. The concert violinist can reverently place his Stradivarius in its case and look at it. The master mechanic can clean up and then go back to look over the engine. The writer can flip through the pages and read the product. As an actor, you *are* the product.

I once worked as an assistant to a brilliant, eccentric, but somewhat out-of-touch professor, who worked herself into a frenzy one day trying to get her students to experiment with new vocal and physical techniques. She shouted during a lecture, ''You each need to go out and play with yourself!'' The whole group fell apart laughing, and she muttered confusedly, ''I mean play with your . . . [interminable pause here] . . . instrument!'' And the class again collapsed. This communication breakdown was a perfect example of the actor's dilemma. The very stuff you need to work with is tied to private matters. So the most innocent suggestion may seem suggestive. And the most professional advice may sound personal.

Your body, your voice, and your mind are your materials for acting effectively offstage and on. Your inventory will be more accurate if you allow yourself the same measured objectivity any craftsman would give to examining the tools of his craft—even when it's just your own thighs you're examining.

BODY AWARENESS

Public interest in the body and health is at an all-time high. Never have so many studied so much about diet and exercise. This awareness is good for an actor, but he needs to move beyond the body-as-machine to body-as-interpretive-instrument. Our focus here will be on the constant interpretive choices you make just by standing, sitting, walking, or gesturing. And on your own particular mannerisms.

There's nothing inherently wrong with a mannerism. The acting profession is packed with successful and mannered artists. Performers like Katharine Hepburn and James Stewart are almost too easy to imitate, their quirks are so pronounced. But you want to be aware that you have them, and that sometimes they are distracting to the observer. No one wants to lose a role (a client, a scholarship, an interview, a job, a date) because of a nervous gesture or the way you shift your weight. These are tiny things, but they may get in the way of an audience's capacity to believe you. And they can be modified.

Check your own body in these overlapping categories: habits, adaptations, and cultural binding.

Habits

When you are in no particular mood, simply passing through the day, what choices are you most likely to make? No matter how these personal tendencies first came about, they are now habitual—happening without thought or effort, automatically. Habits can be subdivided into *still* (you caught in repose, in a photograph) and *active* (you caught in motion, on film).

Consider both the whole package and isolated body parts, any of which may acquire a life of its own. From foot-tapping to knuckle-cracking, from teeth-grinding to shoulder-shrugging, an isolated movement may be a response to stress or just an unconscious, acquired taste. Some heads may lean in suddenly on every key word spoken (''chicken neck,'' many actors call it), others tilt to one side when listening, toss their hair back suddenly, nod repeatedly, or sink down so far into the torso that the neck disappears. And this is just the start of a *head* list.

Adaptations

When you add stress or stimuli to an otherwise average day, how does your body respond? Alone or in a group, as you're touching someone or being touched, as your mood changes, how do your responses change? Note yourself adjusting to *space invasions*. You have an amount of space that you like to keep between you and others. It is as if you carry an invisible bubble around you. It may be larger or smaller (or more or less flexible) than someone else's. It is your desired distance for most interaction. If you're on a mountaintop or in a crowded elevator, your bubble adjusts in size because you know what to expect. But your bubble bursts and you become unhinged when someone unexpectedly invades what you regard as personal space.

Space Invasions sounds like a sci-fi horror flick title, and some people do respond with genuine horror to the most accidental violation of their bubble, forgetting that it's invisible. Others are mindless invaders, forgetting that just because they like bear hugs and pats on the fanny doesn't mean everyone craves that kind of contact.

You can invade another's space by moving in very close without touching (as in certain South American cultures, in which people like only three or four inches between them for conversation), by enveloping or trapping them, by grabbing hold, by gentle touching in an area the recipient considers off limits, or simply by staring so that your eyes invade. Omitting overtly violent or sexual moves (in our culture someone three or four inches away may indeed have one or both of these in mind), there is still a wide range of invasions. It is easy not to share the same covert limits as someone else.

Cultural Binding

Any group whose members share the same behavior is called a culture. Behavioral scientists call it *binding* when you're tied so strongly to the group that you have trouble breaking away from group limitations, even when you need to do so. You can be bound to a culture like a prisoner bound to a stake. All of us are group members. Membership not only helps define who you are, but can give you a sense of pride, especially in your heritage. You may be bound emotionally, even spiritually, but you may also be unaware of binding by geography, conditioning, age, sex, family, and personal interests. Such binding becomes a problem when you want to be believably cast as a member of another group.

Go through the list of questions on the following pages. When the question seems to make no sense or you draw a blank, get up and move around. Take a look in a full-length mirror. Skip over questions that remain puzzling, but jot down responses when you think you know how you fit into the category. Study yourself. Ask people who've been around you for a while. If you haven't got a clue now, give yourself permission to start noticing. It's time to do some research, and what could be a more interesting research topic than yourself? You don't even have to go to the library. You *are* the library. Start watching other people in repose and in action to see ways in which others use their bodies like or unlike you.

Expect to be overwhelmed by more questions than you can answer and more categories than you can immediately comprehend, but also expect everything to get easier and clearer the more accustomed you get to studying you.

HABITS

Answer as many as possible of the following questions about you *still* and you *active*.

Still

Standing

1. Where is your weight placed in your typical silhouette? Which part of your body really carries the load?

2. Where are you centered? Does energy start from one spot?

3. How close to symmetrical is your stance? Do you lean, cross your arms or legs, or favor one side?

4. What is your posture like? Does it vary? Do you slouch?

5. Does any part of your body seem to dominate or draw focus?

Sitting

1. How slouched or erect are you when sitting or reclining? How much do you sink or release into the chair or floor?

2. Do you lean? In what direction?

3. Are your legs or arms crossed? How tightly? Do you appear to be covering yourself anywhere? Are you sitting on any part of yourself? Your leg? A hand?

4. How much space are you taking? Do you thrust out or exhibit any part of yourself? How open and expansive is the spread of your arms and legs?

5. What curves are present? In the spine? The appendages? The tilt of the head? In more than one direction?

Expression

1. What is the typical look you tend to have on your face? And the three runners-up? What range of facial change do you habitually go through?

2. Is your eye contact with others usually direct or not? How intense? How long before looking away? Do you squint, narrow your eyes, droop your lids, or open your eyes wider?

3. Any changes in other parts of the face? Do your eyebrows move? Do you wiggle your nose? Purse your lips? Suck in your cheeks?

4. Do expressions generally linger, or disappear abruptly? How are they timed? Does your smile appear suddenly, or slowly expand?

5. Are you easy to read or somewhat poker-faced? Are your expressions pronounced or subtle and muted? How lively and open is your face?

Figure 3–1 Habits (Sitting)
What information do you convey simply sitting still?

Active

Tempo and Rhythm

1. Are your movements fast, slow, medium? What is your basic rate?

2. How constant is your tempo? Are you fairly predictable or do you change radically?

3. Do you land with full weight, or glide, making only minimal contact with the ground? Are your steps heavy or light?

4. Do you punctuate or stress each move with any part of the body as you walk? Could someone tap your movement patterns like playing a drum?

5. What is the relationship between your speed and your rhythms? To what extent do they affect each other? Are you fast and erratic? Slow and steady? What combination?

Motion

1. When walking, sitting, or leaning, where do you make contact with the surface below? Is the contact flat and solid, or gradual and curved?

2. Do you prepare to move (shifting weight, adjusting clothing, swaying slightly) or do you just take off? When you stop, is there a recovery period of similar adjustments? Do you settle (or even squirm) into stillness, or just land and stop?

3. What kind of support do you give yourself? Do you reach out with your hands to furniture before you sit, lean on walls or corners as you round them, grab railings on stairways?

4. Is your pattern of movement fluid, smooth, and effortless, or is it jerky and labored? How obvious is the changing of gears as you accelerate or change direction?

5. Are the moves straight and assertive? Do you face your target directly and shoot for it, or approach indirectly? Do you ease into furniture sideways, sidle up to people, curve across a room, insinuate yourself into a space?

Gestures

1. Are your arm and hand movements expansive and wide? Or do you work tight to the torso and economically?

2. How frequently do you gesture? Can you sit on your hands without going crazy with the need to use them? Or are your gestures occasional and selective?

3. Do you have moves that are predictable and repetitive? How standard are they? Shared by many, or unique to you? Do you have props you always seem to be playing with?

4. Do you literally demonstrate your feelings or experiences physically? Could someone who doesn't speak English figure out what you are saying from the mimetic pictures you draw? Or are your hands more likely to move in abstract, less literal ways?

5. Do your shoulders get engaged? Do you lean in to make points? Does your head join in? How connected are your gestures to the torso? How free or independent from the rest?

EXERCISE 3.2

ADAPTATIONS

Identify how you react when external elements change.

Public vs. Private Behavior

Do you react differently when the crowds come? When the focus of a large group of people turns to you? Do you find yourself shifting posture, relating to furniture in a different way, walking more or less lightly, changing your timing? Are you consistently yourself in intimate groups, or are you one of those people who only really come alive when there is an audience?

Space Invasions (Initiating and Receiving)

What if actual physical contact with others is involved? Are you more likely to be an invader and receiver? To initiate physical contact? What is your own desired distance? How unsettled are you when others close in? Do you adapt well? And are you more likely to touch a particular place on another person?

Mood Shifts (Up and Down)

To what extent does your physical life express your emotional one? Is the receipt of good or bad news likely to show in your body language while you adjust to what you've heard? Does the kind of day you're having affect your posture, eye contact, the freedom of your gestures? Does intense feeling explode into movement of some kind? Or are you unlikely to change at all? To mask shifts in feelings?

EXERCISE 3.3

CULTURAL BINDING

Try to identify these influences on your physical life.

Geography

Does everyone guess where you were born? Even if they don't hear you speak? Do people know you are from the city or the country without having to ask?

Family

Is your ancestry obvious? Do you share a set of moves with other people whose parents were the same nationality, religion, or any other dominant affiliation?

Conditioning

Do you send out the information that you have been told for years not to assert yourself in groups lest you be thought overbearing? Or do you signal that you've been taught to push, shove, shout, get seen, grab attention—whatever it takes to get what you deserve? How evident is the rewarded behavior and the punished behavior that was part of your home, school, or church?

Interests

Can others tell your special skills and favorite activities? That you are a dancer, athlete, pianist, body builder, scholar? Have you picked up all the trademarks, along with the love of the activity?

Age

Do people get your age right or wrong, and can this be because of how you carry yourself?

Sex

On a scale of extreme sexual stereotypes, where are you? Do you fall into a traditional masculine/feminine image? An androgynous mix? Neutral or ambiguous? How flexible and changeable are you?

I Am What I Am

If your emotional response is like mine, you may look at a list like the Body Awareness Checklist that follows, say "I am what I am!" and reject the idea of changing. But remember that adjusting and changing are not the same thing. The truth is cultural binding limits your casting. If you're "a nice Jewish girl from the Bronx," you are three wonderful things. But imagine yourself cast as Antigone, one of the great tragic heroines. She is "a nice Greek girl from Thebes." The performer cast in the role must achieve a classic, universal quality. Too much Bronx in her stance, gestures, or eye contact, and there's no way the audience will successfully place her in the ancient world. You cannot get in the way of the audience's imagination. You want to *unleash* that imagination.

So how can you win? Learn to recognize your own cultural binding, and modify it when appropriate, but don't lose it! First, you never want to lose your own heritage, because it is precious and important. Few things are worse than going home and finding you have forgotten how to be at home there. Second, the minute you wipe out all the Bronx from your body and voice, guess what the next part to come along will require? Guess what kind of accent and physical life? And guess who will have conditioned herself out of consideration? What you want is control and flexibility. Being other people does not need to mean losing who you are.

EXERCISE 3.4

USING THE BODY AWARENESS CHECKLIST

Make a copy of the worksheet that follows and jot down notes to help you remember information gathered about your physical life. If terms are not clear, go back over that section in this chapter. There are probably far more categories here than you can handle. Fill in what you can. See if a clear physical profile emerges. If there are a lot of empty spaces, promise yourself to start observing you closer in those areas.

BODY AWARENESS CHECKLIST
HABITS (STILL)

Standing	**Sitting**	**Expression**
1. Carriage _____	1. Release _____	1. Typical _____
2. Center _____	2. Leaning _____	2. Contact _____
3. Symmetry _____	3. Crossing _____	3. Parts _____
4. Posture _____	4. Space _____	4. Timing _____
5. Focus _____	5. Curves _____	5. Clarity _____

HABITS (ACTIVE)

Tempo/Rhythm	**Motion**	**Gestures**
1. Rate _____	1. Contact _____	1. Expansiveness _____
2. Changes _____	2. Preparation/Recovery	2. Frequency _____
3. Weight _____	3. Support _____	3. Predictability _____
4. Punctuation _____	4. Pattern _____	4. Demonstration _____
5. Relationship _____	5. Assertiveness _____	5. Connection _____

ADAPTATIONS

Groups	**Contact**	**Mood**
Public Behavior _____	Receiving Invasion _____	Up _____
Private Behavior _____	Initiating Invasion _____	Down _____

CULTURAL BINDING

Geography	**Family**	**Conditioning**
Interests	**Age**	**Sex**

So far you've looked at your offstage life and your potential casting. Take another look at the list, imagining that you've already been cast and are beginning to put together a characterization. Pick any role you ever wanted to play. Ask yourself about the character's center, gestural range, personal bubble, adaptations, and the rest. Find concrete ways of building a full performance. Consider the range of options open to you. Find ways of building on pure intuition with tangible technical choices.

> *I usually collect a lot of details or characteristics,*
> *and then I find a creature swimming about*
> *in the middle of them.*[3]
> —LAURENCE OLIVIER

Imitation for Double Awareness

Actors are observers. They ride the bus or wait in line and watch. They note a walk, a nervous gesture, a set of eyebrows knitting close together. They use the people they see as a limitless encyclopedia. They store, translate, imitate, and interpret what they've observed. And often they learn more about themselves in the process. Actors develop that highest form of flattery, imitation, to an art form.

> *If an actor can find the personal rhythm of a character, he's home free. And one of the best ways to do that is to follow a person down the street, unbeknownst to him. Pick up his walk, imitate it and continue it, even after he's out of sight. As you're doing it, observe what's happening to you. By zeroing in on a guy's personal rhythm, you'll find that you've become a different person.[4]*
> —DUSTIN HOFFMAN

Physical Life Project

Everyone will be a spy in this next assignment. Do this research without consulting anyone. You'll be observing, on the sly, two other actors in class for about two weeks while actual class time is devoted to other activities. You are capturing the physical life of two other people.

Your mission is to observe these two performers in as many different contexts as you can: officially "acting," just "being," in groups, alone, one to one, calm, excited, going through their behavioral repertoire.

Step 1.   You draw a slip of paper which will have on it two names which you will show only to the teacher. These same two names will also have been drawn by another classmate, but for a while you're on your own. Your espionage career is launched.

Step 2.   Everyone comes to class prepared to complete the following self-imitation exercise, designed to help the people who are observing you.

EXERCISE 3.5

SELF-IMITATION

Place two chairs at the front of the room, leaving some space between them. Both chairs face the audience. Everything else you fill in, drawing on your past or imagination. Carry with you as props whatever everyday objects you usually carry.

1. Enter an imaginary classroom.
2. Look for a place to sit.
3. Move past imaginary others to sit down.
4. Once seated, change your mind and move to the other chair.
5. Interact with an imagined classmate.
6. Take notes on a lecture or demonstration.
7. Attempt to get the teacher's attention, but fail.
8. Do something interesting!
9. Let something in your circumstances make you angry.
10. Leave the imaginary classroom.

You'll wish to run through this sequence a few times before doing it in class, so that it comes easily and believably. Use a situation drawn mostly from your own life. If the class isn't made up primarily of undergraduates, any shared activity (grocery-store trip, sale at the mall, some kind of registration hassle) can be substituted.

Remember, you are completely yourself in a typical but intensified situation. Make no effort to entertain or charm the audience. In fact, let yourself be boring. If your concentration is complete, even in this simple set of tasks, you will probably be fascinating. Questions to consider:

1. **Enter the classroom.**

How large is it?

How light or dark?

Cold or warm?

How many people in here?

Where are the authority figures located?

How closely are the authority figures observing?

What time of day is it?

Are you late or on time?

Where have you been just before this?

What is your attitude toward this class?

What do you expect to happen here today?

What are your plans once the period is over?

2. **Look for a place to sit.**

   How crowded is it already?

   Is your favorite place gone?

   Do you hope to sit next to someone in particular?

   How close to starting or long past starting is the lecture?

   Was there a crowd jammed up at the door?

   How easygoing or rude were they?

   How relieved or indifferent are you to have just arrived?

3. **Move past others to sit down.**

   How difficult is this task?

   How narrow are the aisles?

   How cooperative are those you need to pass?

   Do you have to ask anyone to clear your path?

   How self-conscious are you?

   How likely is it that you're being observed?

4. **Once seated, change your mind, move someplace else.**

   What is your motive for moving?

   Something puts you off where you are?

   Something attracts you over there?

   Something beyond your control?

   How much of an endeavor is this going to be?

5. **Interact with another classmate.**

   Do you need this person's help?

   Does he or she need or want yours?

   Is it related to class, or personal?

   How much do you enjoy this interaction?

   How well do you know this person?

Remember, this is silent. Say real words and hear real words, but silently, so that to the audience it looks like the sound has been turned off but everything else is realistic. Make us read your lips if we want to know exactly what's being said.

6. **Take notes on the lecture or demonstration.**

   How do you go about getting out notebook and something to write with?

   Do you need any other supplies?

   What is your attitude toward material presented?

   Is it clear, fascinating, obscure, boring?

   How urgent is your need to understand this stuff?

   How crucial is this class to your survival?

7. **Attempt to get teacher's attention and fail.**

   Why do you make the effort?

   What exactly do you do?

   What's going on up there that makes the prof ignore you?

   How aggressively do you pursue this objective before giving up?

   How devastating or inconsequential is being ignored to you?

   How often does this happen to you?

8. **Do something interesting.**

This part is up to you. You can have some fun with it or agonize over it. Try to find the something interesting from the scene you have created, so that it moves organically out of the situation. It may be an extreme reaction to being ignored, or a mischievous impulse springing from you or motivated by someone else in the imaginary room. There are infinite possibilities.

Actors, especially at auditions, are always being given impossible tasks like "Do something interesting." The best solution is always to go back into the situation instead of worrying about imposing something clever from the outside. These tasks are chances to explore your own creativity and capacity to discover everything a situation has to offer.

9. **Let something make you angry.**

   The teacher?

   The person next to you?

The chair?

Your broken pencil?

Your frustration at what just happened?

An entirely new atrocity?

10. **Leave the classroom.**

Let's assume the bell has not rung, so class is not over. You *decide* to leave.

How has your life changed since you came in here?

What do you know now that you didn't before?

What do you care more or less about?

How much of what you hoped for has happened?

How much do you care who notices you leave?

How much do you want to make a disturbance?

What is the next objective you are shooting for?

Interlude   Now, while the class officially turns its attention to other matters, embark on your spy mission. Start by making comparisons between your two subjects and yourself. Use the checklist to help you organize your observations.

Step 3.   After you've been working alone for a while, your teacher will reveal the name of the other student who is spying on the same twosome you are. Meet your partner and compare notes. Begin working together, checking in with each other daily, alerting each other to new developments in the case. ("Did you notice how X stands when he's coming on to somebody?" "Look at how Z's expressions change when she talks to the teacher." "I think he's going to be at Y's party tonight. See if you notice anything different when he's just hanging out, having a few beers.") The research should be enjoyable, even addicting.

Interlude   As the time to present your findings in class approaches, you may have reservations about "doing" another actor. Will it seem cruel or condescending? No. When the time comes, everyone enjoys this activity. The observees get so much new information (remember all the blank spots on your self-observation sheet?) that they're actually grateful. Why not just videotape actors and have them watch themselves? Because they don't see what you see. Early in their training, actors watch videos of themselves, focus on their noses, moan at the size of their hips, and discover resemblances to Aunt Harriet they never noticed before. Their vision is scattered and personal. (Video can, however, be a great tool later on, once some self-awareness sinks in.) The real, valuable lessons for your subjects will come from seeing their physical tendencies through you. It helps objectify the experience and systematize the information. The habits themselves are what come to the foreground.

Remember to identify what you see without passing judgment. You will not go into class and say, "You have this weird walk and this bizarre gesture you do," but rather something like, "You land heavily with the full foot, especially when you're preoccupied. And your right fist sometimes opens and closes when you grasp for ideas or words." No mannerisms are inherently positive or negative. They just are.

It helps if some written report is turned in and eventually read by the observees. (See Appendix C, "Physical Life Observation," an optional, more streamlined version of the checklist, with more room to write.) If words fail you, you may draw (stick figures sitting, a facial expression, a diagram of a series of gestures) to clarify points you want to make.

At some point in the work with your partner you will decide which of you will be the Primary Presenter of which observee, because one of you will probably have more of a knack for one subject than the other. You and your partner (A and B) have drawn names of two other actors (C and D), but even though you're both working on both, each of you will gradually take more of the responsibility for one of them. The Primary Presenter will be the first one to demonstrate what he has discovered.

Step 4.   Results are due and this is what happens:

EXERCISE 3.6

IMITATION SEQUENCE

1. Let's say A is specializing on C and B is specializing on D. A gets up and walks through a silent imitation while the class calls out their guesses. A ignores the guesses until someone gets it right (and shouts "C!"). A nods to show that the guess was correct but continues until the planned imitation is completed.

2. A then restarts the imitation, this time adding narration ("When you walk into a room you always look around and then down at the floor. You tug your book bag back up onto one shoulder and walk in, putting your weight on the balls of your feet and bouncing slightly, keeping your eyes on

the floor . . ."). The execution of the imitation is exactly the same, but this time A is telling C the details while doing them.

3. B now joins A up front and adds any pertinent details A may have left out ("You often swallow just before starting to move into a room and you place both hands around the handle of the bookbag when you tug at it . . ."). B may also share an area of disagreement with A or a different observation ("I really think you put your weight more on the outside of both feet, not toward the front").

4. A and B now talk their way through the list on the observation sheet, making sure each relevant category is covered, if possible, through both demonstration and description.

5. Once the work on C is completed, A and B reverse roles and cover D. B first does the imitation silently, then with narration; A adds details for D; then the partners once again work their way through the list. It is the same procedure, but with B leading the way this time.

6. The class may wish to add the occasional two cents, and C and D may have a few questions based on the information they have gotten.

After a few imitations have been completed for the class and the procedure is clear, it is possible that only parts 1 through 3 may be done in front of the whole class. Breaking into smaller groups to go through the checklist can save a lot of time and still give both observers and observees the benefit of the experience.*

ALTERNATIVE IMITATIONS

If time doesn't allow the full spy exercise, any number of reduced versions are possible where both the act and the observation are abbreviated. Classmates might be imitated

1. walking to the front of the room and writing names on the board.

2. raising a hand and participating in class discussion in a typical manner.

3. performing in any other assignment presented in class so far.

*Note to teachers: After watching a few complete demonstrations all together, the class can benefit from working in smaller groups, although for this to work it will take some figuring on your part pairing up partners. Actors rarely shortchange each other on this assignment. They feel a strong responsibility for a complete and systematic observation. Your only real monitoring need will be in checking the extremely subjective or naive observation and to suggest other alternatives.

4. sharing brief examples of the biggest differences between their onstage and offstage personas.

5. doing just a few assigned categories from the checklist, instead of the whole thing.

Smaller imitations can also be used to warm up for the big one. While some of the suspense is lost, it can help actors check in with the class at various stages in their observations. If the class stays together for a year or more, additional imitations can be blended in, adding layers of sophistication.

Imitation Pay-Offs

What has all this accomplished?

1. You've looked at yourself in quite a few physical categories, and have begun to get a sense of the kind of figure you cut in space and how you use the space around you.

2. You've presented yourself in an everyday situation to the class, demonstrating basic acting principles firsthand. You've performed realistically with a heightened reality.

3. You've observed other actors (and others have observed you) going through self-imitation to get precise information and personal insight.

4. You've spied on your subjects in every possible situation to sharpen your sense of detail, of nuance of movement, and of sophistication regarding the body.

5. You've partnered with someone, making all the negotiations and compromises that always need to happen between sets of actors.

6. Two people closely watching you have helped you recognize, for better or worse, many of your own tendencies.

7. You've been able not only to watch, but to organize what you see, so that a system of physical characterization is available to you.

8. You've given a gift to other actors by mirroring them, so they experience a friendly but revealing reflection.

9. You've experienced the sensation of performing with both involvement and objectivity, of becoming someone else, but then removing yourself and describing the event. You've maintained that balance, essential for an actor, between being onstage and in the audience at the same time.

10. An exchange of mutual benefit has happened between a group of actors starting to trust and support one another.

Applying Body Awareness

What do you do with this information now? It depends on how close or distant your ''mirror'' was to what you'd expected. How pleased or distressed are you by what has just been reflected back to you? A beginning acting class aims to enlighten, not necessarily to change. Ask yourself if any of your mannerisms interfere with the effectiveness of your communication. Don't do anything without reflecting. What you communicate may be just fine, and you now have self-awareness to add to self-acceptance. Or you may choose to gradually proceed with some changes. If you want to change, you can apply some of the skills you developed in imitating others.

VOCAL AWARENESS

Body work comes before voice work because it's easier. You know your body better. You can see it and feel it. You can look at most of it, even while you read this page. The rest you can see in the mirror. The family album is full of you in various sizes and shapes. Now imagine the family *voice* album. The body is out there to be counted. You have known yours for years; you may not like it, but you know it. The voice can't be seen or touched. It's hiding. Your own voice may still be a stranger to you.

The result? A whole society of people who have no idea how they sound. The world is full of women who spend many hours daily working to look breath-taking but still sound like Bambi; of men who pump enough iron to look like warrior chiefs but still talk like Thumper. They don't seem to notice. It's as if they think like a silent film.

> *You see women who are absolutely stunning, in $10,000 worth of clothes and jewelry. And they are at Spago [an exclusive Los Angeles restaurant] and they say, ''Well, I'd like a prosciutto pizza'' [said in a Minnie Mouse voice] and you think, Oh shit, what did they waste their money on* this *for [pointing at some imaginary Balenciaga gown]? I think it's very ugly. I mind it very much.*[5]
>
> —KATHLEEN TURNER

Countless crucial moments depend on the voice. Onstage, the action of the play stops, an actor sits on the edge of the stage and beautifully speaks a soliloquy that may be the heart of the whole evening. Offstage, speaking on the phone, reading aloud to a group, talking with a lover in the dark of night, or encouraging hope in a friend whose eyes are closed in anguish, over and over again the full expressiveness of the voice is essential to acting your own life.

Body work also tends to precede voice because the body *houses* the voice. If the body is free and aware, the chances are better for the voice to follow. The good news is that much body awareness is transferable. The bad news is that you probably have a lot of catching up to do. You may be starting with twenty years of voice habits and no voice *thought*. But you can work on your voice in the grocery store, the car, the shower—wherever you have the inclination. First, some basic terms.

Quality

Your voice has a tone and texture unlike any other. Quality is the feeling of the sound you produce. It's determined largely by a combination of surfaces inside you (facial bones, nose, sinus cavities, mouth, pharynx, chest) where sound resonates. Voices are traditionally described as harsh, mellow, thin, full, light, dark, husky, nasal, strident, resonant, large, small, breathy, hoarse—or in more metaphoric terms, like silken or velvet.

Tempo and Rhythm

You have a rate of speaking and a stress pattern within that rate. The relationship between speed and emphasis has been explored in the body section of this chapter. The tempo and rhythm of the voice use the same principle, frequently with surprisingly little connection to the timing of the body's physical movement.

Articulation

How crisply or precisely do you form sounds? Articulation is determined by how your consonants are completed, where the articulation organs are put (placement), how long the contact is sustained (extent), how much force is behind it (pressure), and whether your vocal folds are engaged (vibration). When someone says he can't hear you, most of the time he actually means that he can't *understand* you because of your poor articulation.

Pronunciation

How close to standard is the way you speak? How close to the speech heard most often in performance, which does not seem to come from a particular, recognizable region or social group? Some confuse pronunciation with articulation. Pronunciation has nothing to do with how precisely you say something, but rather with how closely the way you say it resembles the way most other people say it. The standard pronunciation of a word may actually be quite slurred.

Pitch

Your manner of speech could be written out on sheet music, identifying the various notes employed from the top to the bottom of your own register. Your tendency to repeat certain pitch patterns is like having your own theme song. Research shows that people respond more positively to the lower pitches, and yet most speakers restrict themselves to the upper half of their range.

Volume

Most of us are aware of tendencies toward loud or soft (Are you someone who is always asked to speak up? Someone who is always shushed?), but it takes a sophisticated understanding of projection to adjust to varying listeners and spaces.

Word Choice

Do you tend to use primarily complex, four-syllable words? Or explicit, four-letter ones? Or both, depending on the occasion? Because any event can be described with infinite variety, the choices you make strongly define you.

Nonverbals

No one utters words alone. There are countless noises or spurts of sound beyond recognizable language. These express emotion beyond words. Nonverbals add color and interest to vocal life. Oddly enough, beginning actors frequently fail to use them in scene work, in part because the playwright usually leaves it up to the performer to add them. A scene will often seem too *clean* to be real, but once sprinkled with nonverbals it will breathe with a whole new believability. Nonverbals are used heavily off-stage, especially when we're surprised and thrown off by the cue we've just received. They help fill our evaluation period while we recover. ("Hmmmm . . . I . . . uhhh . . . *[sigh]* . . . think we . . . ummmm . . . *[tiny laugh]* . . . need to talk about this.")

Influences

You can look at your vocal life from the same perspectives we used for your physical life.

Habits: What are the characteristics of your voice in standard, low-key, daily circumstances?

Adaptations: How does it change in public, when your bubble alters or your mood swings?

Cultural binding: Which of the influences of geography, family, conditioning, interest, age, and sex figure strongest in what other people hear from you?

The Voice Awareness Checklist that follows the next set of exercises will help you remember all these terms and categories.

EXERCISE 3.7

BASIC PARTS OF A VOCAL LIFE

Unlike that for the body, the simplest vocabulary regarding voice may be unfamiliar or puzzling to you. You may need to track down some of the terms below in the dictionary. In each of the following categories, jot down one– or two–word responses as they come to mind.

Quality

1. What is the basic tone or texture of your voice?
2. What adjectives or abstract words best describe the feeling of your voice?
3. Where do you primarily resonate?

Tempo

1. What is your standard rate? Fast, slow, medium, or somewhere between?
2. How does your vocal tempo connect with your physical movement?
3. Are you constant or do you use different tempos? When do you change?

Rhythm

1. Do you really stress certain words or give all relatively equal value?
2. What kinds of phrasing patterns do you use to separate parts of your statements? Where do you take pauses or breaks?
3. Is the overall impression smooth or jerky and erratic? How fluid is your speech? What does it sound like if you try to capture your own timing by tapping out what you consider typical?

For *tempo* and *rhythm* together: What does it sound like if you try to tap out your own timing like beating a drum?

Articulation

1. How precisely do you shape each sound? Is it crisp? Do you mumble? Or have lazy speech?
2. Are there particular words and sounds that always give you trouble? Which challenge you most?
3. Do you drop consonants or syllables? Swallow endings? Which sounds do you tend to omit?

Pronunciation

1. Is your way of pronouncing words standard? If not, how far off? In what way? Regional? Ethnic? Idiosyncratic?
2. How easy is it for you to slide in and out of various accents, dialects, mimicry? How sharp is your ear?
3. Are you aware of substituting one sound for another? Which ones?

Pitch

1. Is your voice higher or lower than most people's in the range used in everyday speech? Where is your basic placement?
2. Do you have a regular melody pattern, so that graphing your pitch would show repetitions?
3. How close to the top and bottom of your range do you venture? What restrictions do you place on pitch? Are you locked into one half? Do you explore without strain? What is your range?

Volume

1. Are you basically loud, soft, or where on the continuum? Do you project or fill a room effortlessly?
2. Does your voice seem to have power or are you aware of needing to push in large space?

3. Under what circumstances does your volume knob get adjusted? Are you sensitive to being too loud or soft for others' comfort? How adjustable are you?

Word Choice

1. Is your working vocabulary relatively large? Is your language formal, casual, full of slang, big words, fad words, meaningless phrases?

2. How do you arrange your words—in sentences or thought clusters? Verbs first? Non-sentences? Your typical syntax?

3. Are certain words and phrases definitely yours? Specific vocabulary choices (like computer language or theatre terms) used no matter what the circumstances? Do you show a fondness for certain kinds of images? Personal favorites? Your own lingo?

Nonverbals

1. How many stalling sounds do you make when you are pondering a question? What kinds?

2. How likely are you to sigh, groan, growl, moan, chuckle, pop your lips, or yawn audibly? To hum, whistle little snatches of tunes, or make percussive sounds? Which sounds dominate your communication?

3. What is you laughter like? Squeals of delight? Guffaws? Snorts? Does it gurgle up like a pot boiling over? A sudden, brief explosion? Little titters?

VOICE AWARENESS CHECKLIST

HABITS

Quality	**Tempo**	**Rhythm**
1. Tone _____	1. Rate _____	1. Stress _____
2. Description _____	2. Connections _____	2. Pausing _____
3. Resonance _____	3. Change _____	3. Fluidity _____
Articulation	**Pronunciation**	**Pitch**
1. Precision _____	1. Standard _____	1. Placement _____
2. Challenges _____	2. Ear _____	2. Melody Pattern _____
3. Omissions _____	3. Substitutions _____	3. Range _____

Volume	**Word Choice**	**Nonverbals**
1. Projection _____	1. Vocabulary _____	1. Stalling _____
2. Power _____	2. Syntax _____	2. Dominance _____
3. Sensitivity _____	3. Favorites _____	3. Laugh _____

ADAPTATIONS

Groups _____	Contact _____	Mood _____

CULTURAL BINDING

Geography _____	Family _____	Conditioning _____
Interests _____	Age _____	Sex _____

Noticing voices starts for almost all of us much later than noticing bodies. Try these awareness exercises.

EXERCISE 3.8

USING THE VOCAL AWARENESS CHECKLIST

Use the Vocal Awareness Checklist exactly as you did the body chart. Analyze yourself, then listen to others, using what you hear and imagine when putting together a character so that you *hear* the character speak. Sharpen your skills with imitation each time you recognize a new vocal twist.

EXERCISE 3.9

RESONATORS

The sound of the voice is strongly influenced by the place where someone resonates. Here are dominant locations and the resulting almost stereotypical sounds:

Head: ''Heidi's head voice gives me heartburn and a headache.''
Mask: ''Max's mask makes for major magnification.''

Nose: "Norm's nasality and neckties are noticeably nerdish."
Sinuses: "Selma's sound search settles sharply in her sinuses."
Mouth: "Thelma's throat thrashes, throttles and throbs."
Pharynx: "Phil's FM fullness comes from his pharynx."
Chest: "Charles' chest sound challenges, charms, and takes charge."

EXERCISE 3.10

CLASSIC VOICES

Use the same approach to this list of standard voice descriptions. Start close to the stereotype the line suggests, then move away to subtler variations. There will be some inevitable overlap with the resonator list.
Harsh: "Hey, Harry, how come Helga hates your hide, huh?"
Mellow: "May tomorrow mean more music and magical memories."
Thin: "Think thankful thoughts throughout your thrashing, Theodore."
Full: "Ferdinand's final fanfare filled and overflowed the farthest foothills."
Light: "Lovely Lili looks luminous in lace and lurid in lamé."
Dark: "Don't dare doublecross Dolores or you die."
Husky: "Hey, hot stuff, how's about holding hands?"
Nasal: "Nadine is nowhere near normal."
Strident: "So far, season sales simply suck, Sam."
Resonant: "Raoul reveled in Rio with the ravishing Ramona."
Large: "Laurence loves to laugh and longs to live."
Small: "Silly, shy Suzy sat stiffly at sorority sing-along."
Breathy: "Baby wants a big blue Buick, boys."
Hoarse: "Watching Harry's horrible Hamlet hurt. It gave me a hernia."

EXERCISE 3.11

AROUND TOWN

Find examples of extremes in each category and on each item on the Vocal Awareness Checklist while on trips to the bank, the grocery store, a restaurant or bar. Learn to recognize when you are hearing an especially low voice or a distinct regional pattern.

MOSTS AND LEASTS

Who in class has the highest and lowest voices? Who is loudest and softest? Work your way through the list. If there are disagreements, discuss differences in the way you hear people. Have an election with winners in the following categories:

Quality: most mellow, huskiest, most nasal, breathiest, most strident
Tempo: fastest, slowest, most varied, most consistent
Rhythm: most predictable, heaviest contrasts, most fluid, least expected pauses
Articulation: most crisp, most slurred, least consistent
Pronunciation: most standard, most unusual, best ear, most regional
Pitch: highest, lowest, most use of range, least use of range, clearest melody pattern
Volume: loudest, softest, most varied
Word choice: most formal, most casual, most idioms
Nonverbals: most distinct laugh, most stalling sounds, most unusual nonverbals, least use of nonverbals

Announce the winners with much applause and fanfare for all recipients.

DO THE TEACHER

You observe the teacher (and any teaching assistants) long and hard day after day. Try to capture their vocal lives. Work as a class trying to top or outdo each other, referring back to the list so you don't just mimic but identify what you've done. Try to do other members of the faculty as well.

CELEBRITIES

Who in the class does a celebrity voice? Everyone try your best one and let the natural mimics do several. Then go through the chart and state what happened when the new voice was created. Identify the physiological changes which create the new voice.

VOICE–OVERS

The following are standard voices used by people who work in commercials and narration. The list represents our own cultural stereotypes. We recognize each one after a few words of dialogue—a necessity since radio spots are brief. The more of these and other voices you have, the more usable you are to a recording studio or agency. Try each. Consider taping them.

You probably have more voices in you than you think. Try to identify vocabulary, what you do to achieve any of these sounds:

tough guy (detective, sergeant)	AM radio frantic announcer	fairy tale characters
starlet	FM radio mellow announcer	Dracula
sick person (cold, sore throat, fever, headache)	farmer	witches
cowboy	country (C&W)	Impersonations:
snob	deity	movie stars
wimp	romantic	comics
executive	vivacious	politicians
secretary	little kid	Dialects:
homemaker	adolescent	Regional American
cultured	grandparent	British Isles
sexy	old–timer	Middle Eastern
greaser	animals	European
airhead	Santa Claus	Slavic
	Disney characters	Asian

Vocal Life Project

This time you're not a spy, you're an investigative reporter. Your subjects know you're after them. You might draw new names or keep the old ones, depending on the time available. In either case, build the vocal work on sound physical observations. If time allows, everyone in class might read the same paragraph aloud and describe the same event, so you have a ready comparison of the group's different vocal lives. Like any good reporter, you'll uncover and even invent ways of studying these voices, but here are some standards.

1. Call them on the phone. Experience the voice in isolation.

2. Interview them on tape and study it, replaying each phase until it's yours.

3. Tape them when they perform in class, so you can hear the differences between regular conversation and acting.

4. Determine other voices that are similar—not only among classmates, but among teachers, well-known actors, and other public figures.

5. If possible, listen to someone from these actors' families, hometowns, or any social groups you suspect may have a binding influence.

Here are two possible ways to approach this assignment, one solo and one with a partner.

Solo Vocal Imitation

Come up with five sentences that this person speaks or probably would speak. Try to capture the person in a variety of circumstances and moods. *Presentation:* Make an entrance as the person and let your "character" be present physically before you speak. Introduce your "self," say the five sentences, and make an exit.

Partner Vocal Imitation

Use the same basic rehearsal process as the Physical Life assignment, only this time you're putting together a *scene* in which both of your observees appear. Where might these two meet? What would they be likely to talk about? What kinds of conflicts might be present? What strategies and tactics would each employ with the other? Cast yourselves according to your aptitude for imitating one of the subjects. Do whichever one you are better at doing. Be sure to switch roles at some point in your rehearsal to experience what your partner does and so you don't get too locked into your own assumptions.

Pick a scene which is *physically varied*, so you have a chance to base your vocal work firmly in their physical lives. The less you choose to do with your bodies in the scene, the less chance you have for capturing the home where their voices live. Your bodies will reveal vocal choices once you are carrying yourself the way your subject does. It's also more fun to explore the space between these two people. Each person wants a clear objective in the scene. Don't just feature them sitting around, shooting the breeze. Idle chitchat can be part of the scene, but for dynamic acting, each person is there for a reason and with a strategy.

Since everyone knows the subjects this time, the game is not one of who it is, but *what* it is. There is still a strong sense of recognition, this time of vocal tendencies heard all term, but never really recognized until they come from another actor. Perform the entire scene first. Then go back over the checklist. Walking through a narrative is not really possible, but do get up, move around, and actively demonstrate every chance you get.

Applying Vocal Awareness

It's important to leave this class understanding the vocal instrument you have and what you do with it. It's far beyond the capacity of this class to bring about sweeping vocal changes. Be patient with yourself. You are already far more vocally sophisticated than you were a few weeks ago. All the material in the body section can be applied here as well. For now, be content to listen more carefully and to master even small changes. And begin to recognize elements of the voice as ingredients for character recipes. ("If I lower my pitch and use a slightly more nasal quality, then slow down and smooth out my delivery, then the character can express . . . '')

PERSONAL AWARENESS

You enter the stage with your body and voice as your primary tangible equipment. They're what you use to communicate in the offstage world, too. But you're obviously no robot or mere machine. You have a whole complex personality with a fascinating history, some of which you've already explored. You have dreams, memories, and textured experience, which the finest actors and most fascinating people manage to bring into their performances. Your personality allows your own spirit onstage, just as it allows it to be shared offstage. However, if the voice is less tangible than the body, then the spirit is even more elusive than the voice.

*You have to live in order to act and
what you put into your performance is
what you've learned from life.*[6]
—PEGGY ASHCROFT

Examine the following incomplete statements. Some you could fill in now. Other statements you'll just want to think about for a while. These are all questions you'll ask later about a character in a play, when you prepare a standard character analysis. Some you've already considered. The best answer to each question is usually the first one that comes to mind.

EXERCISE 3.16

YOUR PAST

Complete these basic statements, making no effort for answers to make sense to anyone but you:

1. I come from . . .
2. My childhood was . . . Family conditions were . . .
3. Major influences on me include . . . Experiences making the most lasting impression on me were . . .
4. Five people whose opinions are most important to me are . . . My outlook on life was primarily determined by . . .
5. Ten facts most important about me are . . .

Areas to consider in answering each of the above:

Early years (Happy? Forgettable? Terrifying? Ideal?)

Home town (Influence? Roots? Memories? Sense of connection?)

Parents (Living? Married? Rich? Poor? Happy? Successful?)

Brothers, sisters, caregivers, companions (Bonds? Influence? Significance?)

Family offerings (Affection? Rejection? Overprotection? Drive? Discipline?)

Home conditions (Divorce? Alcoholism? Religion? Illness? Wealth? Poverty?)

Education (What level? Specializations? Skills developed? Areas omitted? Subjects hated?)

External influences (War? Travel? Political climate? Exposure to other worlds and perspectives?)

Lingering forces (Image of God? Role models or idols? Best friend and worst enemy? Important fantasy or literary figures? Chief nurturers or authority figures?)

EXERCISE 3.17

YOUR PRESENT

At the exact moment you are reading this and jotting down responses, the past, while influential, is not immediate. What's going on in your life right now?

1. I am basically . . . Other people tend to describe me as . . .
2. My physical appearance is . . . My usual style or clothing and type of accessories include . . . My physical and vocal lives are . . .
3. My temperament could be described as . . . For example, . . .
4. My lifestyle involves . . .
5. I am most and least interested in . . . Above all else, I believe . . .

Suggestions for identifying your present:

self-descriptions (Healthy? Ill? Bright? Rich? Independent? Thoughtful? Cute? Confident? Troubled? Powerful?)

appearance (Style choices? Way of wearing/handling clothing? Hair? Amount of artifice? Neatness? Colors? Degree of awareness?)

choices (Foods? Music? Pastimes? People? Places to go?)

EXERCISE 3.18

YOUR FUTURE

A large amount of anyone's time is spent planning things. Or day-dreaming. With the world waiting before you, what do you see now?

1. What I want most to achieve in life is . . . If I have a life plan, it is . . . Other important objectives would include . . . Obstacles I face are . . .

2. My strategy could be described as . . . Specific tactics I am most likely to use in my life are . . .

3. In five years, I see myself . . . In ten years . . . In twenty . . . If I work hard, I believe I can have a future where . . .

4. If I am remembered, it will be for . . .

5. In my darkest fears, I'm terrified that I end up . . . In my wildest fantasies I . . . If all my dreams come true, I will . . .

This future list will need contemplation and imagination. You're not just trying to figure out information. Here you're dealing with dreams.

Bringing Yourself Onstage

Consider the list above for things you are ready to share with new friends and with the audience, if the role warrants it. Which of your own answers surprises you? Note but file away experiences too raw, new, or uncertain to use. Later this checklist will be helpful to compare yourself with a character you play. It will give you a clearer idea of where you stop and the character begins.

> *Whoever I play, whoever I become, I must*
> *have a starting-off point. I must be sure of*
> *who I am, so sure it doesn't worry me,*
> *before I become someone else.*[7]
> **—BOB HOSKINS**

One of the biggest problems any actor faces is acting more onstage the way she does off. Actors are always being critiqued by those who know them with lines like these:

"I've heard you do very forceful things with your voice. Why are you whining so much in this scene?"

"You personally have a wonderful stillness, but you're too busy in the part."

"Why isn't any of your joy and vivacity in the scene? No one is more fun than you, but this character is stiff right now."

"You're so bright. Please don't deny the character's intelligence."

"Get some of that urgency you've just shown me discussing politics into the character discussing her marriage."

Undeniably some of your own qualities will work for a given role, and some could use alterations to suit the character. Edit those parts of yourself which would be imposing your own experience and vision of reality onto the role. Find as much of yourself in the role as you can. Offer as much of yourself to any important life encounter as you can. Don't edit at random. Make the performance yours, not someone else's.

EXERCISE 3.19

ACTING JOURNAL

One of the most effective ways of recording and keeping your individual inventory is an acting journal. Sometimes this is a class requirement, sometimes an option. It's always useful in later years to look back on, and it feels good to have a place to store your acting experiences. Having been recorded, they seem more concrete. Find something small enough to carry around with you all the time, but sturdy enough to hold up to being banged around.

The following is a standard format, which may work for you. Consider dividing your journal into three parts:

1. **Acting Class**

    How are you feeling about it? How is class going for you?

    How are you enlightened? How confused? Any suggestions?

    Are you getting enough (or the right kind of) attention?

    What is helping you most? Least?

    What would you like to share with your teacher that is somehow easier to write about than talk about?

2. **Acting Observed**

    What are you noticing about actors you see in live theatre, film, or TV? At auditions you watch or rehearsals you visit?

    How are your critical responses changing as you see more?

    What do you notice about people in the world that might help your acting?

    What are you discovering about yourself, both in assigned projects and your own imagination?

3. Acting

What happened at your rehearsals for class work this term? How did you feel about each session?

When did you audition, and what occurred? What did you find out that you can take to the next audition?

Which of your offstage performances might apply directly to your work onstage?

Which of your life experiences would you "play" differently, given the chance to repeat? What have you learned from them to prepare you for the future?

Within any structured journal format, try to personalize the whole document so it becomes a real tool for your growth and a reflection of you. If your journal is turned in for class but there are entries which you wish not to be read, indicate that. Trust that your privacy will not be violated.

A journal has a very simple purpose. It helps you capture what you live and act. Theatre is the most ephemeral of arts. You invest months of your life in a show, then one day it's over and this big piece of you is just a newspaper clipping, a telegram, some opening-night good-luck notes, and maybe a pressed dead flower, all in a drawer. The journal makes memories tangible. It revives them. Actors have a tendency to repeat the same old bad habits. Some always get paranoid the second week of rehearsal, some always get morose once the show opens. If you have a record to read over, you can catch yourself falling into old patterns and even stop before you sabotage yourself one more time. The journal helps you trap moments. It gives you a better chance to avoid repeating the bad moments. It gives you a shot at repeating the good ones.

Choosing for Yourself

By now you have a clearer idea of how others see you, whether that is the person inside or not. *You're foolish to fight your type, and you're foolish to accept it.* Work toward a never-ending expansion of your range and power. But work in a way that lets you grow step by step.

> *I was always a character actor. I just looked like*
> *Little Red Riding Hood.*[8]
> —PAUL NEWMAN

The best scenes and monologues for Acting I are those that allow you to focus on the truth of the moment, to concentrate fully, to commit with all your energy to what the character wants. If you have to keep remembering to be anorexic and aged 62, you are unlikely to accomplish the more important objectives above. That's why your first choices in acting class should be close to type and why you should not let type upset you, or in any way stop your desire to change and grow.

Getting yourself onstage, just the right amount, so the performance has a sense of sharing and intimacy without self-indulgence, is an important accomplishment. Once you have been completely who you are onstage, who you are can be limitless. The very best means of being yourself in front of an audience has been designed by Stanislavski. Ironically, it involves finding yourself by forgetting yourself.

> *I'm interested in getting out of my own way and letting the character happen.*[9]
> —SHIRLEY MacLAINE

> *First I'll learn Polish. Then I'll forget me. Then I'll get to her. That's my plan of action.*[10]
> —MERYL STREEP (before starting work on *Sophie's Choice*)

> *I most enjoy the loss of self that can be achieved only through detailed understanding of another life.*[11]
> —DANIEL DAY LEWIS

Notes

1. "Mel Gibson," *Entertainment Weekly,* September 17, 1990.
2. Gordon Hunt, *How to Audition* (New York: Harper & Row, 1979).
3. John Cottrell, *Laurence Olivier* (Englewood Cliffs, N.J.: Prentice Hall, 1975).
4. Douglas Brode, *The Films of Dustin Hoffman* (Secaucus, N.J.: Citadel Press, 1983).
5. Brad Gooch, "The Queen of Curves," *Vanity Fair,* September 1986.
6. Interview by David Jones, in Hal Burton, *Great Acting* (New York: Bonanza Books, 1967).
7. "Bob Hoskins," *People,* January 5, 1986.
8. Maureen Dowd, "Testing Himself," *New York Times Magazine,* September 28, 1986.
9. J. Rovin, "Shirley!" *Ladies' Home Journal,* August 1985.
10. John Skow, "What Makes Meryl Magic," *Time,* September 7, 1981.
11. Matthew Gurerwitsch, "Risk Taker Supreme," *Connoisseur,* December 1989.

4 STANISLAVSKI'S SYSTEM

*Understanding the Only Complete
Process By Which Actors
Build Characters*

> *I think a lot more attention could be paid
> to Stanislavski, as there is still a great deal of
> very messy acting.[1]*
> —VANESSA REDGRAVE

"I really don't believe in all that Stanislavski stuff."

One hears this statement often. The person who says it does not *know* the Stanislavski "stuff." The speaker has almost certainly picked up some distorted version indirectly from someone who didn't know what he was talking about in the first place. The speaker has neither read Stanislavski's works nor studied his actual precepts. No one has contributed more to our progress as actors, and no one has been more misunderstood for it, than Stanislavski.

Stanislavski created the only known complete system for putting together a character, and it is used to some degree by every reputable acting program. Programs expand and vary the System, but always acknowledge the sound principles he gave us. So why all the bad-mouthing?

MYTH AND REALITY

Information about the System came to America in scattered doses. Just as you can quote one piece of scripture and distort the Bible, people have been quoting this particular genius out of context for decades. He suffered from unclear translations of works which reached these shores out of sequence and decades apart. His complete vision took quite a while to get here. (We still do not have many of the 12,000 documents found at the time of his death,[2] and there are major differences between Russian and English language editions of his works.[3]) Stanislavski's ideas suffered at the hands of American acting studios, which took bits and pieces of his work, formulated something called the Method (a term he never used, and a concept with only marginal resemblance to Stanislavski's Method of Physical Actions), and watered down his vision. The Method was nothing more than shorthand for the System.

> *I'm a Methodist, but not in acting.[4]*
> —JAMES GARNER

Even *Reader's Digest*-type versions of Stanislavski, however, worked well for certain scripts, particularly for film, where sustaining, repeating, and projecting performances were not always necessary. Even Stanislavski in shorthand can have merit. But after a while people began to realize that the Method could lead to the worst kind of self-indulgence, self-absorption, muddiness, mumbled communication, and a general confusion of the actor's feelings with those of the character. Guess who got the blame?

> *I don't believe in Method acting, where you*
> *walk around in character all the time. I still retain*
> *a part of myself when I come home and I still*
> *talk to my dog the same way.[5]*
> —KELLY MCGILLIS

In recent years, the full range of Stanislavski's contribution has been acknowledged. But there are still quite a few people who haven't gotten the message.

Who Was Stanislavski?

Constantin Stanislavski (1863–1938) was a brilliant actor, director, and teacher who co-founded the Moscow Art Theatre in 1898 and forever changed the way actors worked. He did as much for performance as Darwin and Freud (his contemporary) did for biological science and psychology. In fact, there are similarities in the way these three helped open new ways of understanding human behavior. Stanislavski wrote four great books (*An Actor Prepares, Building a Character, Creating a Role,* and *My Life in Art*) which eventually make their way into the personal library of almost every serious student of acting. In the first three of these, he uses a brilliant literary device: A master teacher, called Tortsov, takes a group of acting students (including the book's eager narrator, Kostya) through several years of classes. Both Tortsov and Kostya are really Stanislavski at different points in his life. (Kostya is the common nickname for Constantin.) So the elderly Stanislavski meets the young actor he once was, and the books distill his own learning process.[6] There is no relaxation, concentration, or imagination exercise, no warm-up, no improv, and no script experiment currently practiced for which the basic principle and at least the germ of the exercise itself does not appear in these works.

Fortunately for us, when Stanislavski started acting, he was not a natural. He was awkward, ungainly, and ill at ease, so he was motivated to study what all the great performers did to calm and focus themselves, and to then report the results in a systematic way. He later found himself working with new plays (by writers such as Anton Chekhov and Maxim Gorki) that cried out for truth in acting instead of the more extravagant and bombastic attacks many actors then used. He found a system, now taught all over the world, to achieve this calm and truth. Since organized classes and degrees in acting were unknown when Stanislavski started working, it might be argued that without his contribution, your class might not even exist today. Many of the spiritual gifts you will receive as you train as an actor come indirectly from him.

Basic Ingredients

You already experienced the basic Stanislavski System in chapter 1 when you identified these crucial ingredients:

1. Relationship	6. Text
2. Objective	7. Subtext
3. Obstacle	8. Interior Monologue
4. Strategy	9. Evaluations
5. Tactics	10. Beats

Go back and review any of these that fail to come immediately to mind. This is the actor's fundamental vocabulary. You want it secure and working for you. (For simplicity and clarity, the terms on this list are those most widely used now by actors, whether they were part of Stanislavski's original working vocabulary or not.)

Stanislavski determined that in any life situation (or theatrical encounter), the person (or character) always determines her choices based on her feelings about others around her. She has something she wants, and although something stands in the way, her plan constantly changes to get what she wants. She experiences words spoken, but also other meanings implied; in fact, a constant stream of words goes on in her head. She and her partner each consider saying a number of things that they actually end up rejecting along the way. Stanislavski recognized that any encounter between humans could be broken down into sections, marked by the occurrence of changes (a shift in topic or method of persuasion, someone arriving or leaving, an uncovering of new information). Therefore, the encounter, instead of being one long, confusing blur, may be seen in easily understood parts. (The acting terms have been deliberately avoided in this paragraph. Can you substitute acting words for the ones used?)

The Legacy

What is so magical about all this? Well, like most brilliant discoveries, it seems like common sense once you think about it. If an actor really does each of these things, his attention will be fully engaged, his instrument will respond honestly, and he will be compelling to watch. Certain actor blocks, like tension, stiffness, and self-consciousness, tend to fall away because the mind can only hold so much. (Researchers say seven separate categories are the maximum, at any moment, for most people.) If the thoughts "I don't know what to do with my hands" or "I hope the critique isn't devastating" enter your head, you aren't concentrating in the mode above, so you aren't using the System.

The elements above identify only a single interlude in the whole major event that is a play or a life. They help you enter an isolated encounter, while the total System helps you put yourself in a character's complete world. The list above addresses only those facts of which each person is consciously aware, but the System involves the subconscious as well. The System embraces a larger picture and multiple levels. Stanislavski has summarized his vision into three broad ideas he called propositions, which are paraphrased here.

Proposition 1

The actor needs to achieve a state like that of a normal person in life. To do this, he must be:

1. *Physically free and controlled:* His instrument needs to be available to him and under his control.
2. *Alert and attentive:* Combined with freedom, this amounts to the state of relaxed readiness.
3. *Listening and observing:* He must be in genuine contact with the actors opposite him.
4. *Believing:* He must accept and live inside the reality of the character.

Proposition 2

If the actor puts himself in the place of the character, he will then be able to achieve honest action onstage by combining:

1. *Psychological action:* Strong motives drive the character forward toward his objectives. An involved, feeling actor automatically executes organic physical actions.
2. *Physical action:* Feelings are powerfully sustained and expressed through movement. Physical actions support psychological states.

The beauty of the Method of Physical Actions is the way the ingredients sustain each other. You see a symbiotic relationship between them. On a very simple level, let's say you achieve a state of anger and forcefully grab the back of a chair. The movement is just right, and you may never have discovered it without immersing yourself in the character's perspective. In performance, even if you are not always fully angry, the power of the move as the body remembers it and anticipates it is likely to help you generate anger and consistently communicate it to an audience. Stanislavski understood very clearly that the body was more directly reliable and available than the emotions, which "run through your fingers like water," and that the body should therefore be used as a pathway to elusive feelings. Of course, your likelihood of discovering both the physical and psychological actions is greater if you are truly sharing in the character's own perspective.

Proposition 3

The organic action that results from the combination above will give rise to sincere, believable feelings on the part of the actor, but only if he has thoroughly researched and analyzed the role. The actor's meticulous preparation ensures he is in the play, not some fantasy of his own, and his homework frees him to experience "metamorphosis."[7]

Most Misunderstood

In all fairness to his adapters and simplifiers, Stanislavski's writing style is dense and florid by today's standards, his sentences are intricate and complex, he does not always name each concept, and sometimes he appears to call the same idea by different names. He also changed his mind continually as his system evolved, and much incomplete information was passed on by various disciples who worked with him at one point in his life, then went their own way, and didn't grow as he did. As one of his most celebrated spiritual descendants, Jerzy Grotowski, has said, "Stanislavski's method evolved, but not his disciples. Each disciple is limited to his particular period."[8] Yet there are five widely accepted myths presented as his ideas for which there is no sustained support in his work:

1. Since truth is what it's all about, you don't need to bother with technical work.

2. You should be yourself, instead of bothering to develop a characterization.

3. You should use all your own memories and feelings onstage and think about your own past.

4. You should forget the audience altogether.

5. You should wait until you really feel it before you do it or say it.

You can see why lazy, narcissistic actors would grab at these half-truths, and why conscientious artists would be appalled. The fallacious five constitute a license to follow your whims without working. You can also see why even these System distortions might succeed in isolated contexts. In filming, all you need is one good take. There is an old Hollywood story about a ruthless director who supposedly would walk up to his little child star just before shooting a heart-rending scene, and say something like, "Someone just killed your little dog," and then direct the crew, "Okay, roll 'em!" Let's hope that this sick, funny story is *just* a story, but regardless of how he got the tears, the director did get them. Once. The audience seeing the film would never know whether the child was crying about something related to the plot or not. And there would be no need to repeat the scene on Thursday, as there is in the theatre.

Nevertheless, all five myths above are false.

1   No Need for Technique?

Stanislavski was so convinced of the need for painful, meticulous technical work that he often didn't always write about it. You know how you assume certain truths to be self-evident? He was working in a culture and for a company where discipline and lengthy daily classes were so standard that he probably never dreamed that some jerk would presume to walk in front of an audience raw and untrained. The actors described in his books are, in addition to their sessions in the System, taking classes in dancing, gymnastics, fencing, other swordplay, tumbling, voice placement, diction, movement plasticity, boxing, and mask work. There are constant references in his writing to daily "drill sessions." He maintained consistently that the actor needed to be *tuned* to induce the desired automatic responses. Otherwise it just wouldn't work. The vessel would be too weak to carry the water.

2   Yourself Instead of Characterization?

Where does the actor stop and the character start? Stanislavski's concept of the Magic If suggests that the actor imagine herself in the character's *place*. The charge is not to imagine yourself there *instead of* the character. There is a crucial difference. The character's place is her whole life. It is all her training, all her fears and prejudices, all her habits. You do not ask, "What would I do if I were there?" but "What would I do if I had experienced this person's entire life up to this moment?" If anything, this technique assures that you will *not* impose who you are on the character's life. This concept is often not just misunderstood but entirely reversed.

3   All Your Own Memories?

Perhaps the most controversial technique in the whole System is called *emotional memory,* where actors summon up feelings from their own pasts to achieve emotion onstage. It is, however, recommended as a rehearsal rather than a performance device, and then only with experiences which are not so raw that they threaten your sanity and control. Actors should use everything they have, but only when they are masters of the emotions instead of vice versa. Everything onstage is under control. Or, as Stanislavski puts it, ''It is only permissible for an actor to weep his heart out at home or in rehearsals.''[9] What the actor uses in performance is simply triggering impulses and images discovered in rehearsal, not detailed summonings of his own past.

Dwelling on the past? The System asks the actor to dig deeply into the character's past to determine reasons for his behavior and help clarify motives. But Stanislavski never suggests that any of this is what the actor thinks about onstage. It is part of the process. The System demands enough present and future thinking to occupy the actor. But without the past research, the future thinking might be empty. You've been asked in this book to dig back into your own history. But that was to give you self-awareness and a sense of all you have to work with. You don't think about those things at the moment of performance, but they help clarify your thinking at that time.

4   Forget the Audience?

Stanislavski helps the actor keep the audience from invading the actor's work. He never suggested the audience be excluded. He suggested that you keep yourself busy and focused enough that the audience can't inhibit you. His operative word is *concerned*. ''As soon as the actor stops being *concerned* with his audience, the latter begins to watch the actor.''[10] The actor performs as if he were alone and in a state of public solitude.

His tool called *Circles of Concentration* identifies a way of working the audience in and out of your consciousness as necessary. You focus on a specific task in front of you whenever you feel your concentration or involvement wavering. The smaller and more physical the task, the better (sort of a tiny Here and Now). You spiral out your circle to include your acting partner, when the two of you need to interact. You spiral out further, to include the entire stage at the appropriate moment, and further to take in the audience, when there is a specific audience response to deal with, or when you know there is a difficult moment of projection. Basically, these circles widen and narrow according to the needs of the moment. Stanislavski has described them as ''elastic,'' letting the actor's awareness stretch, expand, and contract with minimal effort as is necessary. Clearly, the actor does not wish to be preoccupied or obsessed with the audience. But he wishes to have at his disposal the means of widening and narrowing his perception because ''the audience constitute(s) the spiritual acoustics for us. They give back what they receive from us as living, human emotions.''[11]

5 Wait Until You Feel It?

Not on your life. Stanislavski suggests taking action aggressively onstage because it is likely (although not certain) that feeling will follow. His writings are filled with concern for maintaining the right tempo and rhythm, and he would probably have wanted to assassinate contemporary actors who indulge themselves by taking huge amounts of time to summon up feelings from some dark hiding place while everyone else waits. The investment of time, for the System, is in actor homework and careful rehearsal, all geared toward making it unnecessary for the actor to stumble around in front of an audience searching for his lost emotions.

Leaving behind the five fallacies, let's consider the fundamental truths of the System.

Empathy

If one had to summarize the whole Stanislavski approach in one word, I think the best choice would be *empathy*. You empathize with someone when you so completely comprehend what that person is going through that you share his feelings, thoughts, and motives. Empathy is a far more powerful connection than sympathy or pity. It generates an involuntary physical response, beyond an intellectual or emotional one. Empathizing, you may watch a fight and actually feel a blow being struck with your whole being. Depending on which fighter you identify with, you may feel the blow received or the one given. This is empathy on the simplest level. You may also empathize to the degree that you can comprehend actions which most observers would find inhuman and beyond justification.

EXERCISE 4.1

COMPREHENDING

What would it take to get you to empathize with the following people?

1. A woman who would steal another's child.

2. A terrorist who would try to assassinate the pope.

3. A dictator who would order an entire race of people exterminated.

4. A mother who would murder her own two children.

5. A spy who would betray his country and family for money.

When in your own life have you found an act or a person beyond comprehension, but then something happened to you that made you empathize with the person you used to despise? On a personal level, developing empathy is a profound, troubling, deeply humanizing experience. It feels wonderful to be able to stop judging others, but disturbing to find your crisp black-and-white world turning muddy and full of maybes. On an acting level, empathic response is essential. You may be cast as any of the five people in the exercise above. Those parts are all written and waiting.

Stanislavski showed us that actors are nonjudgmental, totally compassionate artists. You play any role, saint or demon, with an equal amount of involvement. You play Hitler or Gandhi with empathy. It prevents you from presenting a generalized performance full of vague attitudes. You play everyone as the everyday hero of his own life. You play everyone as just some guy doing the best he can with what he's got, since that's the way most guys see themselves. Gandhi didn't view himself in a celestial glow. He was just getting on with life, doing what he had to do.

If there is any part of the System that might be said to possess magic, it is that point where you immerse yourself so thoroughly that appropriate, involuntary actions occur. This is empathy, and if it is a miracle it is also, as Stanislavski was the first to point out, simply a law of nature and an everyday experience. Humane, loving people experience empathy all the time. As do sensitive, responsive actors.

> *You've got to find out how to love her, because you*
> *can't play a character that you don't love.*[12]
> —RICHARD DREYFUSS

Once you understand, not just intellectually but deep within, you're not just on your way to a decent performance, you're also freed from your own prejudices. And, in the words of Stanislavski, "Prejudices block up the soul like a cork in the neck of a bottle."[13]

> *The great gift of human beings is that we have*
> *empathy. We can all cry for each other and sense a*
> *mysterious connection to each other. If there's hope*
> *for the future of us all, it lies in that. And it happens*
> *that actors can evoke that event between hearts.*
> *They can make us feel enhanced. In the audience,*
> *I can be drawn out of myself into someone else's*
> *life and yet suddenly I myself feel more alive! I'm*

*pulled out of what I do every day into something
larger and more lasting, into humanity.
That's what an actor can do.*[14]
—MERYL STREEP

How do empathic responses get started when you have a role in which you feel you hardly know the character, much less function deep within his being?

TEN SYSTEM STEPS

Add to the ten ingredients you experienced early in this book ten more, which embrace the entire system. If you wish to inhabit someone else, you:

1. Learn all the relevant facts that influence this person's behavior *(given circumstances)*.

2. Use these facts to place yourself inside his life perspective *(Magic If)*.

3. From his point of view, determine what he wants most in life *(super objective)* and his range of lesser but still important goals, both conscious and unconscious *(objective hierarchy)*.

4. Experience his particular way of dealing with a variety of obstacles and setbacks. Find the connection between all the moments when a psychological motive prompts a physical impulse, through rehearsal experimentation, until a pattern emerges *(through-line of actions)*.

5. Write down the results in manuscript form and mark the script into workable units *(score)*.

6. Project onto people and objects, real and imagined, qualities from your imagination and experience that bring them to life *(endowment)*.

7. Use your five senses to awaken memories of both physical sensations and emotions that can be filtered into the character's feelings *(recall)*.

8. Add to your constantly playing interior monologue a film of the mind, then speak not to the ears of your partner but to her eyes, trying to get her to see what you see *(images)*.

9. Alter your own tendencies (physical and vocal) to suit those of the character, particularly your sense of time and intensity of experience *(tempo and rhythm)* so that none of your inappropriate mannerisms are imposed on the role *(external adjustments)*.

10. Allow yourself to use all the previous research to free your entry into the heightened reality that allows you both to discover and control simultaneously *(creative mood)*.

The ten steps come in the order above, but one does not stop while another takes over; each is layered in, as the others continue to be actively engaged. Take a look at each of them as they operate in your own life.

Step 1. Given Circumstances

Those details you considered in the previous chapter regarding your own past and present are your own given circumstances. They are life factors that influence how you now behave. Relationships, training, conditioning, social life, financial status, age, and period of history—all shape behavior. Your life has provided you with these circumstances, for better or worse. The playwright gives some of them to a character to help you inhabit that character's world. You fill in the others. You ask all the basic journalist's questions: *who, what, when, where, why,* and *how.* Then determine which of a multitude of circumstances are most important. Almost always there are a few given circumstances that are breakthroughs in your understanding.

EXERCISE 4.2

OTHERS' GIVENS

What are the seven most important given circumstances of:

1. One of the actors you imitated for class?
2. Your best friend?
3. The person you most admire?
4. Someone you dislike intensely?
5. The historical figure you find most fascinating?

Step 2. The Magic If

Next you take the given circumstances and ask yourself how you would respond if you were in his shoes. The American Indian adage to hot-headed young warriors, "Do not judge another brave, my son, until you have walked in his moccasins," is probably repeated in some fashion in all cultures by the wise, experienced, and forgiving to those too ready to fight. It is the capsule Magic If. You step into the other brave's moccasins and try to walk around for a time. The Magic If is the means of entering the character's givens.

You particularly employ the Magic If in those areas in which you have the least in common with your character. If you are an agnostic cast as a Bible-thumping revival tent preacher, you engage that character's early literal visions of God the Father, the prayer meetings that were the source of great thrills and visions, the time he was literally spoken to by Jehovah and told to spread the Word, the triumphant cleansing he feels every time he leads another sheep back to the flock. You leave behind your own experiences of disillusionment and scientific detachment. You do this as much as is necessary to stop feeling superior or judgmental, and to play the character from a full heart, in his own vision of reality. You end up feeling that in his place (his *total* place) you would be bound to act as he did.

I think all good actors use the Magic If.[15]

—JANE ALEXANDER

EXERCISE 4.3

PLANTING

1. Pick anyone from the last exercise and "plant" his given circumstances on yourself, replacing your own when they're incompatible.

2. Spend half an hour giving yourself over to the Magic If.

3. Perform any simple physical task (sweeping, setting the table) entirely from the character's perspective.

4. Observe an event (a TV show, a ballgame) and see it from his eyes.

EXERCISE 4.4

CLASS IFS

1. Imagine three classmates, each cast as you. Where would each of these actors need to use the Magic If to play you fully?

2. Reverse the process for three other classmates, imagining yourself being cast as them and playing them well.

3. Pick the one of the three most removed from you. Use the Magic If to act out any event which would be more comfortable for the person you're playing than it would be for you.

Step 3. Super Objective

We have already examined the objective involved in a single encounter, but everyone has something she wants more out of life (or in the course of the play) than anything else. For most of us this is the driving force, the cause for which we would go to the mat or even to war. By moving through the character's given circumstances and immersing yourself in the Magic If, the super objective may become clear. This usually requires detective work, because playwrights rarely come out and state it. The objective should always be emotional rather than intellectual, and strong enough to involve ''our whole physical and spiritual being.''[16] It should be stated in the simplest, most active terms. The super objective unifies all the tiny objectives that occupy moment-to-moment living into a major motive for living.

Objective Hierarchy

From the super down to the smallest, our lives are full of objectives pursued. Some objectives you consider for super but do not choose. These go right near the top of the list as finalists, because they are still very important. Some are not conscious, but are very strong motivating forces. Strong unconscious objectives should be considered as well as conscious ones. A character often has dominant objective for each act, and always for each scene, in the play.

EXERCISE 4.5

HIERARCHIES

1. Try to put into simple phrases what you (a) want most out of life; (b) want very strongly but not quite most; (c) wanted most during each of the past four weeks; (d) wanted most during each of the past four hours; (e) wanted most (if your objectives changed) during the last four minutes.

2. Try to review and uncover several moments in your life when you thought you were pursuing one objective (conscious), but then suddenly realized you were unconsciously pursuing another.

3. Recreate one of these scenes. Have classmates act other participants, based on your description of the rough scenario. Hierarchize the objective you had and let them all work to motivate you.

CLASS OBJECTIVES

Discuss as a group, with someone writing choices on the board, the shared class super objective for the term, other contenders, the class hierarchy for the term. Do the same for each week so far and for today's class meeting up to this moment. Conjecture about hidden or unconscious objectives which also may be shared by more than one person in the class.

Step 4. Through-Line of Actions

Each isolated action you perform in life has an inward (the need to do) and an outward (what is done) dimension. Whether you need to quench your thirst, so you get a glass of juice, or you need to validate yourself as student, so you get a Fulbright, large or small actions all combine the psychological impulse with the physical attack. The actor needs to discover both elements for a character.

The physical action, discovered through rehearsal experimentation, is "the bait for the emotion,"[17] aiming to "rouse your subconscious."[18] While emotions cannot be directly summoned (trying to do so is usually disastrous), the body can plant conditions and open doors in the hope that "the spirit cannot but respond to the actions of the body."[19] This physical action may be overt, violent, extravagant, or it may involve no discernible movement at all. "Action, motion, is the basis of the art followed by the actor," writes Stanislavski, but "external immobility does not necessarily imply passiveness. You may sit without a motion and at the same time be in full action."[20] In such a case the tension in the body, the light in the eyes, the *commitment* to stillness is likely to communicate at least as strongly as a large sweeping movement.

Over an entire play or life, patterns recur as the character keeps running various obstacles, which Stanislavski calls "counteractions." People tend to repeat choices. When confronted with obstacles, some people give in all the time and even change their objectives rather than fight. Some employ

largely threat tactics: yelling, physically intimidating, and presenting themselves as irrational, confrontational, and disrespectful. Others always
smile, nod, laugh appreciatively, charm, seduce, or gently lure to get what
they want. Some always work indirectly and never say what they really
have in mind. Some stick relentlessly to the same strategy, while others
change easily, making adaptations as they go along. Look for patterns of
behavior through the role that tie the whole together just as your life patterns begin to define your own through-line of behavior. The through-line
ends up like the spinal column, with each action finally connecting to its
neighbor in one continuous, fluctuating organ, which is why the through-
line is often called the spine of the role. No action is too small to con-
tribute.

The very smallest actions are often called *bits*.* Not to be confused with
"doing a bit" or engaging in a piece of stage business of some kind, the bit
is like the smallest piece of information which can be contained in a
computer (byte). I return home from a walk and the first bit might be hoping I have remembered my keys. I hear them jingling, so that objective is
achieved. I reach into the right pocket of my jacket, hoping the keys are
there, but they aren't, so that bit did not end with an achieved objective. I
reach into the left. They're there. Achieved. I hope the house key is easily
accessible on the ring. It's not. It's not even close to the top. Not achieved.
I get the key after sorting through several, and, because I'm entering a door
I don't usually use, I hope I have it inserted at the right angle, and I have!
The door opens and life goes on! These silly, tiny triumphs (sometimes
called moment-to-moment victories) are the way we get through life.

Actors often fail to break down the role into near enough bits and the result is a performance that is too general. Stanislavski says that "in general" is the worst enemy of the actor. Most people playing the admittedly
less-than-riveting scene I starred in above would do a very "in general"
looking for the keys thing (one muddy bit, tops) without getting it bit by bit
(there are six separate ones described) the way we actually do in life.

If you are cast as Hamlet, you can be overwhelmed by the size and the
grandeur of the role, and by all the great "others" who have played it. Or
you can break it down from his super objective to the smallest victory. In
your first scene, all you have to do for a while is avoid your Uncle Clau-
dius. Then your mother approaches you, and you just have to hide from her

*There is some controversy over Stanislavski's use of *beat* and *bit*, partially due to translation
confusion and to the fact that they are pronounced the same by Europeans teaching Ameri-
cans. For our purposes, bits are always smaller and it takes a number of them to constitute a
beat or a complete transaction.

how distraught you are. She speaks to you, and all you have to do is think of the briefest possible answer to get the conversation over with. And before you know it, you're dead and someone else is saying, "Good night, sweet prince." You work your way bit by bit, objective by objective, and the role is not frightening, because each unit in it is manageable, and then you move on to the next. "Proceed," says Stanislavski, "bit by bit, helping yourself along by small truths."[21]

EXERCISE 4.7

TINY TRIUMPHS

Break down the following experiences into the smallest bits possible:

1. The next time you arrive home.
2. The next time you arrive for acting class, the period from entering the building to taking a seat.
3. The first two minutes after you wake up in the morning.
4. The last two minutes before you go to bed.
5. Any short excerpt from a rehearsal with a partner in which the text is not involved.

EXERCISE 4.8

TRIUMPHANT ENTRIES

Volunteers enter the room in one of the situations above. Class members call out identifications of each attempted small triumph, then "yes" or "no" if it was successful or not. Cheer the actor each time one is achieved.

Variation: Act is performed silently with each observer jotting down victories. See if all agree on the total attempted, lost, and won.

Remember that all objectives from super to bit are positive. Even characters who appear bent on self-destruction are usually acting in order to still some demons inside themselves. A wino lying in the gutter, reaching out to the bottle on the curb for one last swig of rotgut *vino,* isn't trying to make himself sick; he's trying to achieve peace, to sleep, to settle nagging self-doubts, at least for tonight.

As his work progressed through the years, Stanislavski preferred attempting to define the role in larger units and breaking the performance into bits only when a section was not working. The through-line of actions represents the total effort at achieving objectives, the various sections of the character's struggle.

Step 5. Scoring the Role

Stanislavski recommends that you score your script and accompanying notebook much as a musician sits down and notates a musical score, with important things like super objective at the front, probably in big letters. Then each scene has its own means of being highlighted. You take each of the ingredients listed in this chapter and find a way of notating them, perhaps drawing a line where each beat begins and ends for you, so that what emerges is like "a long catalogue of minor and major objectives, units, scenes, acts"[22] designed to "draw the actor as a human being closer to the real life of his character or role."[23] Many actors end up doing a great deal of scoring in their heads, but I recommend that you do it on paper at least a few times, to lock it in place for yourself. It also takes a while to work out your own codes, to determine how best to lay out information for yourself.

The score relates to the acting journal and may be combined with it. While no one else should tell you how to prepare a document this personal, and a great deal of what you write may be virtually incomprehensible to others, there is enormous value in the process of writing (sketching, drawing, coding) it down. Actors who score, go back over and over for help and inspiration from the document. And, of course, it is one more way of making a very elusive art form, recorded and concrete.

The first thing I do with a script is divide it up into beats and measures—a measure being a sequence of beats—to get at the fundamental rhythm of the part before playing it in rehearsals.[24]
—JACK NICHOLSON

I secretly structured myself to play Ripley like [Shakespeare's] Henry V *and like the women warriors of classic Chinese literature.*
*[*Adds her director: *"Her copy of the script was marked with 17 different colors of ink. In her margin*

notes, she got the dramatic significance of almost
every line of dialogue and how each one might
tie in with a later scene."][25]

—Sigourney Weaver (on her role in the *Alien* films)

What I remember most is how knowledgeable
[Denzel] is. He does incredible, almost
intimidating amounts of research. When
he gets there, he's there.[26]

—Morgan Freeman (describing Denzel Washington)

You don't complete the score before rehearsals begin and then keep it perfect like scripture. You revise and alter it throughout the whole rehearsal process and even during the run of the show. It's usually messy-looking, with lots of erasing and crossing out. It is a dynamic, ever-changing work, always in progress.

Step 6. Endowment

You had no problem, as a child, with making a stick into a magic wand or into Excalibur, with taking an old sheet and endowing it with great beauty, weight, and even ermine trim as it became your cape. Onstage now you endow plastic swords and capes trimmed in rabbit fur or cotton batten. Props and set pieces tend to be lightweight, cheaply made, and unreal. You endow a glass of tea, which is supposed to be bourbon, with aroma, a burning sensation as you sip, a rush of lightheadedness as a possible aftermath. You endow some stiff plastic flowers with invigorating scent, softness, freshness, and the cheap plastic vase you are putting them in, with the weight, coldness and smoothness of porcelain or crystal. You endow a partner with great beauty in order to find him irresistible.

Endowing something or someone requires a clear memory of the original. If it's not in your experience, you do research. Actors need to keep all their senses awake with each new experience, for the possibility of having to recreate the sensation. They also need to go beyond the obvious, into creative conjecture. The bourbon may be a rare vintage given to you for your twenty-first birthday and sipped on the rarest of occasions. The flowers may be a hybrid developed by a gardener who worshipped you and was sent away by your snobbish parents. The vase might be something your mother brought back from a trip to China, quite expensive, but a color you abhor and she knows it. The cape may have been sewn by angels.

Some endowment will be suggested by the script but the majority of it is up to you and full of creative possibility. The audience will never know the details as you are sipping bourbon or arranging flowers, but there will be a sense of depth, of texture; you will look as if you really live in that space, and the performance can take on the qualities of a tapestry.

Stanislavski divided endowment into *external*, where feelings are used to give imaginary life to tangible existing objects, and *internal*, where your own memory is used to create altogether imaginary objects, such as those that might appear on the fourth wall or in the character's offstage life.

EXERCISE 4.9

ADDING CONSEQUENCE

1. Try wandering around the house and endowing objects that are of no consequence to you. Stop and note those that have great sentimental value and study what happens to you as you contemplate, savor their history, flash on the relationships they symbolize. Go back and endow one to which you have been largely indifferent.

2. Pick some objects that are available in large enough numbers so that everyone in the group can endow them (empty paper cups, coins, notebooks). Work on adding physical properties and then layer in emotional ones.

3. Each person brings an object to class. Working with a partner, first take the other person's object and endow it from your own imagination. Then compare your own addition of consequence to that of the person who brought in the object.

Step 7. Recall

Repeated feelings, according to Stanislavski, "are the only means by which you can, to any degree, *influence* inspiration." He also warns: "The moment you *lose* yourself on the stage marks the departure from truly living your part."[27] The primary tool for untapping controlled, repeatable emotion is memory of the senses. Although sight is probably the most powerful, all five (visual, aural, smell, taste, touch) can be released with great strength. You need to stay alert for any untapping of your own life that might intrude on the character's experience rather than help you connect to it.

On a simpler level, each of the actual five senses is used onstage to assist in endowment where the theatrical object lacks the fullness of the real thing or where the real thing (an actual blow forcefully struck, a genuinely repulsive smell) would be dangerous to the actor or beyond the tolerance of the audience.

EXERCISE 4.10

BRINGING IT BACK

Let each of the suggestive phrases below hit you with the first memory to come along. Let the image expand to include the given circumstances, and allow the feelings to return.

1. A landscape where you felt small and lost

2. A song that used to get to you

3. The voice of a lost loved one, soothing you

4. Something baking at your grandmother's home

5. The perfume or cologne of someone with whom you were infatuated

6. Your father's handshake or hug, your mother's embrace

7. Your first taste of an alcoholic beverage

8. The taste of your favorite birthday cake

Release Pictures

When calling on emotional memory there is often a single lingering image, like a photograph in the mind, that summons back all the feelings in a rush and opens that emotional vein. Finding these images (once the experience is repeatable) can be far more effective than trying to recall the entire lengthy experience, which can get muddied by sheer overload of material. You may recall a romantic summer affair by the image of one sunset watched while seated quietly behind your lover. The tanned back of your lover and the colors in the sky reflected on the loved one's skin can be so vividly etched that the rest unlocks. You may recall your attachment to a favored grandparent by the image of a rocking chair with an afghan thrown over it. The icons of our times (a flag, a cross, a swastika) serve as release images for many every time they are viewed.

Sometimes when you look through a photo album you stumble across such a release shot unexpectedly, after pages and pages of photos that were enjoyable but did not unlock any emotional memory. Suddenly you are flooded with feelings.

RELEASE ALBUM

Identify a release photo for an emotional memory for each of the following. Experiment with variations of long shots, close-ups, slow motion, and other visual alterations to make the image even more evocative for you.

childhood delight	triumphant accomplishment
awakening sexuality	humiliation
inspiration	utter insignificance
romantic love	complete freedom
heartbreak	selfless compassion

TOTAL RECALL

Select a moment where you know there was a strong, genuine emotional response on your part. Instead of trying to summon the feeling, go through all your senses for the occasion.

1. What you were wearing, down to your underwear
2. What you were touching and what it felt like
3. What you were smelling
4. What tastes were in your mouth
5. What sights, other people, images jump out
6. What sound, including background or white noise

7. Any muscle tension or physical sensation
8. The way your were breathing

Step 8. Images

Thinking in images, instead of just words, is exciting and evocative. If you have a definite picture in your head as you speak a phrase, and try to get your listener to see the picture, your words are more likely to be vividly expressive and your connection with your partner more intense. It is as if you are plugging your energy into your listener and causing him to catch your vision. You have a film of the imagination, for which your interior monologue is the soundtrack. Here are some examples of the way Stanislavski uses images:[28]

Excessive gestures	"trash, dirt, spots on a performance"
Involuntary, nervous movements	"convulsive cramps" causing "blotches on a part"
Sloppy pronunciation of a word's beginning	"a face with a bashed–in nose"
Swallowing a word's ending	"a man minus a limb"
Dropped letters or syllables	"a missing eye or tooth"
Actor who speaks well	"a phonetics gourmet, savoring the aroma of each syllable and sound"
A comma	"the warning lift of a hand, making others wait for you"
An unfilled pause	"a blank hole in the fabric of artistic creation"
Accenting a word	"a pointing finger singling out"
Use of an adjective	"to color a noun and set off this particular 'individual' from others"

You see how much more exciting these standard suggestions for stage movement and speech become when a picture is painted? The mental picture increases the chances for intense partner connection.

IMAGING

1. Working with a partner, speak the following lines with Stanislavski's corresponding images in mind.

   "You need to get rid of all those extra gestures."

   "I don't think you mean to make all those nervous little movements, but they are distracting."

   "I can't understand the beginning of your first three words."

   "What happened to the last part of what you were saying?"

   "You're just not saying everything, so I can't get what you mean."

   "You speak well. I love to listen to you."

   "You made it clear to me where the punctuation, especially the comma, was."

   "You took pauses, but I couldn't figure out why or what for."

   "You need to show which words and phrases are important, which need to stand out for attention."

   "Those adjectives are there to help you. Try to alert the dark, shadowy, reticent recesses of my sluggish, tired imagination by the way you use descriptive words."

2. Describe any brief experience you've had in the past few days, first with just the words, then with the movie of the experience (and occasional striking still photographs) in mind, trying to get your partner to see the same movie and notice the same still shots. Discuss the comparative "look" of your and his films.

Step 9. External Adjustments

No matter how much of yourself you find in the character, some altering of your own habits will be needed to portray this other human being. Some adjustments will have occurred automatically in setting up each of the previous conditions, but others can be layered in from the outside. These externals may involve any of the physical or vocal tendencies explored in earlier chapters. Where is your body and voice just not right for this character? Now is the time to adjust them. Stanislavski believes above all else in experimenting with various tempos and rhythms. The character ''in time'' is crucial to untapping who he is. Character detail is liberating. ''A characterization,'' says Stanislavski, ''is the mask which hides the actor-individual. Protected by it he can lay bare his soul down to the last intimate detail.''[29]

TIME GAMES

1. Take the lines in the exercise above and try to get your listener to change mood just by your changes in tempo and rhythm. Try to get her to:

   fall asleep   beg you to stop

   get angry   get sad

   giggle   leave the room

   get inspired   feel sexy

2. Perform a simple pantomime of any basic household task, first in a neutral state or in your own habitual tempo and rhythm. Then repeat with the following adjustments:

   rapid, low intensity   medium external, slow internal

   rapid, high intensity   erratic, internally and externally

   slow external, rapid internal   extremely slow external, high intensity

   Discuss both the way the change made you feel and the impression left on observers. Take other suggestions for adjustments from the class.

3. Keep the same task but add accompanying narrative, first where you describe what you are doing, then where your conversation is unrelated to your activity. Experiment with vocal tempos and rhythms which match your physical choices as well as those which contradict them.

Step 10. The Creative State

When an actor is able to pull together all the elements above, he has an excellent chance to enter a state in which he's open to inspiration. Stanislavski compares the creative state to ''the feelings of a prisoner when the chains that had interfered with all his movements for years have at last been removed.''[30] In this state of metamorphosis, he is able to think as the actor *and* as the character without either interfering with the other. The performer functions simultaneously on two planes, with actor perspective running parallel to role perspective "as a foot path may stretch along beside a highway."[31]

Far from being naive or mystical about this state, Stanislavski is quick to point out that you have a shot at achieving it only if

> you have understood the play correctly, analyzed the character accurately, have a good appearance, clear and energetic diction, plastic movement, a sense of rhythm, temperament, taste, and the infectious quality we often call charm.[32]

He does not claim that the mood will come whenever called, but rather it will emerge between stretches of struggle. Much of the time an actor on-stage isn't functioning in "a second state of reality," but wavers back and forth between actor and character awareness. The creative state is always worth pursuing. The careful preparation involved will ensure that decisions made will be honest ones. "Plan your role consciously at first, then play it truthfully."[33] If the internal and external work are both "based on truth, they will inevitably merge and create a living image."[34]

OPEN SCENES

One of the best ways of applying the basics of the System is the open scene. It is called *open* because the lines of dialogue are essentially nothing, waiting to be filled. Here is a sample.

EXERCISE 4.15

OPEN DIALOGUE

This dialogue is so open that the characters are called One and Two:

One: Ah.
Two: So?
One: All set?
Two: No.
One: Well.
Two: Yes.

Try it in class or simply imagine it with the following contexts:

1. Leaving home for a very long time (parent and child)
2. A drug bust (dealer and narc)
3. Revealing notice of academic probation (parent and child)
4. Picking out a new outfit (two friends)
5. Answering an ad in the classified section (advertiser and customer)

Repeat with the class suggesting more specific given circumstances to alter the scene.

Open scenes provide a comfortable introduction to the System because you are allowed to make up things. You get to be a little bit of a playwright as you master the basic terms. Later, when you approach a work scripted in greater detail, you're able to respond more sensitively to the playwright's vision as you investigate the same elements you created for your open scene.

Closing Scenes

You can tell already that no scene is completely open. Even in one as simple as in the exercise above, one character is obviously more aggressive, the other more defensive or indecisive, one inquiring, the other responding. This and every scene is to some degree closed by information implied. Some open scenes are put together by a random computer search of short lines of dialogue. No matter how objective the process, an implied relationship always emerges in the resulting text. There is also no such thing as a closed scene, where everything is defined. No matter how simple-minded or explicit the material, there's still a dimension left to the performers. All scenes are only relatively open or closed. Look at any script, asking yourself right away how open the material is. How much information has the playwright provided or closed for you, how much needs to be inferred, then invented by you?

The following open-scene script is a favorite because it is so potentially complex in its twists and turns. It is a classic used in many theatre classes, for both directing and acting projects.

One: Oh.
Two: Yes.
One: Why are you doing this?
Two: It's the best thing.
One: You can't mean it.
Two: No, I'm serious.
One: Please . . .
Two: What?
One: What does this mean?
Two: Nothing.
One: Listen . . .
Two: No.
One: So different.
Two: Not really.
One: Oh.
Two: You're good.
One: Forget it.
Two: What?
One: Go on.
Two: I will.

What can we close at a glance? Two seems determined to do something. One tries, with various tactics, to discourage Two. By the end, however, One is encouraging Two to do something, which may or may not be what Two originally set out to do. Are there any other implied closures on this scene? Let's look at two of many possible interpretations of these lines.*

Open Interpretations

Setting: A bedroom.
Characters: A young married couple.
Script: Given above.

The three elements above are the only things shared by the following two scenes.

---

*The two scenes are adapted and extended from directing projects first presented under the supervision of Wandalie Henshaw, now artistic director for the Clarence Brown Theatre Company and professor at the University of Tennessee, and were published in an article entitled "The 'Open Scene' as a Directing Exercise" in *The Educational Theatre Journal.* Professor Henshaw in turn wishes to acknowledge Kathleen George, professor at Pitt University and author of *Rhythm in Drama,* for basic concepts and dialogue.

Example 1   The couple lost their only child before the baby reached three. The death occurred about six months ago. Lately, the wife has often been found sobbing hysterically over the child's basket of toys. The day has come when the husband is determined to get rid of the toys because of the way they haunt his wife and himself.

Example 2   This couple do not get along well because their sex life is unsatisfying to both of them. The wife usually takes a book to bed, and tonight it happens to be a *Love Without Fear*-type manual. The husband often wakes the wife to have a go at it when he can't sleep. She hates these sessions, and does her best to discourage him.

Set and props   Both scenes require something to represent a bed and both can share the same book, if its cover is plain. *Also needed for Example 1:* Basket containing a variety of toys, including a doll and a music box. *Also needed for Example 2:* Sheets and pillows, water glass, aspirin bottle, cold cream jar, any invented props for first beat.

Example 1:   Time To Let Go

Activity	Intention
1. She enters bedroom	*to find something to distract her.*
2. She finds and opens book	*to grab first available diversion.*
3. She sits on bed	*to calm herself.*
4. She pages through book	*to occupy her mind.*
5. She hears noise, starts, recovers	*to suppress her fears.*
6. She crosses to door	*to somehow stop what she expects.*
7. He enters with basket	*to make her understand his plan.*
8. She says, "Oh"	*to get him to stop.*
9. He says, "Yes"	*to make her understand he will not back down.*
10. She touches the toys	*to somehow touch her child as well.*
11. She asks, "Why are you doing this?"	*to cause him to change his mind.*
12. He says, "It's the best thing"	*to persuade her that he is doing this because they need it.*

13. She takes the basket	*to stay close to the toys.*
14. She says, "You can't mean it"	*to intimidate him.*
15. She kneels, puts toys on the floor	*to keep them near her.*
16. He moves to put a hand on her shoulder	*to comfort her.*
17. He says, "No, I'm serious"	*to get her to comprehend he will not be dissuaded.*
18. She picks up doll from basket	*to cling to it.*
19. She says, "Please"	*to get him to back off.*
20. He says, "What?"	*to force her to at least speak of it.*
21. She holds the doll like a baby	*to bring back the feeling of comforting.*
22. She says, "What does this mean?"	*to arouse his grief.*
23. He turns away	*to find a less devastating sight.*
24. He says, "Nothing"	*to maintain control of his emotions.*
25. She picks out music box	*to find a more powerful weapon.*
26. She plays it	*to pull him into her perspective.*
27. She says, "Listen"	*to remind him of better times.*
28. He says, "No"	*to fight the music's effect.*
29. He crosses to other side of room	*to regain firmness and purpose.*
30. She rises and faces him	*to confront him combatively.*
31. She says, "So different"	*to accuse him of insensitivity.*
32. He turns to face her	*to stop the charge.*
33. He says, "Not really"	*to accept his own vulnerability.*
34. She says, "Oh"	*to acknowledge his feelings.*
35. She goes to him	*to make peace.*
36. She embraces him	*to apologize and comfort.*
37. They hold each other	*to gain strength.*
38. He looks at her	*to check if she is ready.*
39. He holds onto her, says, "You're good"	*to assure her she has the strength to give the toys up.*

40. She slowly returns to the toys	*to say goodbye.*
41. She stands up, looks away	*to end her attachment.*
42. She says to herself, ''Forget it''	*to discipline herself.*
43. She picks up basket	*to test herself.*
44. She hands it to him	*to free herself from any temptation to change her mind.*
45. He says, ''What?''	*to get a verbal commitment from her.*
46. She quietly says, ''Go on''	*to encourage him to do it quickly, before she weakens.*
47. He says, ''I will''	*to accept the offer firmly and close the discussion.*
48. He exits with toys	*to accomplish his task.*
49. She listens to music box fading as it gets farther away	*to linger an instant longer in the past.*
50. She sits on the bed	*to support herself.*
51. She lies down and curls up on the bed	*to comfort herself and to help her resolve.*

Example 2:   Try It, You'll Like It

Activity	Intention
1. They enter from opposite sides	*to go to bed.*
2. They stop to glare at each other	*to keep the other at a distance.*
3. They go through separate preparations (he rubs feet, stretches; she applies cold cream, takes aspirin)	*to avoid contact of any kind.*
4. They get into bed	*to go to sleep.*
5. They fight over the sheet	*to spite each other.*
6. She immediately falls asleep	*to forget she married him.*
7. He tosses and turns	*to find some position to get to sleep.*
8. He sits up	*to admit he can't sleep.*

9. He looks at her   *to decide whether to try or not.*

10. He looks away   *to find courage.*

11. He shrugs   *to persuade himself to go for it.*

12. He nudges her awake   *to warn her.*

13. She groans   *to avoid being awakened.*

14. He clears his throat   *to signal her.*

15. She says, ''Oh''   *to wither his resolve with her sarcasm.*

16. He says, ''Yes''   *to double his determination.*

17. He attempts passionate kiss   *to emulate screen lovers.*

18. She stops him   *to avoid being smothered by him.*

19. She asks, ''Why are you doing this?''   *to distract and discourage him.*

20. He answers, ''It's the best thing''   *to appear confident.*

21. She says, ''You can't mean it''   *to remind him of past times.*

22. He kisses her   *to encourage her participation.*

23. He says, ''No, I'm serious''   *to stop her protests.*

24. She picks up the book   *to seek mental diversion.*

25. She reads while he carresses her   *to entertain herself.*

26. She pushes him away   *to free herself to concentrate.*

27. She says, ''Please''   *to keep him off while she studies a passage that interests her.*

28. She slams book shut, stunned   *to grasp fully what she has found.*

29. He says, ''What?''   *to find out what is so interesting.*

30. She shows him page in book   *to share her discovery.*

31. She asks, ''What does this mean?''   *to get help comprehending.*

32. He takes book, reads   *to mollify her.*

33. He slams book shut   *to suppress shocking information.*

34. He says, ''Nothing''   *to cover his amazement.*

35. She says, ''Listen''   *to suggest book's suggestion may be worth trying.*

36. He says, "No!"	*to free himself from experimenting.*
37. She reads passage again	*to memorize procedure.*
38. He lies down	*to protect himself.*
39. She looks at him	*to plan her attack.*
40. She grabs him and they disappear beneath the covers	*to act out passage in book.*

Blackout (May be accomplished by couple just flailing beneath sheet, out of audience view, for a while.)

41. They emerge from covers	*to come up for air.*
42. They sit up smiling	*to glory in their success.*
43. She says, "So different"	*to express her appreciation.*
44. He says, "Not really"	*to persuade her he is fully capable of this and more.*
45. She pokes or tickles him	*to make loving contact.*
46. She says, "Oh"	*to tease him.*
47. He says, "You're good"	*to praise her prowess.*
48. She says, "Forget it"	*to acknowledge praise.*
49. She taps him on the shoulder	*to seduce him.*
50. He says, "What?"	*to play coy, to encourage her aggression.*
51. She points to bed beneath them	*to show him the way.*
52. She says, "Go on"	*to get him to take the initiative.*
53. He says, "I will"	*to accept the challenge.*
54. They disappear again beneath covers	*to pursue their mutual pleasure.*

EXERCISE 4.16

MOTIVATION UNITS

1. Go back over each scene and mark where you feel changes in beats occur. Then discuss to see if your choices matched others.

2. If time allows, two couples should volunteer to present the scene regarding the dead child, and two other couples the sex problem scene, trying to follow closely the motivational units on the list.

Discuss the differences between each couple doing the same scene. Which elements of subtext will vary, simply because of what any single actor will bring to a role?

OPEN SCENE PROJECT

1. Stick with the sample script and format, but devise two new scenarios. Working with a partner, begin brainstorming various situations that contrast as strongly as the examples.* For each scene, turn in a tentative title, conflict, description of the action, and a statement about how each character is different at the end. (See Appendix E, Open Scene Scenario, for suggested form.)

2. Look for opportunities to explore the power of subtext. While a comic scene and a serious one have immediate contrast, consider all the other ways contrast is possible.

3. This is one of the few times in your life when you get to cast yourself any way you want. It may be your only chance to play Abraham Lincoln, Pooh, a talking horse, Mother Teresa, Mother Nature, a hustler, God. Consider the possibilities.

4. Plan to present both of your scenes in class and to turn in a written breakdown of the scenes into beats and bits just prior to performance. (See Appendix F, Open Scene Score)

Start by looking at situations and characters instead of moods. At least one of the scenes above could be played in an entirely different mood. A couple having an unsatisfying sex-life is not inherently amusing, certainly not to those involved. While in questionable taste, ''dead baby'' jokes have been around for years. Sometimes an idea that starts as funny develops sad. The scene switches emotional gears so that the final product has tragicomic balance, beginning in one mood and moving into another. Start with interesting people in intriguing predicaments, and then let them respond honestly. No character or encounter is too outrageous if the responses are truthful to the people and the event. Stanislavski says that acting is behaving truthfully in imaginary circumstances. This is a chance to let your imagination fly, free as a kite. The string is truth.

As you work on writing motivational units, concentrate especially on what happens between each line of dialogue. Notice there are only 20 lines, but over 50 bits, in each scene. In both examples, there are more

*Four to Avoid: Because no scene is truly open, four ideas should be mentioned because they lend themselves so obviously to the lines and offer little challenge: (1) suicide, (2) substance abuse, (3) leaving home, (4) visiting a new hairdresser who is trying kinky techniques. Try to stretch your imagination beyond these first obvious choices. You are more creative than this.

nonspeaking motivational units than there are speaking ones. Novice actors tend to rush open scene work, particularly the first beat, and to neglect the tiny stages (remember the door example?) that make up real lives. Don't ever neglect subtext, particularly when your text is as negligible as the one above. Each line in the motivation column should begin with the preposition "to" followed by an active (or actable) verb.

Since you will probably be revising your score right up to the last minute, work with pencil and expect several rough drafts. If you prepare a document that looks too finished too early, you will be tempted to make yourself stick to it. Wait to complete what you turn in until after your last rehearsal. Determine the ten basics for each character, plus the ten more advanced ingredients: given circumstances, the Magic If, super objective and objective hierarchy, through-line, score, endowment, sense and emotional recall, images, external adjustments, and an open, responsive attitude toward the creative state.

As with the imitation assignments, this is a collaboration, but you may find it easier if you and your partner each take primary responsibility for one scene, from conception through writing the score. There should still be maximum input from both actors, but the process itself is simplified if each partner focuses on the *mechanics* of one scene only.

Rules for the Open Scene Project

1. Because this is an exercise in *subtext*, the text, such as it is, should remain absolutely intact.
2. Actors may switch who is One and who is Two between scenes, but no other switches are possible. No person ever gives two lines in a row and no reversals in the middle of the scene are fair.
3. Actors have complete freedom of line delivery, but are not free to change wording. By all means, put in unexpected pauses, change a declarative statement to a question, change the intent of a line right in the middle, add numerous nonverbals—those are all actor tools. But do not turn "You're good" into "You are good" or "Yes" into "Yeah," and so forth. Dealing with a difficult line by changing it is always a last resort. In this exercise, it's cheating.

> *I can't understand actors who learn their lines*
> approximately. *If it's a good script, the writer*
> *has sweated over every part of it and a single*
> *word can throw everything. If it's a bad script,*
> *you shouldn't be doing it.*[35]
> —KATHARINE HEPBURN

Open Scene Presentations

If time allows, scenes should be presented twice in class, to allow the actors to go back and rehearse between showings. When it's your turn to present, give the audience no more than a title or a headline (''TYCOON WEDS MARTIAN'') by way of introduction. If any more background is necessary, you haven't done your homework. Every other piece of information needs to be on the stage. You're seeking strong, clear physical actions which reveal strong, committed psychological states. If two characters share a long friendship and you can't get that into the title, explore ways in which that friendship may manifest itself in their behavior.

It's a good idea to use props and costume pieces in an assignment of this kind. Your attention needs to be on the truth of the moment, not on the precision of miming. Keep all these things restricted, however, to just what is actually used. Not set decor. In your last few rehearsals before the day you present in class, start rehearsing setting up the stage, introducing your material, getting quickly from one scene to the other, shifting props and costume pieces, and clearing the stage. I have seen actors, otherwise well prepared, simply collapse on the *bookends* of their presentation because they forgot to work on how to get up there, how to switch from scene to scene, how to get off. You work on these things not to achieve some slick level of polish but to put your mind at rest, to keep yourself from being unnecessarily distracted or scattered, and to avoid wasting the time of your classmates who otherwise must sit and wait while you fuss over your scarf. If you can avoid it, why do this to yourself?

Remember that the System is all preparation. Don't get bogged down with your homework when it comes time to perform, but give yourself permission for freedom, earned through your homework. As the inventor himself said, ''You cannot act 'The System'; you can work on it at home, but when you step out onto the stage, cast it aside, there only nature is your guide.''[36]

STANISLAVSKI EXTENDED

Much knowledge has opened up since Stanislavski worked and wrote. Acting has benefited from sources as diverse as the behavioral and computer sciences. Stanislavski was in favor of anything that worked. In fact, one of his admonitions was that each actor should move beyond him to his own discoveries.

If anything would upset the great man as much as the degree to which some of his concepts have been misunderstood, it probably would be the degree to which they have been slavishly imitated. There are disciples who refuse to tolerate an exercise or a phrase not dropped from the master's lips. But his System is open-ended. At no point does it close off expansion and change. That is why it has emerged as the reigning school of acting in the world. Like democracy as a political system, it grows, suffers, adapts, gets battered, and survives.

The following techniques are in the Stanislavski way of thinking and are worth attention.

Private Audience

Your own private audience is that group of people whose opinions are important to you, those to whom you have always felt the need to prove yourself. They influence you so strongly that you can't get them out of your head, as least not easily. Imagine that you are walking along, dragging your feet, shoulders slumped, and you hear your mother (who lives 500 miles away) tell you: "Stand up straight and walk right." Now, you may automatically straighten up, or you may mutter "Buzz off" and keep slumping, but she remains very much present in your audience in either case.

This group also includes supporters and nurturers, as well as major detractors, competitors, and those who have abused their authority over us. So some members are not friendly at all. When you have a triumph, and you think of someone and mutter to yourself, "I wish the s.o.b. could see me now," you have acknowledged a member of your private audience. Ex-husbands and ex-wives are always private audience members. I keep waiting for the day when someone wins the Oscar or Tony and instead of thanking the world, says something like, "I won't bore you with thank-yous, but I do have a list of people who tried to stop me. I'd like to name them. First, there was my terrible second grade teacher, Miss Markowitz, who didn't cast me as Cinderella. Then there was . . ." and so on. The winner would be acknowledging those truly unsung members of the private audience.

Your own vision of God, too, has membership, whether it is abstract (such as "The Force") or literal (an elderly, bearded man carrying a scroll and seated on a throne, or like that of Jerry in *The Zoo Story,* who maintains that "God is a colored queen in a kimono."[37]). A variation involves those you idolize but have never actually met, such as a favorite author or actor.

NAMING MEMBERS

1. Jot down at least two names or incarnations in each of these categories for yourself:
   1. Family
   2. Nurturers
   3. Detractors
   4. God
   5. Idols
2. Replace your members with those of your open-scene characters. Run each scene, leaving your character open for any of the members to make an appearance in her mind and influence her decisions.

The identification of the character's private audience helps you with the Magic If. It also clarifies where you stop and the character begins, which influences you share, and which ones you, the actor, need to take on to perceive the world as the character would.

Grouping

Grouping involves looking at others in general terms, instead of as individuals. It is a way of endowing in large numbers. Bigots are the worst groupers, branding all members of a particular race or creed with the same qualities, seeing cultural binding where it doesn't exist. But everyone groups to some degree. Theatre majors and business majors tend to view one another as aliens. Liberals tend to view all conservatives as selfish, whereas conservatives tend to categorize all liberals as irresponsible. No one is entirely guiltless of the sweeping label.

Grouping others (as powerful if you are cast as a timid soul, as ignoramuses if you are playing an intellectual snob, as thieves if you are playing a miser) helps you actively use all the other people onstage and in the character's world in a collective Magic If. It also helps you avoid playing an "attitude." You can't play "timid," "snob," or "miser" as isolated clichés. The more eccentric or unbalanced a character is, the more essential this technique becomes, so you aren't tempted to play the character's zaniness or craziness, but instead let yourself see people as she does. If you place these qualities on others, quite a bit of behavior is likely to be automatically appropriate and free of stereotyped choices.

GROUP BIAS

What groups do you view in the most sweeping way? Write the name of the group and the one or two words you would use for them. Consider people who differ from your convictions in each of these areas.

1. Politics
2. Religion
3. Pastimes or Recreation
4. Attractiveness
5. Discipline

Imagine someone whose views are the polar opposite of your own. What terms would he or she use to cluster you and those who feel as you do into a single group?

Substitution

While actually inserting your own experience in the place of the character's seems thoughtless and shallow, there are certain rare instances where you may have no choice. Something in the character's life may be wholly outside your experience. Now, nothing should be outside the spiritual or imaginative experience of an actor. You certainly shouldn't have had to rule a kingdom in order to play a king. But you may not have a frame of reference. Uta Hagen uses two of the best examples when she writes about shooting someone and being shot. Killing and being killed are experiences that are, one hopes, foreign to you. She suggests that stepping into the shower expecting warmth but being stunned by ice-cold water instead is a reasonable analogy for the sensation of a bullet hitting you. And, while you may never have hounded another human with a pistol, you have probably pursued, swatter in hand, a fly or wasp that has been driving you crazy, stalking it with genuine menace and malevolence.[38] Her suggestions act as triggers for the imagination. I think some actors would categorically deny that a character's actions are in them to perform. Substitution is a superior solution to denial.

Conditioning Forces

Isolate from the given circumstances, which influence a character's general behavior throughout the play, factors influencing the character's behavior of the moment, which may change from beat to beat. Conditioning forces are immediate, physical, and sensual. If it's raining outside and you enter the stage wet, this force conditions at least the first moments of the scene, influencing each decision you make. Standard conditioning forces include:

1. *Temperature or weather*
   How hot or cold, wet or dry, constant or changing? This force may include variable conditions, as in a cold palace room with one fireplace, so that proximity changes feelings.

2. *Light*
   How bright or dark, and what kinds of difficulties do you have as a result? Are there pools of light and shadow, so that your vision and sense of security vary from space to space?

3. *Comfort*
   Any irritating little aches or pains? Any discomfort that comes and goes, depending on how you move? Any stiffness? Do your clothes fit? Do you need to go to the bathroom? Is your foot asleep? Are you hungry or thirsty?

4. *Time*
   Actual hour? Are you running late? How late? How long have you been up? How fatigued or energized? How anxious are you to get this over with? How willing to play around and sustain the encounter?

5. *Space familiarity*
   Who owns it? How much right do you have to be here? How well do you know the space? How curious are you about it? Who do you know here? Has it changed since your last visit?

6. *Distractions*
   Is there loud noise from the street outside? From the next room? Is there an unpleasant, intriguing, or tantalizing odor in the space? Are your senses diverting you from your objective? Are you terribly curious about something? Terribly aroused by someone? Is any force or activity making it hard to focus your attention?

Actors often mistakenly play in a space which seems utterly neutral, without any discernible physical influences. They also tend to play only two physical states: vibrantly healthy or dying. Consider the effect on the scene if your character had one glass of wine too many last night, and while not truly hung over, feels this tiny irritation at the side of his temple and is just a bit sluggish. Then there's that silly cut on your little finger where the Band-Aid won't stay on. And the neon light above is a bit glaring, but you don't have the energy to turn it off and a lamp on instead. But there is a nice breeze coming in the window, relieving the heavy humidity in this room, and so on. Our state of well-being is relative, not perfect or terminal. Like endowment, a conditioning force may or may not be read by an audience, but the sense of a complete human being in crisis probably will. Conditioning forces are especially important as you enter the scene because it is here that they often change (moving from dark movie theatre into glaring sunlight, heat wave into air-conditioning, space uncertainty into relieved familiarity), and their effect on you may then modify as you grow accustomed to the new environment.

EXERCISE 4.20

ADDING CONDITIONS

1. Run the first several beats of one of your open scenes, adding a strong influence from one of the six forces listed above, then one from another force, until you've tried all six separately. Now go back and layer in all six, one by one, so that all are finally working at once.

2. Have volunteers improvise situations where the audience identifies a basic relationship for the actors to start with. Do the scene first in a neutral state, then select two crucial conditioning forces to add.

EXERCISE 4.21

CRAZY CAR CONDITIONS

Set up four chairs in two rows like the front and back seat of a car. Three actors get in and assume an identity, driving along. A fourth is a hitch-hiker, who, upon entering the car, brings in a distinct conditioning force, which everyone catches. Another actor hitchhikes, and, when he is picked up, one of the first actors leaves. The new actor brings in a conditioning force which everyone also catches. After the group gets the idea of taking on the force, be sure that a conditioning force does not leave the car until the person who brought it on leaves the car.

Rehearsed Futures

In the same way that actors rehearse for the opening of a play, most of us rehearse our futures in our heads, thinking about some moment when our lives will come together, or, possibly, fall apart. There are three kinds of rehearsed futures: best possible, worst possible, and wildest dream come true. Most of us feel that our present circumstances will somehow change. Rehearsing your future is a way of holding onto your sanity and surviving present misfortunes. The future can be freely fantasized about in both practical and possible terms, and in wild and unlikely terms requiring windfalls or even miracles to transpire.

For many actors, a best possible future would include getting a Master of Fine Arts degree from a respected program, working for some regional repertory companies, and perhaps doing some successful runs on Broadway. A worst possible future might include flunking out of your undergraduate program, never getting the courage to leave town, and spending the rest of your days busing tables. A wildest-dream-come-true future might include being discovered tomorrow; becoming a household word overnight; winning the Oscar, Tony, Emmy, and Grammy awards all several times over; having all the great writers of the world beg to create vehicles for you and all the great lovers of the world beg to sleep with you; somehow managing to create peace and harmony among the peoples of the world with your art; and having a newly discovered planet named after you in honor of your accomplishments.

Taking the time to develop your character's rehearsed futures adds to the liveliness and energy of your performance, beyond the obvious additional dimension to the Magic If. Knowing your character well enough to fantasize from his perspective gives great confidence. Thinking about and yearning toward his future tends to make your performance alive with anticipation.

EXERCISE 4.22

OPEN FUTURES

1. Identify all three rehearsed futures for both of your open-scene characters.

2. Run the scenes, keeping yourself open to moments when the character might fantasize about the future.

3. Discuss any immediate impact on the scene.

Suppression

Much of our energy during time spent with others is devoted to trying not to reveal how we feel or how strongly. This suppression of emotional display helps us avoid making complete fools of ourselves, but it can also stifle our freedom and spontaneity. (Review the section on offstage suppression in chapter 1.) Research has shown that instead of trying to cry, if you can identify, as Stanislavski has suggested, the conditions of the body that lead to crying (maybe you start to pause at odd places, your voice moves back into the throat, your fingers begin small spasmodic moves of their own), and then play directly *against* revealing those symptoms, the result will be either tears or a truthful struggle. (Most actors who attempt to cry approach the phenomenon exactly backward.) Having planted the character's given circumstances, next plant physical symptoms he wishes to avoid revealing. Remember, what is hidden just under the surface, what is not fully shown, is often what is most interesting.

> *As an actor, you tend to want to show everything—but that's not true to life. What's compelling is the sense that something isn't being revealed—you just see little flashes that give you a hint as to why somebody is acting the way he is. That's what draws people to characters—that mystery or possibility. Will we know? Will we be shown?*[39]
>
> —GLENN CLOSE

EXERCISE 4.23

PLAYING AGAINST

1. Observe yourself for the next week, whenever you are trying not to show your feelings but are not entirely successful. Note your physical symptoms. Put these in your mental acting file to employ when needed.

2. Go back to your open scenes and identify each point where your character wishes to suppress emotion. Plant the symptoms to be avoided. Rehearse the scene with the focus on playing against what the character fears to reveal.

OBSERVING THE SYSTEM

Attend a performance and identify each of these techniques for an individual performer (see Appendix E, Open Scene Scenario).

1. List ten of the character's most significant *given circumstances.*

2. Specify *conditioning forces* at work at the character's first entrance, and describe how and when these changed throughout the evening.

3. How would you, if cast in this role, employ the *Magic If* to help you absorb yourself convincingly in the character's perspective?

4. How would you employ *grouping* if cast in this role?

5. Write three paragraphs or three different versions of the character's *rehearsed futures:* (a) best possible, (b) worst possible, (c) wildest dreams come true. Write as the character in his own words.

6. Find three instances where the actor was required to use *endowment* to make use of props or set pieces effectively. Do the same for the character's view of three others in the play. Extend at least one of these endowments into detailed conjecture.

Working with a Partner

Stanislavski suggests that one must learn to touch a partner with one's very soul. Never one to understate, he establishes throughout his works the need for complete respect, trust, and connection between acting partners. You share so much responsibility with and for your partner that the working relationship should be one of self-disclosure, nonpossessive caring, trust, risk-taking, mutual acceptance, and open feedback. Stanislavski calls this working relationship a state of ''communion,'' which is a step higher than simple communication toward complete sharing.

> *Acting is an intimate thing. You entrust your partner*
> *with something very private, a tremendous bond*
> *develops and that intimacy is like love.*[40]
> —KEVIN KLINE

We have already discussed certain basic rules of courtesy, such as never standing your partner up, and always getting a message to her if you're unavailable to rehearse. Here are some other accepted guidelines:

1. Never direct your partner. This is a collaboration. Neither of you is in charge.

2. Ask for help from your partner instead. Remember the problem is always yours. If you need a response, state it as exactly that, something you need and she can give you.

3. Endow your partner shamelessly and allow yourself to fantasize about him, but keep this information to yourself. A lot of your ideas can be rendered ineffective by sharing them when there is no real point and only potential embarrassment in doing so.

4. Try to bring a contagious, supportive energy into the rehearsal.

5. Your relationship is like a small, short-term marriage, with all the give-and-take and need for mutual support which that implies.

The two of you need to know each other better than can usually be accomplished accidentally. The following exercise imposes some structure and speeds up the process. It does not force an artificial, instant intimacy, however, because you always have the freedom to reveal only as much information as is comfortable. Stanislavski and his company had the extraordinary luxury of working and living together for many years, so that members of the Moscow Art Theatre were like family to one another. This is the best exercise I know for gaining some semblance of self-disclosure between people who have no choice but to trust each other.

EXERCISE 4.25

PARTNER SHARING

Decide who will speak first and take turns answering each question. Whenever possible, the listener should repeat in her own words what she has just heard. It is sometimes helpful to say ''What I hear you saying is . . .'' and then complete the statement. If the speaker agrees that this was what he intended, then it is time to go on. Don't look ahead and do not plan or ''rehearse'' any answers, but respond in the moment.

In each statement, such as item 2, you have the freedom to reveal as many nicknames or titles or as few as you want. This way you are not forced to share more than you want. When a statement (as in 6 and 15) is repeated, answer it for the specific moment at which the statement is made. This exercise takes most people about an hour. If you are given some class time but do not finish, why not begin your next rehearsal by completing it together?

1. My name is . . .
2. My other names are . . .
3. My romantic status is . . .
4. I come from . . .
5. The reason I'm studying acting is . . .
6. Right now, I'm feeling . . .
7. When I am in a new group, I . . .
8. When I enter a room full of people, I usually feel . . .
9. When I'm feeling anxious in a new situation, I usually . . .
10. In groups, I am most comfortable when the leader . . .
11. Social rules make me feel . . .
12. If a situation is ambiguous and unstructured I . . .
13. I am happiest when . . .
14. The thing that excites me the most is . . .
15. Right now, I feel . . .
16. What concerns me most about the theatre is . . .
17. When I am rejected, I usually . . .
18. To me, belonging means . . .
19. The thing most difficult for me to do in public is . . .
20. Breaking rules makes me feel . . .
21. I most like to be alone when . . .
22. The thing that turns me off the most is . . .
23. I feel affectionate when . . .
24. Toward you, my partner, I feel . . .
25. I cry most easily when . . .
26. I laugh most easily when . . .
27. When I have a day to myself, I am most likely to . . .
28. As a performer, I feel most insecure about . . .

29. I am most likely to get very angry if . . .

30. If I believe anything strongly, it is . . .

31. The thing I am most curious to know about you is . . .

After completing the list, take a few minutes to discuss the experience generally, and to discuss anything that may have come up during the rehearsal period so far that you would like to explore.

EXERCISE 4.26

PULLING IT ALL TOGETHER

Review the next three paragraphs, which summarize the basic vocabulary of the Stanislavski System. Go back and review any idea still not entirely clear to you. Promise yourself not to reject any of these actor's tools until you know you have tried them.

Begin by determining the *given circumstances* of your character and using the *Magic If* to place yourself inside those circumstances, including *endowment* of real and imagined objects and people with physical and emotional qualities. Explore the character's *relationships* with everyone he encounters, developing his *private audience* and his *grouping* of others. Use your five senses to *recall* impressions, with *sense memory* adding detail and texture. You sometimes tap *emotional memory* to connect with the character's feelings. *Release pictures* can be especially powerful in this process. Explore not just the character's past and present but his *rehearsed futures* including his fantasies. Each time the character appears, identify *conditioning forces* which may influence his behavior in an immediate, sensual way.

As you explore the *text*, seek *images* to bring each line to life in order to connect fully with your partner. Work closely and in sufficient trust with your partner for mutual *communion* to occur. Discover the text's underlying *subtext*, including the character's *interior monologue* and *evaluations* where *alternatives* are explored. In each scene, find his *objective*, the *obstacle* in the way, and general *strategy* and specific *tactics* employed to make it happen. Find many small *actions* or *bits* where any inner impulse has an outer execution and you experiment with the *method of physical actions*, balancing the psychological and physical ingredients of each action.

Instead of trying to feel the emotions for each moment, concentrate on *planting* the physical symptoms of emotions, sometimes including *suppression* of emotional display. Section the role into *beats*, changing as individual transactions are completed.

Attempt to identify the character's *super objective* and to find the *through–line of actions*, connecting all of the strategies, tactics, and individual maneuvers executed by the character along the way. All this work is placed in the *score* to guide the process. While a number of changes in your own habits have occurred automatically, some *external adjustments* are likely to occur as your own body and voice change to suit the character. Attention to *tempo* and *rhythm* is especially important in entering the character's experience. If all these ingredients have been carefully pursued, you have a good chance of entering the *creative state* and are almost certain to achieve a performance based on *truth*.

Taking the Gifts

Stanislavski created an acting system as flexible and misunderstood as any political system, including our own. It is based on behaving truthfully in imaginary circumstances. His contribution was summed up by the most renowned actress in the history of the Moscow Art Theatre (who was also the wife of Anton Chekhov), Olga Knipper, who said that Stanislavski "summon[ed] us all to be scrupulous and honest in our approach and understanding of art. His name is our conscience."[41]

The System includes looking closely and carefully at the world of the character, and then gradually entering the character's perspective. It is composed of *objective* means for taking on the *subjective* views of the character. It allows the actor to portray any person, however despicable at first glance, without judgment. It is based on the most humanizing trait, empathy. Any actor who chooses to reject the gifts of the System has a minimal obligation to do so on an informed basis, rather than out of ignorance. It is Stanislavski's System that is likely to provide you with the basis on which you develop your own. It is his contagious spirit that may give you the courage to change.

> *Create your own method. Don't depend slavishly*
> *on mine. Make up something that will work for you!*
> *But keep breaking traditions, I beg you.*[42]
> —Constantin Stanislavski

Notes

1. Interview by Clive Goodwin, in Hal Burton, *Acting in the Sixties* (London: BBC, 1970).
2. Constantin Stanislavski, "The Evolution of My System," in Toby Cole and Helen K. Chinoy (editors), *Actors on Acting,* 1st edition (New York: Crown Publishers, 1970).
3. Jean Benedetti, *Stanislavski: An Introduction* (New York: Theatre Arts Books, 1982).
4. "The 128 Best Things Anyone Ever Said in *People,*" *People,* March 6, 1989.
5. Dan Yakir, "Surprise, Surprise," *Cabletime,* November 1987.
6. See Note 3 above.
7. Constantin Stanislavski, *An Actor's Handbook;* Elizabeth R. Hapgood, translator (New York: Theatre Arts Books, 1963).
8. See Note 3 above.
9. Constantin Stanislavski, *Building a Character* (New York: Theatre Arts Books, 1949).
10. See Note 2 above.
11. Constantin Stanislavski, *An Actor Prepares* (New York: Theatre Arts Books, 1948).
12. Gordon Hunt, *How to Audition* (New York: Harper & Row, 1979).
13. Constantin Stanislavski, *Creating a Role;* Hermione I. Popper, editor; Elizabeth R. Hapgood, translator (New York: Theatre Arts Books, 1961).
14. Brad Darrah, "Enchanting Manipulative Meryl," *Life,* December 1987.
15. *New York Theatre Review,* March 1979.
16. See Note 11 above.
17. Sonia Moore, *The Stanislavski System,* 1st edition (New York: Viking Press, 1965).
18. See Note 7 above.
19. See Note 7 above.
20. See Note 11 above.
21. See Note 11 above.
22. See Note 13 above.
23. See Note 13 above.
24. Ron Rosenbaum, "Acting: The Creative Mind of Jack Nicholson," *New York Times Magazine,* July 13, 1986.
25. Richard Corliss, "The Years of Living Splendidly," *Time,* July 28, 1986.
26. "Denzel Washington," *New York,* August 13, 1990.
27. See Note 11 above.
28. See Note 9 above (pages 69, 71, 82, 87, 126, 135, and 146).
29. See Note 9 above.
30. See Note 2 above.
31. See Note 9 above.

32. Christine Edwards, *The Stanislavski Heritage* (New York: New York University Press, 1965).

33. See Note 11 above.

34. See Note 13 above.

35. Alvin H. Marill, *Katharine Hepburn* (New York: Galahad Books, 1973).

36. See Note 9 above.

37. Edward Albee, *The Zoo Story* (New York: Dramatists Play Service, 1960).

38. Uta Hagen and Haskel Frankel, *Respect for Acting* (New York: Macmillan, 1973).

39. Michael Bandler, "A Star Who Learned to Be Happy," *Parade,* March 26, 1989.

40. See Note 14 above.

41. See Note 32 above.

42. See Note 17 above.

5 TRUTH/TECHNIQUE

Balancing Open, Honest Spontaneity
With Steady, Polished Consistency

If you learn to be truthful first . . . it's terribly hard
to learn to be heard. And if you learn to be heard
first of all, it's terribly hard to speak truthfully.[1]
—GERALDINE PAGE

Being bone-real is not the big problem in
acting in the theatre. The problem is to express
what you are expressing at close distance, fifty
yards away—that is the problem.[2]
—LAURENCE OLIVIER

Which Way?

Is it better for an actor to work from inside out or outside in?
Is it preferable for a performance to have emotion or precision?
Should the actor show the audience his face or a mask?
Should the feelings be real or calculated?
Which is needed most, external form or internal conviction?
Is it more important to be honest or interesting?

''Which way?'' is everyone's favorite debate topic in acting. It is no less interesting for being unresolvable. Like most debate topics, you can learn without settling the issue.

Why don't we just ask the great actors and get it over with? Because *they* can't agree. From Eleonora Duse (for truth) and Sarah Bernhardt (for technique) in the past century, through countless others in this one, there have been celebrated advocates for both sides. Great actors, like all geniuses, skip steps, so their work processes and statements can be deceiving. And many of them simply will not speak of what they do, lest they lose the magic.

Not only do actors work differently from one another, but the same actor will work differently depending on the medium, the space, and the script. Is there a microphone? Is my partner a camera or a person? Are there 50 people out there or 5,000? Is it intimate, or do I need to fill a barn? Am I playing someone like me, or am I Mephistopheles, Hercules, the Mad Hatter, a potato chip? The same actor will work differently even from scene to scene. I was once in a musical in which I had a scene that always came straight from the heart, but minutes later was involved in a dance routine where my interior monologue never got beyond "Step–ball–change. Step–ball–change. Don't forget to smile." The same actor may work differently even from moment to moment. Ultimately the first steps will probably depend on the role.

> *My character in* Beetlejuice *is clearly an outside-in,*
> *with a walk and voice coming before an attitude.*
> *In* Getting Straight, *it was an inside-out. Who*
> *is this guy and where is he in me?*[3]
> —MICHAEL KEATON

As True As Possible

I believe that most actors, if pressed, would say they prefer to work internally, if possible. It is more fun to dig inside and tap real emotion, to cry genuine tears, to summon laughter that isn't forced. It's more of a genuine rush to share the character's feelings. It simply isn't always possible. How can you enter the character's soul if you can barely remember his dance steps? You could risk bumping into the other dancers, but there would be consequences. Nearly every actor, early in his training, experiences something like the following:

> You're in performance and it all seems to be happening for you. In your big scene, the tears come out in floods, everything is real, you're inspired, you're absolutely in-the-moment. You know you are at last an actor in the fullest sense. Later, the director comes backstage and says something like, "You know in scene 7, when you started blubbering, not only could I not understand a word you said, but you personally added five minutes to the

running time of that act. What's wrong?'' Others come backstage and do not praise. They give you sympathetic, curious looks, or they look away. A few also inquire about your health.

You have just learned firsthand one of the classic truths of acting:

An actor's first obligation is to be seen and heard.

To be ''heard'' here, of course, means to be *understood*. Emotion, when it overtakes you completely, overrides clarity of communication. Especially if you are trying to speak.

Of course, many actors also encounter the reverse of the above situation:

You give a performance which to you seems calculated and hollow. You feel you were too aware of each effect and probably were stiff as a result. Afterward, people come backstage. *They* are weeping. Your performance is eulogized. The director and other company members say you have never been better, that tonight you finally flew.

You have learned firsthand another classic truth:

The audience doesn't care whether or not you are having a personal moment. They care whether or not they're having a personal moment.

The theatre is an art based on illusion, and what ultimately matters to the people out front is what *plays* out front.

Actors prefer to be as truthful as they can be while remaining technically sound. If you can play from deep inside and still hit your marks, project to the back row, and give your partner support, then you have begun to marry these partners in art.

A Marriage of Necessity

Lee Strasberg, though often associated with emotive acting, still criticized actors who were all feeling. ''Blood, without flesh and bones, only spills,'' he noted, and, ''Without will, sensitivity is of no value.''[4] A purely technical performance risks looking like a lifeless, stripped skeleton. A purely emotional performance risks looking like blood with no framework to flow through. Stanislavski demanded a completely trained instrument, with the *technical repertoire* to know how to respond fully to the *impulses from within*.

The actor's task is to become knowledgeable enough in technique to have at her disposal the means of transmitting emotion. A basic technical framework involves:

1. Mastering a working vocabulary of rehearsal and performance communication

2. Being able to execute a variety of physical maneuvers

3. Being capable of vocal experimentation, change, and clarity

4. Adjusting your behavior to suit the needs of the character and nature of the playing space

5. Learning to make decisions quickly and to commit to them with high concentration.

At a later, more sophisticated level, it can include such diverse techniques as speaking dialects, handling rapier and dagger, scanning verse, mastering styles, and a multitude of additional specialty skills—advanced techniques to be called on when you need to tackle characters from other worlds and times.

BODY MANEUVERS

We've dealt with the body in a number of contexts. Now it's time to identify what it needs to do onstage. If you're new to the stage, think of this as a crash course in the jargon used there. If this is review for you, skim the lists quickly to brush up and see if there are any new terms. Try to tour the theatre itself, associating each item with something concrete.

The Acting Space

The following items designate theatrical geography. They name the landmarks on the map, helping you explore this world. Knowing where each is helps communication in rehearsal. If a director asks you to move to the third stage right and face the teaser, you don't want to be looking at real people's legs and searching God knows where to find the teaser.

Above area away from the audience, upstage
Apron part of the stage which projects into the auditorium, close to the audience, downstage of the proscenium arch

Arch short for *proscenium arch*, the frame that defines the stage, the opening through which the audience sees the stage

Arena form of staging in which the audience surrounds the stage on all sides, sometimes called theatre-in-the-round

Backing flats or drops used to mask the backstage area by limiting the audience view through doors, windows, or archways on the set

Batten long pipe or strip of wood on which scenery or drops are hung

Below toward the audience, downstage

Border short curtain hung above the stage, used to mask the flies

Box set standard set for contemporary, realistic theatre, showing a back wall and two side walls, with the fourth wall understood to be the transparent one through which the audience views the play

Callboard bulletin board backstage, where messages for a show are posted

Cyclorama curtain or canvas hung at the back of the stage, usually to represent the sky; also called the *cyc*

Downstage the part of the stage nearest the audience

Drop curtain or flat hung above the stage and dropped, or lowered, as needed

Flat single piece of scenery usually made of muslin, canvas, or linen stretched over a wooden form, and used with other similar units to create a set

Flies the area above the stage from which scenery may be "flown" into view

Forestage part of the stage nearest the audience (see *apron*)

Fourth wall imaginary partition through which the audience watches

Green room actors' lounge backstage

Grid framework of wood or steel above the stage; also called the *gridiron*

Ground plan scaled floor plan that shows the ceiling view of the set, including entrances, windows, doors, and furniture

House all areas of the theatre not onstage or backstage: auditorium, lobby, box office, lounges

Legs flat or curtains at extreme right and left of stage, used to mask wings (see *tormenters*)

Mask (*verb*) to conceal from view of the audience

Props any articles handled or carried by the actor

Proscenium opening through which audience views the stage (see *arch*)

Rake (*verb*) to place the floor of any area of the set on a slant, like a ramp

Scrim net curtain, stretched taut, which can become transparent or opaque depending on how it is lit, so that the audience may or may not be able to see through it

Sight lines areas of the stage visible to the audience

Spill light leaks around the edges of a lighting area

Stage left left side of the stage from the actor's point of view, facing the house

Stage right right side of the stage from the actor's point of view, facing the house

Teaser border curtain just upstage of and in back of the front curtain

Thrust form of stage which thrusts from its fourth side into the house, so that the audience surrounds it on three sides

Tormenters flats or curtains at the extreme right and left of stage (see *legs*)

Wings left and right offstage areas

Acting Areas

The terrain of the stage is mapped out into the major areas labelled in Figure 5–1. Some directors break up the acting area into more or less separate areas, but these are where you move on major crosses when staging a play.

Which of these areas are stronger and which weaker? The center stage areas are relative, but the most commonly accepted hierarchy for the others, from most powerful to least, is shown in Figure 5–2. Can you see why? Areas 1 and 2 are center and framed by the arch. As a culture, we tend to look left first, because we are trained to read that way. Any of these factors may be changed by adding a platform (which puts a character on a much higher, more compelling level) or by any number of other manipulations of the space. The relative power of areas also alters with non-proscenium staging.

Up Right	Up Center	Up Left
Right Center	Center	Left Center
Down Right	Down Center	Down Left

Figure 5–1 Acting Areas

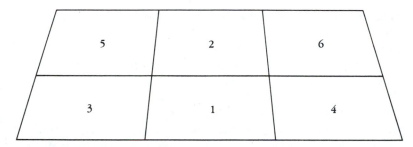

Figure 5–2 Area Power

USING THE MAP

Execute the following basic moves:

1. Walk from the cyc to the apron, then to the down left leg.
2. Stand downstage of the down left tormenter and look at the grid.
3. Start at the border and move in a triangle, with the other points being a tormenter on either side of the stage.
4. Move from the right arch to the cyc, then to beneath the batten.
5. Make up additional problems for individual class members to practice. Have each person write down a three-part problem, and then draw one another's slips of paper, doing the map maneuver written there.

Stage Movement

As anyone who has ever been lost will tell you, reading a map and using it aren't the same thing. Once you have the locations down, there is still a new vocabulary to learn for using the space.

Bit a particularly striking or theatrical piece of business, not to be confused with a single motivational unit (which is also called a *bit*)
Blocking those movements of the actor which are set by the director at some point in the rehearsal process

Break* to drop character suddenly, often by laughing or in some way "breaking up"

Bridge transition from one unit to another

Business pantomimed action with or without props, the smaller movements not involving full crosses

Cheat to turn toward the audience, while appearing to focus on another player onstage, so as to be seen better

Closed turn a turn executed so that the actor turns his back to the audience

Composition stage images created by placing actors and properties in various arrangements

Counter small move made in the direction opposite a move made by another actor, done to balance stage composition

Cue final word, move, or technical change which signals the actor to proceed to his next line or movement

Cue-to-cue to rehearse while skipping lengthy passages and running only those moments where change in responsibility occurs, moving from one cue directly to the next

Focus directing attention toward a focal point so that the audience's attention will follow

Front curtain curtain hanging in the proscenium arch, concealing the stage from audience view

Freeze to suddenly stand completely still to form a tableau

Give stage assuming a less dominant position in relation to another actor

Hold any deliberate pause in the play's action

Indicate* to show the audience, rather than let them see; to play actions without intentions

Mug* to exaggerate facial expressions and reactions to the point of caricature

Open turn turning in such a way that the actor always faces the audience during his movement

Places a command to take stage positions for the beginning of the play or scene

Presentational acknowledging the audience, the theatricality of the event, and playing generally toward the house

Read to register with the audience; often used to describe the difference between the way an action feels onstage and the way it actually looks from the house (also called *play*)

*These three terms represent degrees of actor failure in physical reaction. The actor moves increasingly farther away from the character's perspective and truth as he deteriorates from indicating to mugging to breaking, in which complete control is lost.

Representational creating the impression that the audience is not present, that a real-life situation is being enacted onstage so that the audience seems to be eavesdropping

Run-through uninterrupted rehearsal of a scene, an act, or an entire play

Shtick silly or cheap piece of business, usually designed for laughter

Share stage assuming a position of equal importance in relation to another actor

Stretch to take longer to execute something than would normally occur, often done to allow time for a difficult costume or set change

Strike to remove an object from the stage

Take a reaction of surprise, usually involving looking again (a *double-take*) at the source or the audience; takes may be single, double, or triple

Take Stage to draw audience attention, to assume a stronger stage position

---

EXERCISE 5.2

MANEUVERING

Execute the following maneuvers. Two actors together onstage.

1. A cross down right, B counter, both cheat.

2. A and B face each other. A do a closed turn to face the wings. B start an open turn a beat later and A stretch your turn so both finish at the same time.

3. A and B stand down center. A take stage from B through movement. B regain focus by a shtick.

4. A and B move freely, conversing about the theatre in a presentational manner, finding as many opportunities for takes as possible.

5. Add other problems suggested by the class for pairs of classmates onstage, either with the audience calling out directions or by drawing tasks.

Movement as Technique

Once you understand stage vocabulary and maneuvers, you are ready to use the space to achieve effects. The more you know about how stage pictures are continually created and dissolved, the more comfortable you'll be in the space. It will feel more and more like home, and you will look to the audience as if you really live there.

LIVING PICTURES

When you and your partner are onstage, there is the feeling of an active relationship between the two of you, and between each of you and the audience, before you ever physically move to another spot. Try each of the following pictures. Ask yourself what impression is made if:

1. The two of you stand quite close, facing each other, in profile to the audience?
2. Same as above, but with considerable distance between you?
3. Same as above, but with pieces of furniture separating you?
4. You are standing close to your partner, but his back is turned to you?
5. You are standing close to your partner, but *your* back is turned?
6. You are close to each other, but both facing opposite directions?
7. The distance of number 2 (above) and the separations of 3 are added to the relationships of 4, 5, and 6?
8. You are standing close to each other, but both facing full front?
9. Both of you face full back?
10. Both of you are ¼ left or right? ¾ left or right?
11. One of you is ¼ left, the other ¼ right? If you switch?
12. The same combinations of ¾ left and right?
13. One of you full front and the other full back?
14. Any other combination, including profile?
15. You take any of the close-to-each-other combinations and put it up center?
16. Move it down center?
17. Move it to any of the other four major acting areas?
18. Take situation 4, but you are up right and your partner is down center? The two of you reverse?
19. Any other situation with the two of you in different acting areas?
20. Same as 19, but with varying proximities to pieces of furniture?
21. Same as number 1, but this time both sitting?
22. You are both kneeling?
23. You are both on a staircase or ramp? Both up on a platform?
24. Any situation above, with both of you reclining? Both lying down?

25. Any situation listed so far, but with each of you in a contrasting position from the following list:

(a) on platform   (e) kneeling
(b) on staircase or ramp   (f) reclining
(c) standing   (g) lying down
(d) sitting

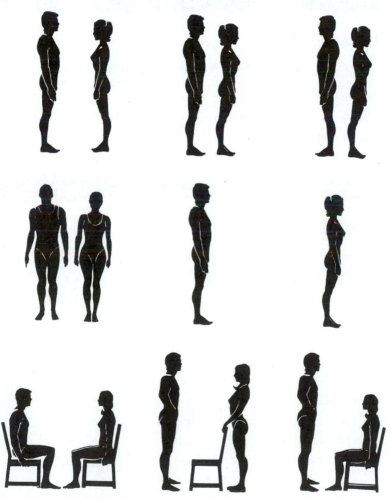

Figure 5–3 Implied Relationships
What seems to be changing besides the picture in each of these situations?

Even before adding business or overt movement, strong messages have been sent about how open the two characters are to each other and to the audience, about how equal they are, or about who is dominant and who subservient, about degrees of dominance, barriers to contact, and about the relative involvement or indifference of each participant.

EXERCISE 5.4

OFFSTAGE PICTURES

1. If you are not already aware from the imitation exercises, try to note whether you have a tendency to face people at ¼ instead of straight on, whether you tend to stand when others are sitting, or which of the combinations above are most and least characteristic of you in life.

2. When you see two people from a distance, note the immediate judgment you make regarding what might be going on between them.

EXERCISE 5.5

ADDING MOTION

When you and your partner stand in profile, as in the first silhouette in Figure 5–3, what impression is made if:

1. You both gesture with full large bubble, extending your arms all the way out and even involving your legs in the conversation?

2. You gesture within a normal, everyday range?

3. You gesture in a tight manner, close to the torso?

4. There is any contrast between the two of you in gestural patterns?

5. You both use hand props to emphasize everything you say?

6. One of you uses hand props, but the other does not?

7. You both make long crosses every time you speak?

8. You both make short crosses of just a few feet?

9. One of you moves a great distance and the other a short distance?

10. One of you moves and the other is always still?

11. One of you moves a lot but does not gesture, while the other stands in place but gestures fully?

12. The movements are relatively constant throughout the scene?

13. Large moves come after at least a minute of no movement at all?

14. One of you moves in an erratic, varying pattern while the other is quite predictable?

15. You both tend to move directly and then stop, or instead both move to an intermediate location, then change directions before you finally stop? If there is a contrast of directness between you?

16. Recalling your basic body positions when static, what if your movements tend to be largely pointed straight upstage or downstage?

17. There is constant countering, with moves going back and forth along the proscenium arch?

18. There is a greater use of the diagonal by both or one of you?

19. There is a tendency to circle each other and to move in curves, S shapes or figure-eights? If one person uses these circular moves while the other is always heading straight for a target?

20. The movements themselves are rapid and darting?

21. All movements are slow, steady, almost lugubrious?

22. There is a contrast in tempo/rhythms between characters or at various moments in the scene?

23. A movement comes just prior to a line?

24. The line comes first, then the cross?

25. The line is broken, with a movement occurring somewhere in the middle? If one character falls into a pattern while the other is quite surprising?

These tools, combined with the prior list, give the actor an almost unlimited combination of ways to communicate a relationship. The more you practice and observe these maneuvers as pure technique, the more responsive the body becomes to discovering appropriate moves in a more spontaneous way. Once you've been exposed consciously to all the modulations, it is amazing how many simply come to you when you are exploring within a scene.

EXERCISE 5.6

EXCHANGES

Use the following brief exchanges of dialogue to explore the staging relationships covered so far. Which changes in basic stage picture, business, stage movement, and timing alter the impact of the lines most significantly?

One: Your place or mine?
Two: Neither.

One: I'm so excited. I'm just going to hold my breath 'til we get the news!
Two: You do that.

One: How cold, crude, and rude.
Two: Yes, those are my lawyers. You'll be hearing from us.

One: How do you like my outfit?
Two: You know, a lot of people couldn't get away with a look like that.

When you get larger groups of actors in the space, many variables are added. The most important principle is *contrast*. Whenever an actor does something different from all the others, it will take focus. So you may be sitting in a weak area of the stage with your back to the audience, but if it is full of actors in stronger areas, all standing and facing forward, *you* will be what we watch. Also, no matter what kind of picture exists, the minute someone moves, all eyes will go in the direction of the moving target.

EXERCISE 5.7

CONTRAST

Go back over the lists in the preceding exercises and find situations in which an actor might position himself in such a way that it would normally be considered a weak choice, but could be quite powerful, simply because of contrast.

Onstage/Offstage Comparisons

Some things that have been learned as simple good manners offstage need to be modified onstage for purposes of audience attention. Most of us have learned to be less assertive in life than is necessary in the theatre just to be seen and heard.

1. Cross *in front* of another character, unless that character is seated and you can be seen the whole time.

2. Generally, look at people who are entering or exiting to help direct attention.

3. Entering characters should move well onto the stage and not linger at the entrance. They also leave completely. Half-moves distract out front.

4. Actors should not often move at the same time unless momentary chaos is intentional. The audience gets confused about where to look.

5. Move on your own lines and, usually, remain absolutely still on those of other actors.

6. Remain as open to the audience as possible when speaking, with particular care to keep your face, especially your eyes, visible much of the time.

7. All other factors being equal, if you are standing and the other person is sitting, you will dominate. Even though possessing the chair may seem the more powerful position, as it would be offstage, the audience, looking through the picture frame, sees one person looming powerfully over another. The possession does not read nearly as strong as the height. All such assessments of dominance need to be seen as through a picture frame.

8. Minimize eye contact. Inexperienced actors look at each other either not at all or too much. Casting director Michael Shurtleff estimates that people in real life look at each other only ten percent of the time.[5] He may be right. Connecting with your partner does not mean staring at her relentlessly. In fact, if there is only one other person in the scene, eye contact tends to lessen, because there is no need to signal to whom your remarks are being directed.

   Offstage, even when you're in a position (like a restaurant booth) which forces you to face another person, note how often your eyes dart away or settle on other targets. When you are outdoors with a companion, note how seldom the two of you lock eyes and how much of the time you focus on surroundings.

VOICE MANEUVERS

While word choice is determined by the writer, the actor is responsible for adjusting the control knob on each of the other categories we have covered (quality, tempo, rhythm, articulation, pronunciation, pitch, volume, and nonverbals). Each of these is worth working on separately offstage. You might pick a day when you listen for rhythm in others and experiment with it on your own. Try working your way through each category on a different day, aiming to expand your range in that particular aspect of vocal life before the day is over.

The most frequent request from directors and coaches is for variety, for the actor to simply use *more* of everything, to break out of a very narrow vocal life. Most actors need to expand their expressive mode by letting their pitch slide into the upper registers and down into the lower; by letting the quality move into different textures as they describe a range of feelings; by speeding up, slowing down, and hitting a middle stride with less predictability. We're not talking so much about changing your own vocal tendencies as *broadening* them. Most of us tend to trap our voices in a tiny expressive mode. Actors learn to use more voice, period.

Vocal Directions

The following terms are used in standard rehearsal requests, during lectures, and in class critiques.

Anticipate to respond earlier than the given cue, revealing that the actor knows what is coming even though the character would not

Build to increase any combination of vocal techniques for a speech to reach a climax

Curtain line last line in a scene, or any other line requiring pointing up; also called *tag line*

Diphthong two consecutive vowel sounds

Drop to omit or to say inaudibly

Dynamics energy, color, and variety of speech

Elongate to stretch out or take longer than usual to say

Emphasize to point, by stress or any other technique, particular words or sounds

Inflection a change in pitch

Intonation a series of pitch changes on a vowel

Melody pattern a predictable use of pitch which can be graphed like notes on a musical scale

Onomatopoeia characteristic of a word that sounds like what it identifies (''slap'' sounds similar to the act of slapping)

Overlap to begin speaking during another actor's speech, not to be confused with anticipating; overlapping may be both deliberate and natural

Paraphrase to say words that convey the meaning of a line but are not those of the playwright

Phoneme any of the basic distinctive sounds of a language

Phrasing sectioning speech into units for emphasis and breathing

Resonate to use as a bodily sounding area, usually a request to change

Setup first of three parts to a comic line, in which subject is introduced (followed by a *pause*, then the *punch line*)

Speed-through to run lines as rapidly as possible while still maintaining sense, mood, and relationships

Stress greater weight placed on a particular portion of a word or phrase (see *emphasize*)

Stretch to take longer with a speech, often by elongating individual vowels

Substitute to insert one sound in place of another

Support to sustain sound, projected from within, without allowing waste of breath

Swallow to fail to project or resonate certain sounds

Tap to hit a consonant lightly, firmly, and briefly

Top to register more strongly than a preceding line, usually by speaking louder and faster

Throwaway to give a line only the slightest emphasis, usually for comic effect, because the words themselves register so strongly

Triphthong three consecutive vowels, employed in few standard sounds, but often true of regional speech or dialects

Voice/Unvoice to vibrate or not vibrate the vocal folds so that a sound reverberates or does not, as in the initial sounds of the words *fine* (unvoiced) and *vine* (voiced); although lips and tongue are in the same position for both words, only in the second do the vocal cords vibrate

Undercut to deliver a line with much less intensity than the preceding one, usually to deflate; the opposite of *topping*

EXERCISE 5.8

VOCAL CHANGES

1. Pick a line of dialogue. Face one wall of the room. Begin the line in your head voice. When you get to the corner, switch to your sinus voice. When you get to the next corner, switch to your throat or pharyngeal voice. At the last corner, employ your chest voice. Change lines and expand to other resonators until you feel aware of the differences.

2. Play catch with sound. Throw a "one" to your partner, with one of you onstage and the other out in the house. Give the "one" definite weight and shape so he knows what kind of ball to catch. Partner repeat "one" as you catch it. Then throw a "two" back. Vary the distance between you, the weight and mass of the sound, and the degree to which the receiver needs to move quickly or some distance to catch the sound where it has been thrown.

Vocal Technique

Even though mastery of your voice starts later and happens slower than mastery of your body, it's worth the daily grind when your sound is finally truly yours. The first step is to expand your own speech repertoire so that you have more choices whenever you speak a line. Every time you hear another version of the ten voice elements (covered in chapter 3) or of the directions above, play with it and try to capture it. The following exercises, if pursued regularly, will offer you a wider range of possibilities.

EXERCISE 5.9

ADDING REPERTOIRE

1. Go back over the two-line scenes employed for movement exercises and use each of the vocal directions above to add yet another dimension to the relationships. Even if the direction appears to imply a negative speech characteristic, see what characterizing it may achieve.

2. In groups of two, draw slips of paper with each of the items on the list above. Quickly improvise dialogue to demonstrate the concept. Class guess which vocal maneuver was being employed.

EXERCISE 5.10

T-SHIRT PHILOSOPHY

These lines appear on T-shirts I have seen. Their humor works without taxing the delivery of the line. Relax and experiment, knowing that variation can only enhance each line's impact:

BETTER TO REMAIN SILENT AND BE THOUGHT A FOOL THAN TO SPEAK AND REMOVE ALL DOUBT.

THE FUTURE ISN'T WHAT IT USED TO BE.

HAVING SEX IS LIKE PLAYING BRIDGE. IF YOU DON'T HAVE A GOOD
   PARTNER, YOU'D BETTER HAVE A GOOD HAND.

LIFE IS A BED OF ROSES, BUT WATCH OUT FOR THE PRICKS.

CONFORM. GO CRAZY. OR BECOME AN ARTIST.

THE DIFFERENCE BETWEEN GENIUS AND STUPIDITY IS THAT GENIUS HAS ITS
   LIMITS.

I REFUSE TO HAVE A BATTLE OF WITS WITH AN UNARMED PERSON.

YOU'RE TWISTED, PERVERTED AND SICK. I LIKE THAT IN A PERSON.

OBVIOUSLY, THE ONLY RATIONAL SOLUTION TO YOUR PROBLEM IS SUICIDE.

A WOMAN WITHOUT A MAN IS LIKE A FISH WITHOUT A BICYCLE.

DON'T TELL ME WHAT KIND OF DAY TO HAVE.

REALITY IS FOR PEOPLE WHO LACK IMAGINATION.

YOU'RE THE REASON MY CHILDREN ARE SO UGLY.

MEN [or WOMEN] SHOULD COME WITH INSTRUCTIONS.

KEEP AMERICA BEAUTIFUL—STAY HOME.

SEX IS LIKE SNOW. YOU NEVER KNOW HOW MANY INCHES YOU'LL GET OR
   HOW LONG IT'S GOING TO LAST.

STUPID PEOPLE SHOULDN'T BREED.

EXPERIENCE IS WHAT YOU GET WHEN YOU DIDN'T GET WHAT YOU
   WANTED.

ONWARD THROUGH THE FOG.

1. Which voice quality best brings out the line's impact? (Review "Resonators" and "Classic Voices" exercises in chapter 3.)

2. Which lines should be rapidly or slowly delivered? Should some alter tempo as the line progresses?

3. Where should pause be used and where should a word or syllable be punched for effect? Where should emphasis be placed, and how strong should it be? What rhythmic variations are possible?

4. Are there specific sounds that can be crisply emphasized as spoken? Any that might be slurred or thrown away? How might articulation alter?

5. Would any line be enhanced by a dialect or accent, by a pronunciation other than standard?

6. Do any lines seem to cry out for a high or low pitch or for a change mid-thought? Where does a change in pitch prove most effective?

7. Does the line work well almost whispered? Bellowed? With the volume knob adjusted as it progresses?

8. Are there any nonverbal additions which might be amusing or enlightening? Any places for a slight stammer, growl, deep sigh, or any other sound beyond the words themselves?

IMPROVISATION AND FREEDOM

In the search for the healthy blending of truth and technique, no activity can be as liberating as *improvisation*. Once the basic language and maneuvers of the body and voice are comfortable, and the actor begins to feel playful again, improvisation can channel that playfulness and help renew spontaneity. Without some playfulness, how can you do plays?

Improv (which is how it's always abbreviated) gets a bad name when the games don't lead anywhere. Some theatre groups spend a lot of time improvising and none of it shows up in the final product. Original works, created exclusively through improv, tend to be amusing, even satiric, but rarely memorable. Some people want *only* to improvise, nothing else, so they drive everyone else crazy with their refusal to set anything. Ever. It is easy to abuse improv, but when properly focused, few activities can be as invigorating.

Improv is aimed at tapping *intuition*, your knowledge that does not rely on reason or rational processes. It can help sharpen *insight*, your capacity for guessing accurately. And it can help you dare to decide quickly, and dive in, without wasting time in speculating or reflecting unnecessarily. All of us would like to make better decisions faster, without mentally debating an issue to death. On the other hand, no one wants to turn into a reckless fool. Improv can help you avoid the extremes of careful and careless, in favor of the carefree.

Improv Ground Rules

Any game needs rules, or there is no structure to the freedom. The more wild and freewheeling the game, the more important are those rules that keep it from chaos. In improv, actors agree to:

1. Participate without evaluating, explore without judgment.
2. Stay involved until the session ends because either the situation has resolved itself or the teacher/coach calls it to an end. Accept side-coaching, without breaking your concentration.
3. Play to solve the problem, not to find the clever line or cute ending, which may be untrue to the character.
4. Remove preconceptions or plans and respond only in the moment.
5. Accept whatever another actor brings into the scene as true. If an actor enters an improv scene, looks at you and shouts "Brother!" with open

arms, you don't answer ''I've never seen you before in my life.'' All new information is accepted. You are his brother. Hug him. If a new actor comes on while you are holding a broom and asks you whether your baby is a boy or a girl, your broom is indeed your baby. You get to decide the sex.

Basic Awareness Improvs

Earlier chapters in this text contain improvs designed to illustrate basic acting concepts. The following improvs are designed to help your concentration and tune up your responses.

Exposure

The following exercise is almost universal in an introductory improv session because its lessons are fundamental to performance situations of all kinds.

EXERCISE 5.11

BEING AND DOING

1. Standing in groups of five or more onstage, look at the rest of the class—and have them look back at you—for at least three full minutes. Everyone should get a turn up there.
2. Repeat the process with these tasks: Count the number of book bags in the room, the number of women vs. men, the number of people with each hair color, the number of people wearing running shoes. Take suggestions from the audience of what to count. Try to beat the other members of your group and shout out the answer when you have it.

EXERCISE 5.12

CHANGING

In the same onstage groups, while remaining up there in a line:

1. Be interesting
2. Be sexy.
3. Appear indifferent.
4. Look intelligent.
5. Be mischievous.

Now replace each of these instructions respectively with:

1. Think of a secret which no one here knows.
2. Quietly scan the room and note those people who turn you on and which qualities especially appeal to you.
3. Count the items of clothing you have on.
4. Decide which controversial topic intrigues you most at the moment. What is the best argument for each side?
5. Find someone in the room on whom you can play a favorite trick.

Discuss the differences in relative relaxation and the reasons. This is a lesson every actor needs to learn deep in his bones.

Reactions

The capacity to respond with all the senses to an imaginary event calls on the full range of your ability to remember, deep inside the mind and body. It also requires a complete return to a state of Let's Pretend. Perform in groups of five to ten the following five exercises.

EXERCISE 5.13

SPECTATOR SPORT

Agree as a group on the sport which is going on at a great distance from you. Watch without interacting with each other, but feel free to speak and move around. Accept whatever changes the teacher adds.

EXERCISE 5.14

SOUNDS OF MUSIC

Same situation as above, but at a concert where you are enthralled by what you see and hear.

SENSES ALIVE

Pick an agreed-on eating or drinking task and concentrate fully on the act, with as many senses involved as are needed.

WEATHER WATCH

Add to the above a change in weather that to some extent breaks your dwelling on the task, dividing your focus between consuming and climate.

FIVE ALIVE

Agree on a specatator situation which will allow you to combine all of the reactions above. Several groups should layer them in one by one. Later groups try to begin with all reactions working, never allowing any single influence to disappear for long from your consciousness.

(Example: group watching square dance at county fair; add sound of fiddler, midway noises, bright glaring sunlight, mix of cooking smells, odors from animal exhibits, eating corn dogs, drinking lemonade, and so forth.)

Joining

Working as a unit, balancing and supporting each other, and using each individual's contribution are what make acting the ultimate collaboration. In groups of five to seven:

WHERE ARE WE?

Focus on establishing an environment. The first actor enters an open space and starts a task. The second actor does not enter until he is absolutely sure where the scene takes place and how he might fit into the space. Public places (supermarkets, student unions, libraries) should be selected so that the second actor can choose any characterization he wishes and still fit it into the location. All interact with the environment and use all the senses.

HELPING OUT

The first person goes onstage and begins an activity, such as yard work or house-painting, which can be done alone, but can also benefit from help. The task should be physically involving and apparent even to someone who speaks a foreign language. Others join, one by one, concentrating on completing the task with free-flowing group interaction. Every person's objective is to effectively accomplish the basic shared task at hand.

BUILDING

The first person enters, assumes an identity, and starts an activity, but he is the only one who knows both of these. Others join as they are called on and given an identity by the person preceding them, until the group is complete and functioning on the task. (Example: A detective calls in an assistant, who calls in an eyewitness, who spots and calls in a suspect, who calls her lawyer.) Everyone is concerned with accomplishing the shared objective, unless the person calling on you gives you an identity which justifies your working against the others.

CHANGING

Variation on the exercise above, with each new person arriving and deciding both who she is and her relationship to others onstage. They don't know until the entering actor reveals her connection to them and the task at hand. The character entering is free to decide whether to help or hinder the task at hand.

Concentration

The double task of pursuing two activities at the same time, or doing one thing while thinking about another, always faces the actor, who is constantly juggling or splitting his focus.

WHO AM I?

(Done with two actors.) The first actor is onstage seated on a bench and the second (the only one who knows their relationship) enters. The first needs to find out who she is and what her connection to the second is by studying the other's behavior toward her, but without revealing her ignorance. If time allows, actors should switch, once the relationship is clear, so each gets a chance to initiate.

EAT, DRINK, AND BE MERRY

(Two to four actors.) Same as Senses Alive (Exercise 5.15), but this time the actors agree instead on a topic of conversation, which engages them as they consume a large meal. Keep all the areas of concentration balanced. Once secure, add sounds, sights, and weather conditions to the scene.

EXERCISE 5.24

PREOCCUPATION

(Two actors.) A shared physical task is undertaken which necessitates that the two people interact, but each is totally preoccupied with his own work and neither listens to the other at all, except for matter related to the mutual task. Alternate which person is chattering and which is silently thinking of something else, with moments when both talk or momentarily drift away. Keep the task active.

EXERCISE 5.25

I'VE GOT A SECRET

(Five actors.) Two actors decide on a topic which they must discuss in the presence of the other three without revealing the topic. They try to mislead the others without saying anything that is actually untrue. Others join, one by one, when they think they know, but never ask if they are right. Two talkers may challenge any participant to a huddle and if the joiner is wrong, she has to leave. Everyone gets two chances to join before being permanently on the outs.

Selectivity

It is important to know what *not* to think about onstage or off, so that distractions do not get in the way of objectives. Because the mind can only hold so much at once, only the essentials can stay.

EXERCISE 5.26

DRAWING AND DRAWING

(Entire class in two teams.) Each team has a pile of scrap paper and pencils. Each team sends forward its champion to be shown the name of an item, written on a slip of paper which the scorekeeper has drawn from a hat. Each champion runs back and tries to draw a sketch of the item fast enough but clearly enough so that his team guesses it first. Get only the essentials on the paper. Keep score between teams until everyone has had a turn.

SLOW-MOTION TAG

(Entire class.) Begin by simply forcing all movement to slow down, even though someone is chasing and others are escaping. Once this becomes comfortable, each person who is "it" sets a particular movement, which everyone imitates, while still trying to keep from being caught. Each new "it" changes the mode of movement.

PASSING SOUNDS AND MOVES

(Entire class.) First everyone stands in a circle and one person starts a peculiar sound, accompanied by a movement. He carries these across the circle, to someone else who catches both, until they are perfectly imitated. When the new person reaches the middle of the circle, both sound and motion evolve into others, which the new initiator carries to another actor. Neither sound nor move should just jerk into a new mode, but selectively move out of the former set, into the new one. Once the group is responding fully, transfer into tag, this time with both sound and movement involved and everyone required to imitate the person who is "it" both vocally and physically, while avoiding being caught.

COMING AND GOING

(Entire class, but one actor at a time.) Each person picks a place she just came from, and another she is headed toward, and all we see is the moment between. The actor tries to be selective enough, that both are clear. (For example, a man zipping up his fly and then pressing an imaginary button on the wall has come from the men's room to the elevator.) Once procedure is clear, actors should draw slips of paper which assign one of the two places, then finally draw both places. Variation: actors work in pairs.

Nonsense

The use of gibberish or nonsense syllables forces you, as when traveling in a foreign country where you don't know the language, to call on the full range of body language and vocal expressiveness. In each exercise below, even your partner will be simply making an informed guess as to the precise meaning of what you have just said. Remember to use sounds with no recognizable meaning (not even letters and numbers), so that all information is nonverbal.

EXERCISE 5.30

HELP ME

Work privately, in pairs. Alternate asking favors of your partner, warming up your sense of freedom from words. Ask for specific physical tasks so that your partner is able to literally help you out.

EXERCISE 5.31

TRANSLATING

One of you demonstrates some product in nonsense, while the other translates to the audience what he believes his partner has just said. Not even the identity of the object is decided on beforehand. The object should have little relationship to its usual function (so a pail may be the latest in hats or an open notebook may be a bathing suit top) but the speaker should try to be as clear as possible about intentions and new function.

EXERCISE 5.32

SELLING

Working in pairs, persuade the audience to buy some product. The two of you alternate physical demonstration with the sales pitch, helping each other out until the end of the commercial.

EXERCISE 5.33

INTERPLAY

Working in pairs, select any of the above conditions—a request for assistance, a demonstration, or a sales pitch. This time the audience is free to ask questions (in English), which you comprehend, but always answer in your own imaginary language.

Calls

A *call* is a signal which is given to you by some other source: drawing a slip of paper, side-coaching, or the audience itself. Calls usually involve the given circumstances of the scene.

EXERCISE 5.34

THREE Ps

(Groups of two to five.) Each group draws three slips of paper from three containers marked People, Places, and Projects. People will be members of the same profession (doctors? hairdressers?) or background (Martians? Elizabethans?). The Place (a stadium? a sauna?) may or may not have something to do with what they share. The Project (spring cleaning? playing poker? a quilting bee?) may also be unrelated to their background. It's all in the luck of the draw. Audience shouts out guesses. Stick with the task until it is finished or well under way.

AUDIENCE COACHES

(Groups of two to five.) Those not in the group decide on the setting, an identity for each participant, the occasion, and the basic conflict, as we have done in earlier chapters. Audience is free to side coach the scene as it progresses.

AUDIENCE HANDICAPS

(Same group sizes as above.) Actors decide on everything except the conflict, which comes from audience. At various points in the scene, the audience layers in no more than a total of five handicaps (someone cannot speak, a dark secret, a case of amnesia) which are incorporated. Keep within the character's perspective and don't succumb to parody.

Transformations

The ultimate effortless skill of childhood, which every actor needs to recapture, is changing whatever you look at by just believing it is now something else.

PLAY BALL

(Entire class in partners.) Begin tossing an imaginary ball back and forth between you. Teacher will call out changes as it turns into football, medicine ball, ping-pong ball, and others as you let size, weight, and attitude influence you. Later, the ball may become other objects of varying shapes, values, and complexity, which are still sent through the air.

PASSING OBJECTS

(Entire class in a circle, sitting on the floor.) First chosen actor creates an object out of air so that her fellow actors can see it, then passes it to the person next to her, who handles it until it transforms into something else, and is passed again.

PASSING MASKS

(Groups of five to seven.) Sit in a tight circle. First person picks up an imaginary mask from the floor in front of him, puts it on and lets it change him, takes it off, returning to himself, passes it on to the person next to him. Each person gets to try on this particular mask and each person gets to initiate a mask of his own.

MAGIC CLOTHES

(Entire class.) Everyone wanders around room, ignoring the others, until discovering before you a magic pair of shoes. You decide what they look like and what their power is, but once you put them on, they control you and change how you move and relate to the world. After a time you spot a magic sash, belt, or girdle, which again takes you over and dominates not only that area of the body, but your entire relationship to the space around you. Finally you encounter a headdress, hat, helmet, or crown which you put on and it sends your energy up while transforming how you move and what you feel about the area around you. After allowing the headgear to dominate who you are for a while, the three garments begin to fight each other and your sense of self is pulled in different directions. You remove the influence you like the least, then the second choice, and finally allow the one discovery which seems to have freed you most to transform you completely.

ON AND OFF

(Groups of five to seven.) First actor begins a task and establishes an identity, which, once made clear, second actor enters and changes by virtue of his first line. Once the two of them fall into the new pattern, actor three enters and again changes everything. Allow each new relationship to function before the next change. Once the entire group is on and involved, first actor finds a reason to leave, which transforms the group again, and each actor departs, leaving a change behind. The last actor transforms himself before leaving.

Blending and Balancing

The marriage of truth and technique, like most marriages, requires time and adjustment, but is worth it. Every conscientious actor experiences moments that in themselves are tiny miracles. There are few things more wonderful than finding yourself in rehearsal with an impulse you know you can support. Let's say your heart wants you to cry out to your partner with a desperation that suddenly seems absolutely right for the character. You know how to extend an *s* sound masterfully, how to support a plaintive vowel sound so it is mournful but not weak. You know how to land on a final consonant like *p* so that it seems to explode. You have learned to focus almost all your energy momentarily in your eyes. So when you call out ''Stop!'' to your partner, the other actor feels a chill, is frozen, turns, mesmerized, and is locked into your eyes. Your sense of truth launched you, and your technique carried that truth to capture your partner. Then you feel a chill. Of power. And then delight.

> *If you want to be able to express the maximum*
> *variety of things, then the more technical*
> *mastery you can achieve, the more* fun
> *you're going to have!*[6]
>
> —GERALDINE PAGE

Notes

1. Harry Hill, *A Voice for the Theatre* (New York: Holt, Rinehart and Winston, 1985).
2. Interview by Kenneth Tynan, in Hal Burton, *Great Acting* (New York: Bonanza Books, 1967).
3. Cathleen McGuigan, "Keaton Plays It Straight," *Newsweek*, September 27, 1988.
4. Chris Chase, "Lee Strasberg," *Viva*, November 1974.
5. Michael Shurtleff, *Audition* (New York: Walker and Company, 1978).
6. See Note 1 above.

SCENE STUDY

Discovering Character Through Script

> *One begins with the text because it's the text that leads you to the character.*[1]
> —PEGGY ASHCROFT

> *I'm not interested in transmitting my pain to someone. I'm interested in transmitting the* character's *pain or joy. That's my job.*[2]
> —GEORGE C. SCOTT

Regardless of where your performance ends, it starts with the script. Actors are recreative artists, not purely creative ones. Actors start with the playwright's vision and attempt to realize or *complete* that vision. A great actor moves beyond completion into extraordinary discovery, but no actor starts with a blank sheet. The work begins with the text.

This chapter deals with working on an excerpt from a play in a class or workshop, and the next chapter deals with working on an entire play in production. Scene study may be broken down into seven steps. You never leave one step behind; you add on new ones.

1. *Scene selection*
   What is the best material for my partner and me? What excerpt is worth several weeks of our lives?
2. *Script analysis*
   What is this play about, and how does our scene fit into the whole?
3. *Cutting*
   How can we edit the scene to serve time and to favor both actors?

4. *Character analysis*
   How can I get to know this character well enough to deserve to play her?

5. *Staging*
   How can we use the stage to tell the story? How can our characters' relationship become clear through space?

6. *Script awareness improvs*
   How can we use improvisation to help us own our roles?

7. *Shaking up the scene*
   How do we keep from getting complacent, bored, or predictable? How do we keep it fresh?

SCENE SELECTION

The following guidelines are the most common for class assignments with scripts. What may appear to be limitations are actually freeing. They get rid of distracting hurdles and allow you to concentrate on the basic truth of your character. The best first scenes are those fairly close to home.

EXERCISE 6.1

SCENE PROJECT

1. Select a scene of no less than five and no more than ten minutes' playing time,

2. by a contemporary American realist (or from another country, if accents are unnecessary),

3. with characters preferably within five years (and always within ten years) of the actual ages of the actors,

4. with neither actor cast against type,

5. with dialogue divided fairly equally between the two (or at the most three) characters.

Scene Suggestions

The two-character scenes in the following plays meet the basic guidelines given above and offer interesting conflicts:

All My Sons, by Arthur Miller (Chris and Ann)
All the Way Home, by Tad Mosel (Jay and Mary)
Am I Blue, by Beth Henley (Ashbe and John)
The Art of Dining, by Tina Howe (Elizabeth and David)
At Home, by Michael Weller (Paul and Carol)
Baby with the Bathwater, by Christopher Durang (John and Helen)
Bad Habits, by Terence McNally (Benson and Hedges)
Beirut, by Alan Bowne (Blue and Torch)
Bent, by Martin Sherman (Max and Rudy)
The Big Knife, by Clifford Odets (Charlie and Ann)
Birdbath, by Leonard Melfi (Frankie and Velma)
Blue Denim, by James Leo Herlihy and William Noble (Janet and Arthur)
Boy's Life, by Howard Corder (Lisa and Don)
Buried Child, by Sam Shepard (Vince and Shelly)
Burn This, by Lanford Wilson (Larry and Burton, Larry and Anna)
Cheating Cheaters, by John Patrick (Angelica and Theresa)
Coastal Disturbances, by Tina Howe (Lee and Holly)
Danny and the Deep, Blue Sea, by John Patrick Shanley (Roberta
　　and Danny)
Days of Wine and Roses, by J. P. Miller (Kris and Joe)
The Death of Bessie Smith, by Edward Albee (Receptionist and Intern)
Dirty Hands, by J. P. Sartre (Jessica and Hugo)
Dolores, by Edward Alan Baker (Dolores and Sandra)
Duet for One, by Walker Owen (Feldman and Stephanie)
Eastern Standard, by Richard Greenberg (Stephen and Drew or
　　Peter and Phoebe)
Echoes, by N. Richard Nash (Tilda and Sam)
Extremities, by William Mastrosimone (Raoul and Marjorie)
Fishing, by Michael Weller (Rob and Mary Ellen)
Fool for Love, by Sam Shepard (Eddie and May)
The Foreigner, by Larry Shue (Ellard and Charlie or David and Katherine)
The Four Seasons, by Arnold Wesker (Adam and Beatrice)
Fugue in a Nursery (from *Torch Song Trilogy*), by Harvey Fierstein
　　(Arnold and Laurel)
Gemini, by Albert Innaurato (Francis and Judith)
Ghost on Fire, by Michael Weller (Michelle-Marie and Julia)
Golden Boy, by Clifford Odets (Lorna and Joe)
A Good Time, by Ernest Thompson (Mandy and Rick)
The Good-bye People, by Herb Gardner (Nancy and Korman)

A Hatful of Rain, by Michael V. Gazzo (Polo and Johnny)

The Heidi Chronicles, by Wendy Wasserstein (Heidi and Sandra)

Here We Are, by Dorothy Parker (He and She)

Hooters, by Ted Tally (Cheryl and Ronda)

Hothouse, by Megan Terry (Jody and Roz)

How I Got That Story, by Amlin Gray (Reporter and Historical Event)

I Am a Camera, by John van Druten (Sally and Christopher)

I Won't Dance, by Oliver Hailey (Don and Kay)

In the Boom, Boom Room, by David Rabe (Chrissy and Susan)

Isn't It Romantic, by Wendy Wasserstein (Janie and Harriet)

Jimmy Shine, by Murray Schisgal (Rosey and Jimmy)

Laundry and Bourbon, by James McLure (Elizabeth and Hattie)

Lemon Sky, by Lanford Wilson (Alan and Ronnie)

Life of the Party, by Doug Holsclaw (Jay and Curtis)

Little Bird, by Mary Gallagher (Maura and Prandy)

Live Spelled Backwards, by Jerome Lawrence (Frank and Woman Who Knows)

Lone Star, by James McLure (Roy and Ray)

Long Day's Journey into Night, by Eugene O'Neill (Jamie and Edmund)

A Long Walk to Forever, by Kurt Vonnegut (Katherine and Nute)

Look Homeward, Angel, by Ketti Frings (Eugene and Laura)

Look, We've Come Through, by Hugh Wheeler (Belle and Bobby)

Loose Ends, by Michael Weller (Paul and Susan)

Love Nest for Three, by John Patrick (Veronica and Norton)

The Loveliest Afternoon of the Year, by John Guare (He and She)

Lovely Afternoon, by Howard Delman (Alan and Pam)

Lovers, by Brian Friel (Meg and Joe)

Lovers and Other Strangers, by Rene Taylor and Joseph Bologna (Cathy and Hal)

Lu Ann Hampton Laverty Oberlander, by Preston Jones (Lu Ann and Billy Bob)

Lunch Hour, by Jean Kerr (Carrie and Oliver)

Mimosa Pudica, by Curt Dempster (Diane and David)

Minnesota Moon, by John Olive (Alan and Larry)

A Modest Proposal, by Selma Thompson (John and Mer)

Ordinary People, by Judith Guest and Alvin Sargeant (Karen and Conrad)

Orphans, by Lyle Kessler (Phillip and Treat)

Out of Gas on Lover's Leap, by Mark St. Garmain (Mystery and Gruper)

The Owl and the Pussycat, by Bill Manhoff (Felix and Doris)

Patio, by Jack Heifner (Pearl and Jewel)

The Paper Chase, by Joseph Robinette and John Jay Osborn (Hart and Ford)

Period of Adjustment, by Tennessee Williams (Isabel and Ralph)

Perfect, by Mary Gallagher (Tina and Kitty)

Prelude to a Kiss, by Craig Lucas (Peter and Rita)

Private Wars, by James McLure (Gately and Silvio)

A Quiet End, by Robin Swados (Jason and Max)

Reckless, by Craig Lucas (Rachel and Lloyd)

Sally and Marsha, by Sybille Pearson (Sally and Marsha)

The Real Thing, by Tom Stoppard (Billy and Annie)

Savage in Limbo, by John Patrick Shanley (Savage and Linda)

Say Goodnight, Gracie, by Ralph Pape (Jerry and Steve)

Seascape with Sharks and Dances, by Don Nigro (Tracy and Ben)

Sexual Perversity in Chicago, by David Mamet (Danny and Bernie)

Shivaree, by William Mastrosimone (Chandler and Shivaree)

The Sign in Sidney Brustein's Window, by Lorraine Hansberry (Sidney and Iris)

The Sorrows of Stephen, by Peter Parnell (Stephen and Christine)

Speed-the-Plow, by David Mamet (Charlie and Bobby)

Splendor in the Grass, by William Inge (Bud and Deanie)

The Square Root of Love, by Howard Delman (Alan and Pam)

Strange Snow, by Stephen Metcalfe (Martha and Megs)

Streamers, by David Rabe (Richie and Billy)

Summer and Smoke, by Tennessee Williams (Alma and John)

Talk to Me Gentle Like the Rain and Let Me Listen, by Tennessee Williams (Man and Woman)

The Time of Your Life, by William Saroyan (Joe and Mary)

Tracers, by John DiFusco (Williams and Baby San, Professor and Doc, or Professor and Baby San)

True West, by Sam Shepard (Austin and Lee)

Two on an Island, by Elmer Rice (John and Mary)

Uncommon Women and Others, by Wendy Wasserstein (Kate and Rita)

Voices from the High School, by Peter Coe (Senior and Freshman)

The Wager, by Mark Medoff (Leeds and Ward)

When You Comin' Back, Red Ryder? by Mark Medoff (Angel and Stephen)

The Woolgatherer, by William Mastrosimone (Rose and Cliff)

The Wrong Man, by Laura Harrington (John and Nadia)

The following plays have three-character scenes for those instances when there are an odd number of students in the group:

Baby with the Bathwater, by Christopher Durang (John, Nanny, Helen)
Blue Window, by Craig Lucas (Bob, Alice, Griever)
Burn This, by Lanford Wilson (Burton, Anna, Larry)
Independence, by Lee Blessing (Sherry, Jo, Kess)
Last Summer at Blue Fish Cove, by Jane Chambers (Rae, Annie, Lil)
Strange Snow, by Stephen Metcalfe (Megs, Martha, Dave)
The Miss Firecracker Contest, by Beth Henley (Carnelle, Delmont, Elaine)
A Thousand Clowns, by Herb Gardner (Murray, Sandra, Albert)
T-Shirts, by Robert Patrick (Marvin, Kink, Tom)

A glance at the list shows that you will have a far easier time finding a scene for a man and a woman than any other combination, so know that if you decide to work with a same-sex partner your choices will be limited.

SCRIPT ANALYSIS

Understanding the text as a whole will help you see how your character fits into the big picture and relates to other characters, the words, and the audience. Here are seven categories to consider in your analysis.

1. *Classification*
   What kind of a play is this? Try to come up with a phrase (e.g., ''a light, romantic comedy'' or ''a raw, slice-of-life drama'') to describe the script. If you do not know dramatic literature terms, find your own words to describe the overall feeling of the text.

2. *Style*
   Although all scenes for this assignment come from contemporary American realists, there are variations in their realism. Is the play more like life as totally uncensored (naturalism), more beautifully extravagant (romanticism), totally out of whack (theatre of the absurd), making fun of certain targets (satire), a largely physical joke (farce), or a series of overblown coincidences (melodrama)? Ask yourself how probable the behavior of the characters is, and, if it is at all improbable, in what

direction does it lean? Are people in this play wittier, weepier, crueler, or clumsier than they are in your offstage world?

3. *Structure*
How is this play put together? Is it a one-act or full-length? If full, how many acts is it divided into? How many scenes within each act? Are these scenes lengthy, short, or some combination? If you had to title each act, what would they be called? Where does *your* scene fit into this overall pattern? How close is it to the climax of the play, and how much new information does it provide compared to other scenes?

4. *Theme*
What does this play say about life? What is the author's message? What issues are raised, and what position does the writer take regarding the human condition? Do you think the writer is trying to change the audience in some way, or just divert them? Try to put the theme in a single sentence. Remember that all plays say something, even if it is only "Isn't middle-class life great?"

5. *Cultural binding*
This play probably was written between the 1940s and the 1990s. When? Do the social customs, attitudes, and language seem tied to the date of writing? Is the play better served by moving it into the present, or by placing it in its own time? Was it written from a strong geographical, economic, or ethnic bias? How do these intersect with those of you and your classmates?

6. *Production history*
What can you find out about this play in performance? Has it been popular? Obscure? Have any well-known actors played your roles? What kind of reviews has it received? Were there any choices made by previous performers that you might also try? Are there mistakes other actors made from which you might learn?

7. *World of the play*
Just as a character has given circumstances, so does the play as a whole. It's important to know not just who your character is but how she fits into the play. If your character is gregarious, bubbly, and personable, it's a lot more significant if all the other characters do *not* share those traits, and if being outgoing is not rewarded behavior in this play. You may have heard a performance described as being "striking, but not in the same play as everyone else." Here are some questions to use to find out what play everyone else is in. Ask yourself how close or far away your character is from the majority.

A. *Time:* How rapidly does it move for most people? What lengths of attention spans do these people have?

B. *Space:* How large a bubble do most people carry around? To what degree are privacy and open space respected?

C. *Place:* Do people feel connected with where they live, or indifferent to it? How aware are they of other places?

D. *Values:* What are the beliefs most widely shared? What ideals? How do people define sin, consequences, forgiveness, ethics?

E. *Structure:* Who rules and who follows? How easy is it to bring about change? How is the pattern of daily life ordered and followed?

F. *Beauty:* What is the look most aspired to in this group? Who are the contemporary ideals of male and female perfection?

G. *Sex:* How is seduction defined and sexuality communicated? How much tolerance exists for deviation, infidelity, promiscuity?

H. *Recreation:* What is most people's idea of fun? What would be an ideal social occasion in this world?

I. *Sight:* How does the world look in shapes, angles, light, shadow, and color? What are dominant patterns of movement and gesture?

J. *Sound:* What is the common mode of speech and use of nonverbals? To what degree are listening and speaking prized? How close is your character to the average member of the group? How likely to defend his right to be different if pressured to conform?

Analyzing the world of the play becomes more and more crucial the farther that world is from the one you live in offstage.

EXERCISE 6.2

ANALYZING THE SCRIPT

Prepare answers of a single phrase or sentence in each of these categories:

1. *Classification:* single phrase capturing what kind of play this is

2. *Style:* degree of probability; types of improbability

3. *Structure:* script length, acts, scenes; place of your scene in the whole

4. *Theme:* author's message on life

5. *Cultural binding:* date written and set; cultural bias present in text; challenges for performance here and now

6. *Production history:* possible lessons from those who have done it before

7. *World of the play:* majority choices made by characters in terms of:

Time	Beauty
Space	Sex
Place	Recreation
Values	Sight
Structure	Sound

FITTING INTO THE WORLD

Create a situation in each of the ten categories above where your character is confronted with a group which conforms to the expected behavior in the world. React as your character would and either give in completely, make an adjustment, or defy the standards altogether. Complete, in some other way for each category, your sense of how your character will or will not blend with all the others.

CUTTING THE SCENE

Time limits on acting class scenes have to be enforced, simply because there are so many people in class and so little time for vital individual attention. If you present a scene that goes way over the assigned limit, you have wasted time in a number of ways. First, you're eating into your own period of getting critiqued or having your scene worked. You're probably eating into other people's time, which is worse. Also, you've spent all these valuable rehearsal hours working on a giant, unwieldy rock of a scene when what was wanted was a little jewel glistening in the sun. You've probably heard the standard theatrical adage: ''Leave them wanting more.'' As advice, it has no peer. It stands to reason that the shorter your excerpt, the more times you can run it, work it, try something else, polish it, right? No epics allowed.

Time the scene regularly while you work. You probably will add time as you get more layers, find inspired pauses, consider incredible alternatives during your evaluations. So if your scene was timed near the limit at first reading you will inevitably have to cut. It is very common for a scene to run fifteen minutes and for the actors to say, ''But it was only ten last week.'' Last week? That was before you found all that glorious subtext.

What can be cut? Every line is perfect? Here are some standard edits:

1. Anything connecting your scene with other parts of the play, but not directly related to the scene. The scene can have a life of its own.

2. Start closer to the climax than you originally intended, or consider ending with more of a cliff-hanger than full closure. Find the portion of the scene that gives you the best acting workout.

3. Any passages you have found that you can imply, or communicate physically, without stating them specifically. Some speeches may be overwritten. Others, you'll find, can be edited once your subtext is clarified.

4. If one character has been given lengthy monologues, cut for balance, so that the scene becomes more of a duet. This experience should serve both partners.

5. Lines you have trouble with—trouble pronouncing, motivating, clarifying. Not until you've tried to make them work, but eventually to relieve yourself from unnecessary pressure. There's no point in approaching a word or phrase with dread because you've rarely been able to say it right.

6. Dated or obscure references which the audience is unlikely to grasp.

7. Bleed the scene instead of looking for giant amputations. Sometimes you do need the entire body of the scene but can ease out a word here, a phrase there, so you have a cleaner script but a complete one.

EXERCISE 6.4

EDIT THREE MINUTES

Imagine that your scene is overtime and must be shortened by at least three minutes. Go over the text in each of the categories above. Find the cuts that will serve both the script and actors best. Get a sense of how each of the categories may create a slightly different piece of work.

Cutting is a valuable skill for actors. Too many leave it all up to directors. As an actor, you are much closer to each line, more intimately aware of potential nuances within each speech. In play rehearsals, if you are able to offer suggestions for cuts, you are also far more likely to be able to keep your favorite lines. Respecting a text isn't synonymous with needing to present it all. Some magnificent texts can be enhanced with skillful surgery.

CHARACTER ANALYSIS

When you take on a character you need to get to know him at least as well as you do a close friend. You need to analyze him enough to understand the choices he makes. Texts offer different amounts of information about the people in them. Some playwrights, such as George Bernard Shaw and Eugene O'Neill, give microscopic character details, right down to the titles of books the character keeps on his shelves. Others simply give your role a name like The Boy, minimal dialogue, and leave a lot for you to discover. To make certain all evidence is examined, go through the following stages:

The Three I's: Investigation, Inference, Invention

1. *Investigation*
   This is just facts. You find evidence in the script. If the character is well known, it's crucial to make sure you are looking at the person the playwright wrote, and are not overly influenced by some famous actor's performance, by an acting tradition for this part, or by the public image of this character. There will still be gaps, so you move to inference.

2. *Inference*
   From facts, you draw conclusions. If everyone keeps calling you "child," you deduce that you're younger than they are. If your stage directions are filled with indirect movements and pauses, you infer that you're hesitant and nonassertive. This is a fascinating process, and easy to confuse with investigation, but inference must be based on facts. Afterward, blanks can be filled in with invention.

> *Acting is interpretive by nature. An architect may*
> *have an overall vision, but it takes the attention*
> *of craftsmen like plumbers, carpenters, sheet-*
> *metal men and roofers to bring it to life. I'm quite*
> *happy being a craftsman. I don't feel lessened by*
> *that at all. It's the facts, Jack.*[3]
>
> —HARRISON FORD

3. *Invention*

Some actors are tempted to skip to this stage without working their way through the first two. Others neglect it, content with unactable generalizations: "She's in her teens," or "She's in high school." Remember, no real person thinks of herself as being simply in her teens; she's concerned with precisely where. Stanislavski admonished that "in general" is the *actor's greatest enemy*. After inferring an approximate age, this is where you *decide* that you are 16 and were born March 4 on a still moonless night, by Caesarean—the whole picture.

Following this progression (from investigation to inference to invention) ensures the actor that the writer's will has been served, and leaves him free to discover. The list that emerges is filled with technical details to rehearse and master, plus emotional conditions to plant and let develop.

The document you prepare is often kept with the score and strongly connected to it.

EXERCISE 6.5

CHARACTER PAST

Complete the following statements from the character's perspective, as if filled with a strong need to tell the truth. Fortunately, you have already done a character analysis on yourself in chapter 3, so you are familiar with the standard questions and can compare yourself with your character. This time each category is phrased with acting vocabulary developed in the past few chapters. (See Appendix H, Script Analysis.)

I come from . . .

My childhood was . . .

Family conditions were . . .

Experiences making the most lasting impression on me were . . .

Ten most important given circumstances are . . .

Five most powerful members of my private audience would be . . .

Crucial actions prior to scene were . . .

The moment before my entrance in complete detail involves . . .

CHARACTER PRESENT

Complete the statements from the character's perspective, with a strong need to tell the truth:

Immediate conditioning forces are . . .

Others in script (and/or playwright) describe me as . . .

I describe others as . . .

In groups I tend to . . .

I would describe myself as basically . . .

My usual style of clothing and type of accessories include . . .

My most distinguishing characteristics are . . .

My favorite things are . . .

My temperament could be described as . . . for example, . . .

I am most and least interested in . . .

My physical life varies from the actor playing me in . . .

My vocal life varies from the actor playing me in . . .

The actor playing me needs to use the Magic If for this role in . . .

Three examples where endowment must be used in the scene are . . .

The location of this scene can be described . . .

The most crucial moment of evaluation (including all alternatives considered and rejected) is . . .

I make the following discoveries in the scene . . .

CHARACTER FUTURE

Complete the statements from the character's perspective, with a strong need to tell the truth:

My super objective is . . .

My intentional hierarchy would include . . .

My immediate scene objective is to . . .

Obstacles I face are . . .

My strategy in the scene could be described as . . .

Specific tactics I employ are . . .

My worst possible future would be . . .

My wildest dreams come true would be . . .

Once you do your homework, build your character's biography, immerse yourself in the period—do all the conscious work—then a moment of ease and effortlessness may come. You are transcended, you lose your self-consciousness. All ego concerns go away and you're free.[4]

—Annette Benning

Abstracting

Because much analysis work is systematic and logical, a useful balance can be achieved by also working in an abstract and fanciful mode. The following questions should be answered, by thinking not of what the character would choose to wear, drink, or drive, but of which qualities sum up his essence.

Barker [the director] said to me, "Lear should be an oak, you're an ash; now we've got to do something about that."[5]

—John Gielgud

A person may choose the finest champagne to consume and still be warm draft beer to those who know him. Someone may drive a truck but clearly be thought of as a Rolls-Royce by everyone she meets.

EXERCISE 6.8

CHARACTER ABSTRACTS

This exercise is based on a party game, sometimes called ''Abstracts'' or ''Essences.'' The class may wish to play. In the first version, one person picks one other in the room and then everyone poses a question until someone guesses who is being abstracted. In another, a guesser leaves the room while everyone agrees on a subject in their midst. When the guesser returns, she questions each person there until she guesses correctly or gives up. It's always surprising how often people agree on these indirect ways of describing others, and how clear the final image emerges. Ask yourself, if the character were actually one of the following categories, which would he be?

1. fabric
2. animal
3. beverage
4. mode of transportation
5. city
6. tree
7. color
8. play
9. scent
10. song
11. type of day
12. decade or era
13. film or TV series
14. landmark or building
15. snack
16. mythological or fantasy figure
17. spice
18. musical instrument
19. painting or photo
20. toy

Abstracting helps you discover some images to snap you into character and to help drop the day's distractions, especially if you're not in the mood to perform. You walk into rehearsal feeling like milk and a bus shelter, but you think of dry sherry and the Taj Mahal, and thereby shift your sense of yourself. It is whimsical, but it works. Abstracting also provides a way of communicating when traditional terms are inadequate. Gielgud the actor *is* an ash, and the character King Lear is truly an oak. There's no clearer, kinder way to make that distinction than in abstract images.

EXERCISE 6.9

CHARACTER'S AUTOBIOGRAPHY

Take all the information you've accumulated and write an autobiography, no longer than one page, in the voice of the character. Keep the following criteria in mind:

1. There's far too much available material to include, so pick what the character would consider important.

2. Take the character only up to his first entrance into the scene, and end the essay by completing the statement: "What I want most out of life is . . ."

3. Give yourself a strong motive for speaking the character's truth as he sees it. Maybe the essay is being written for a psychiatrist, who can only help if the answers are genuine. Maybe for a priest, with the complete conviction that the man of God will see through any deceptions. Maybe for a child, who deserves to know the truth about her parent and you are determined to finally tell it. If the only way the character would ever prepare a manuscript of this kind is to write a letter to someone, then use that format. Try to find a motive and a format that suit who this person is.

4. Use the character's language, spelling, and sentence structure. Experiment with altering your handwriting (if the character would not type this document) to suit the writer. Pick the texture and color of paper and pen this person would choose. The difference between using lavender stationery, purple felt-tip pen, all small letters, and i's dotted with circles, maybe even some smiles in those circles (which would be the right way to express some characters) and producing a legal-size document, in triplicate, from a word processor (which would be right for another), is one vivid way to express differing personal approaches. Enjoy the process of finding the right mode of presentation.

EXERCISE 6.10

ANALYSIS INTO SYSTEM

1. Score the scene based on Stanislavski's concepts.

2. Armed with new information about your scripted character, go back and execute each of these exercises in chapter 4 from the perspective of the person you are playing: Others' Givens, Planting,

Hierarchies, Tiny Triumphs, Adding Consequences, Bringing it Back, Release Album, Imaging, Naming Members, Group Bias, Adding Conditions, Open Futures, Playing Against.

Work with your scene partner when appropriate. Work alone when you need time and space and there is no pressure to react quickly. Make a promise to yourself to let none of your analysis and research remain theoretical, but to apply the results actively in rehearsal.

EXERCISE 6.11

WARMING UP

Pick the most evocative images from your character analysis, those that seem to thrust you most vividly into the character's experience and feelings. While warming up to present the scene, let these particular images drift over you so that as your body and voice prepare, your mind releases your own biases and accepts those of your character.

All this homework finally pays off when the character is an inevitability in your life.

> *It's like a woman getting pregnant. This character,*
> *this person that I am to become, starts to grow inside*
> *me and I listen. If I don't listen, he will die in me.*[6]
> —MARCELLO MASTROIANNI

STAGING

It is not impossible to block your scene yourself. You start with a floor plan as a map and work your way through the scene step by step. Again, some scripts give you infinite details and others only vague references. Write down every item (entrance, piece of furniture, prop) you know must be present. As a shortcut, see if some variation on the generic floor plan presented in Figure 6–1 will work. Though the possibilities are infinite, when you sit in the audience, you will see some version of this set a majority of the time.

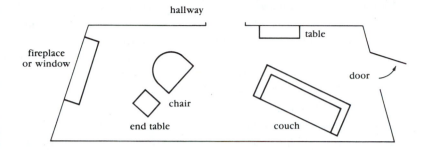

Figure 6–1 The Generic Floor Plan
This stage arrangement is used constantly in the theatre. Why?

Why? Because it is simple, and provides most of the opportunities to explore relationships, while keeping everyone easy to see. It provides:

1. A strong up center entrance.

2. Two "islands" that can become territories, so that any actor may assume one space as his, and his partner the other.

3. Opportunities for actors to play space invasion or space-sharing games.

4. Easy movement around the furniture so that actors can protect themselves at one instant, then step forth the next.

5. A couch and an armchair, which offer the widest possible scope for leaning, sitting, sprawling, and lying down.

6. The smooth and effortless use of figure-eights around the two main sections, as well as other curving patterns.

7. Two isolated areas, up right and left, for retreat and reflection, as well as an alternative, if weaker, entrance and exit.

This is not a bad space to start exploring with your partner as you begin work on a scene, especially if you know little about scene design. Alter it as the scene requires, but try to keep the same opportunities for variety and visibility. What it lacks in originality, it offers in reliability. Ultimately the space is made compelling by what people do there.

1. If your scene has special requirements, make the adjustments from this floor plan on paper, along with a list of what must happen physically.

2. Review the section on stage movement in chapter 5, this time with the context of your scene in mind. What pieces of *business* are necessary?

What *bits* might be fun to try? Where can you tell you will have to remember to *cheat* to avoid closing off a crucial moment from the audience? Are there lines where it feels as if one character is likely to *cross*? Where another should *counter*? Is it evident when and where one of you needs to *give*, and the other *take*, *stage*? Some patterns should immediately emerge to give the scene a rough outline.

3. Review the section in chapter 5 on ''Living Pictures,'' asking yourself if there are moments best served by having one of you sitting and the other standing, where you may not be looking at each other at all, and so on.

4. Review ''Adding Motion,'' also in chapter 5, to see if there are movement patterns that might contrast your characters, where one may be more active generally. Is one more likely to cover space but the other more likely to gesture actively?

5. Remember that the most effective action-generated staging is organic. It evolves as you rehearse and get to know these people and this space better. You need to get on your feet and rough out something that will do early, or you will be tempted to postpone too long. But once the scene has a physical outline, let yourself explore and trust your intuition.

SCRIPT AWARENESS IMPROVS

Anything in your character analysis could become the basis for an improv to help get that information fully assimilated, especially if you wrote it down but you are not yet using it in the scene. Here are some possibilities.

Characters Offstage

EXERCISE 6.12

FIRST MEETING OF THE CHARACTERS

Set up with your partner all the circumstances of the first time the two of your characters laid eyes on each other. Then enter the scene from a point of innocence and discover your partner. Leave the encounter when you have some idea when you will see this person again.

CRUCIAL OFFSTAGE EVENT

Select the single most influential experience in your character's life, either before the play begins or away from the script, and explore a related event. This exercise may or may not involve your partner. Set yourself up simply to respond without scripting the experience. Solo examples: a character anticipating an abortion goes to an actual clinic for counseling, an alcoholic attends an AA meeting, an expectant mother goes to a birthing class. It matters far less how many demands you place on yourself than the range of feelings the experience allows you to share with the character.

CHARACTER WAKE-UP

On the morning of the beginning of the play's action, move from sleep to the character's anticipation of the day ahead. Get a strong sense of the bed (if it *is* a bed), the space, your feelings about where you sleep, the time you wake up, your expectations of the coming day, and all the circumstances that launch you into this event. Go through each detail of bathing, choosing what to wear and eat, what to take with you. Arm yourself with everything the character carries onto the stage.

TYPICAL TIME

With your partner, spend an evening or an afternoon as the two characters, doing something they would likely do together. Agree on the exact point at which you leave yourselves behind and take on the characters. Try to view each event and line heard from the character's perspective and to relish the change. Pick up a sense of how the two of them deal with each other and others outside the script itself.

CHARACTER INTERVIEW

If possible, this exercise should be performed in class, but it can be done with your partner alone or with a friend playing the interviewer. You decide the circumstances. Are you being interviewed for a job, a deposition, a biography, an article, a grant, a TV show? The class is free to ask you any question, and you must answer at all times from the character's point of view.

CHARACTER ENCOUNTER

In character with your partner, go through the list used for the partner encounter at the end of chapter 4. Imagine the circumstances under which these two characters would do this together (e.g., to save their marriage, to satisfy the urging of one of them, to help them get over a misunderstanding). Answer as fully as the character would, and note later where you and the character intersect and where you divide.

Characters Onstage

SCOREBOARD

Place a blackboard (or some other prominent means of visibly displaying who scored the last point) somewhere on your set. Play the scene with particular attention to one-upping your partner. When you know you have scored, walk up to the board and give yourself the point. Take time out if the point is contested. Relish each point you score. At the end, tally who has won and by what margin.

UNRELATED ACTIVITY

As you run lines with your partner, pick a variety of ways to involve your-selves physically at the same time. You might set the table for dinner or do laundry or clean the rehearsal hall or any task that will involve the two of you equally. Let the lines and the activity influence each other so that nei-ther is independent of the other.

STOP PARTNER FROM LEAVING

Imagine that one of you wants to simply leave and not deal with the en-counter at all. Using the actual dialogue, one actor should employ any tac-tic available to keep the other from going. The partner should actually walk out of the space if not stopped by some riveting sense of urgency, need, or power. Reverse positions and run the scene the other way around. Then al-ternate, every four lines, whose turn it is to feel the need to get away.

TALKING BEATS

In character, walk through the scene, negotiating where each beat begins and ends, and what it should be called ("This is the beat where I show what a fool you've been and it should be called 'Sheila's Revenge' "). Disagree as your character might ("What is really shown here is your mindless cruelty and it should be called 'Sheila the Bitch' "). Negotiate until you find a mutually acceptable spot for the beat's beginning and end, and a title that both parties can deal with. Try it with larger clusters of beats (measures or subscenes), giving titles to them as well.

Keys

Actors are always searching for the key to a character. They often discover what they are looking for in a costume prop (a hat, a handkerchief, a pair of shoes or glasses) or some physical characteristic (set of the jaw, hands deep in pockets, feet turned in slightly when walking) or vocal quality characteristic (a slightly nasal quality, a hum, a startling laugh). The actor will talk of searching and searching ''until I put on this scarf, and that was the key''—the moment when suddenly the door to the whole characterization opened.

This search-and-discovery process demonstrates vividly the way in which a single technical element can unlock an emotional awareness. It also shows how much technique the actor needs to experiment with all those physical and vocal traits, to know what to do when he picks up the hat or the cane, to even *recognize* the value in picking it up. Stanislavski refers constantly to ''unconscious creativeness through conscious technique,'' whereby the actor earns the right to discover by carefully opening himself up to possibility. A simple physical object or tiny change can make him suddenly feel like another human being, with detail after detail rushing in to complete the character.

EXERCISE 6.22

KEY SEARCHING

1. Select a character and spend a half-hour wandering around your own room (or, if available, a prop room) trying things on, picking up and handling props, examining small objects, letting each work on the character's sense of self. Keep the best of what you find, but keep your personal antennae out everywhere you go for objects which might open character doors.

2. Do the same thing with isolated physical and vocal characteristics and techniques. Try them on like glasses or scarves, seeing if they fit (or even release) the character.

SHAKING UP THE SCENE

Not all improvisation work has to be done in early stages, as groups begin to form or as the scene is just starting to take shape. Some rehearsal experiments should come later in the process, when the scene is relatively solid and ready for some new life. The following exercises work best when lines and blocking are quite secure. In class, these fit best when the work has been shown once, critiqued, and gone back into rehearsal.

Your teacher and classmates may suggest some specific ones based on the first showing, but all are worth trying. Sometimes that very aspect of the scene about which you feel most complacent turns out to benefit most from a jolt of a different kind of energy. If this experimenting is not done in class, it helps to have some observers at your rehearsal to help you identify your discoveries. It is possible to get so caught up in doing an exercise that you fail to register the benefits. After each exercise below is an indication of what often happens when it is accomplished. Don't force that result, because in your case it may be something altogether different. Or, like any improv, it may fizzle out. Not all mining expeditions lead to treasure. Not all lead to the *same* treasure. Leave yourself open.

Character Explorations

EXERCISE 6.23

SPOKEN SILENT SCRIPT

Actually speak aloud your continuous interior monologue in addition to the lines themselves, so you are speaking both text and subtext. Take all the time you need to recognize inner thoughts and get them into words. Go ahead and overlap with your partner, as your tapes run simultaneously. Remember, a lot of your silent script won't make sense to others, and that's as it should be. Speak the "silent" parts in a slightly less projected voice than the actual lines, which can be more projected for clarity. This exercise starts rough, but once you get it, it rolls. Stanislavski suggests trying it in four stages: speaking the silent script (1) in a lower tone of voice, as above, (2) in merely a whisper, (3) soundlessly, and finally (4) expressing it only with the eyes, moving the benefits gradually back into the traditional performance mode.

What Happens: You find out where your thinking is muddy and some gets cleaned up. Some awkwardness drops away because you are so busy. You discover business and movement as your body takes over.

SHADOWING

Hand two other actors your scripts and have them go through the scene. You and your partner shadow them, telling them where to move, asking to have some words punched, to repeat some lines or moves with greater emphasis, encouraging prior to an important moment and after a maneuver is accomplished successfully, acting as alter ego and coach. When you are ready for your stand-in to read the line, press her lightly on the back.

What Happens: You get a new perspective. Countless little insights come out of just peering over another's shoulder and seeing the scene from another place altogether. You are able to put this alter ego onstage with you in places where encouragement would help.

ISOLATING

Pick any two tactics and use them exclusively in the scene. Don't let your partner know which ones you choose. (This may also be done by simply drawing slips of paper so the decision is made for you.) Make sure every inch of mileage is gained from each tactic.

Variations: (1) Both of you employ the same tactic on each other; (2) both select tactics you are relatively sure your character does not employ in the scene.

What Happens: Focus shifts from lines to maneuvers. Evaluations have more excitement. You see tactics as possibilities that you failed to consider before. The scene becomes more like a game, and partners are studied more carefully.

ROLE REVERSAL

1. Switch parts with your partner and run the scene.
2. Keep the major shape of the scene the same, but feel free to use your own line readings and character business whenever you wish to do something differently.

3. Listen closely for when your partner gives a new and interesting twist to a speech, when it sounds the same as the way you usually do it, and when your sense of timing is altered.

4. Most important, enjoy playing the other role and doing all the things you might wish the other actor would do, but would never direct him to do.

What Happens: You learn immediately how well you know the whole scene and how often you have simply been biding time and not really listening when your partner speaks. There is a therapeutic release in getting to say the words and do the other part the way you want. Whether your partner hears, notices, or decides to use anything of yours, at least you've had the chance. You tend to feel somehow freer. You find places you may have been making the other guy wait forever, or where you may have been anticipating his cues, or a cross you have been making more difficult than necessary. You get all the benefits of the Magic If for your partner: If you are alert, your partner will show you some better alternatives and will give you permission to try things.

So I said, "Okay, let's just switch roles." It's tricky;
you have to trust the other person, because when he
plays your role, he's gonna be telling you how you
should play it . . . Well, we just flew. Raul [Julia]
was the one who took off first. I was dazzled by his
flamboyance. So I took up the gauntlet and made
that revolutionary one tough son of a bitch. We were
giving each other what we needed from each other.[7]

—WILLIAM HURT (on role reversal in rehearsal for
The Kiss of the Spider Woman)

EXERCISE 6.27

PASSING

Start with a simple object, such as a rubber ball, bean bag, or tennis ball, and run the scene, passing it to the other person at the very end of each speech. Use the object to punctuate your lines while you have it, and literally pass it to your partner the way the cue is passed (violently, slyly, flirtatiously, with outrage, etc.). Let the relationship between the characters centralize in the object. Remember, you don't have to just hand it to the other person, you can put in his pocket, on his head, down his pants. You can nudge it over to him with your foot or your little pinkie. You also can do more than hold it while you speak. You can crush it, roll it, bounce it or put it down your own pants. *Variation:* Move to a game that is most appropriate to the conflict in the scene (e.g., ping-pong or croquet if it is witty repartee, boxing if it is all frontal assault, wrestling if it is noncerebral and gutsy, chess if it is sly) and explore in the same way.

What Happens: Line readings tend to have more color. As the energy goes into the object it also goes into the words, so variety and clarity both rise. Individual consonants and vowels, within words, get more liveliness and variety of attack. Both partners become more alert hearing and receiving cues.

EXERCISE 6.28

ANIMAL ABSTRACTIONS

Assume the animal images you have chosen for your characters and perform the scene with all the animal's physical characteristics you can summon, with an animal voice (animal-sounding, but with real words, punctuated by a generous dose of nonverbals). Your animal can be a combination of animals instead of one that exists in real life. Let the blocking of the scene alter in any way that seems right, and go ahead and scratch where it itches. Open up the scene to all the nonintellectual sensory, sensual, sexual, purely physical realms. Repeat the scene immediately without any effort to animalize.

What Happens: A greater playfulness often emerges as well as some pure animal carryover. An effective counterbalance for actors who tend to talk a scene to death or to act too much with the head.

EXERCISE 6.29

CONTACT

Touch your partner at some point during each of your lines in the scene. Take your time and find some way to physically connect with her every time you speak. Touches may be anything from traditional moves (slapping on the shoulder, nudging, pointing into someone's upper chest) to those that are simply discovered (touching elbows, pulling someone's shirt untucked, even pressing your nose to someone's knee). Some combination of the conventional and the new will probably emerge. Don't try to be clever, but let your body tell you some way to connect at the same time your words do.

What Happens: A surprising number of these moves end up being serious possibilities to put into the actual scene. Others provide an emotional memory for the body to suppress interestingly later. The emotional contact is inevitably heightened by the physical contact. And some unexpectedly pointed line readings are discovered.

EXERCISE 6.30

"GIBBALOGUE"

Select agreed-on nonsense syllables and run the scene, using these limited lines instead of the actual dialogue. Make sure you have communicated as fully through the gibberish as you would through the words. To accomplish this you will need to intensify your physical and nonverbal responses. The face will need to get involved and the range of vocal life will need to be more vivid. Do not go on to the next line until your partner has made your cue perfectly clear.

What Happens: Much as when struggling with a foreign language, the body gets engaged. As in the ''Nonsense'' section of chapter 5, the communication suddenly has higher stakes on the part of both participants. Often you decide to keep some of these vivid choices at moments of high intensity.

EXERCISE 6.31

HANDICAPS

1. Play the scene sitting back to back, with your partner's arms and yours locked, and neither of you having any possibility of seeing the other. Communicate everything through your voice and whatever pressure you can manage on the other person's back and your arms, where looped.

2. Sit against the wall, facing each other at opposite ends of a large classroom or rehearsal hall. Communicate over the vast space, keeping the scene intimate and complex, not allowing it to become loud and flat.

3. Invent a handicap for the scene, based on removing anything you agree either of you has grown to rely on heavily. If that is different for each of you, try it both ways.

What Happens: Just as those who are sight or hearing impaired tend to gain, by necessity, a heightening of other senses, adding some limitation to the scene can sharpen the intensity of communication in other areas and get both actors thinking again.

EXERCISE 6.32

COUNTERPOINT

Decide what your character is *not,* and play the scene as if she is just that. Deliberately interpret each line so that it conveys a meaning opposite to that which seems intended by the text. Create a character who would be the polar opposite of yours and relish the difference. You may need to repeat this once, for the obvious amusement you will experience, then for listening very carefully, to determine once and for all what you know is absent from the scene, and also to find the occasional contrast within people, which makes them interesting, the touch of villain in the saint and vice versa.

What Happens: Initially, there is a relief of laughter as in seeing a parody of something taken as deadly serious before. Then a security comes from eliminating some options completely from the scene. Finally, some spice and unexpected twists may be discovered.

There are great lessons in playing opposites. If you've got an unsympathetic role, try playing him like the hero. The script won't let you succeed, but you'll find something worth keeping.[8]
—JEFF DANIELS

LAYERING

Add gradually extreme conditioning forces into the first beat of the scene.
Make the space arctic-cold or swelteringly hot and humid, blindingly light
or all dark shadows. Make the characters dreadfully late or having had to
wait forever. Give yourself an extreme physical condition (a dreadful cold,
the worst hangover of your life, a devastating injury). Manipulate various
combinations, then back off to more subtle, nuanced circumstances, but
ones with constant influence.

What Happens: If you tend to play in a bland, neutral state, this will
shake you out of that quite firmly. It opens up the senses. Even though the
exercise choices will be too extreme to retain, an intense physical awareness tends to linger later. Also, with the concentration so strongly on the
body, some surprisingly natural readings emerge.

RALLY SQUAD

1. Select four class members to serve as a cheering section for each actor (eight altogether). Each
   squad stands in a different part of the room.
2. Perform the scene, returning continually to your squad for encouragement and advice before
   returning to give your next line. Squads should react to the other side much as you did to opposing
   teams in high school. They should cheer their hero or heroine on to victory. They should speak out
   encouragement and comfort to their player. *Variations:* (1) Split the class down the middle and have
   the actors play, each to his own half of the house. If the actors are a man and a woman, let each
   sex root for its own. (2) Divide the class between those over and under age 20, or some other
   group identification that gets the adrenaline flowing.

What Happens: All the competitive elements of the scene are suddenly
quite clear. The scoring of points is sharper. The rally squad can carry over
into the private audience so that each character feels supported in his part
of the conflict. Most important, there is an infusion of enthusiasm. Each

actor savors his chance to play, and the resulting scene tends to have a greater feeling of playfulness once the shouting dies down.

SPEED-THROUGH

Run the scene as rapidly as the words and moves will come, while keeping all the values present and playing it in the same emotional key as always. Save this one for the very final stages of rehearsal, close to the last time the scene will be presented in class. Try to go through all your normal evaluations and interior monologues as well as the script and blocking itself, so that all ingredients are included, only faster.

What Happens: An antidote to potential indulgent pauses or subtext work that has gotten labored. You find places where the lines do work that fast because of the urgency of the moment. You even may find some places to overlap each other's lines in a believable and realistic way. You discover where you can evaluate during lines when you thought you had to isolate your alternatives between speeches. Conversely you find out which pauses and extended evaluations are absolutely essential to accomplish transitions.

ATTACK AND RETREAT

Run the scene, dropping your usual blocking in favor of moving improvisationally. Use the whole space and move in or chase on the other actor when you feel you are in an aggressive, attacking mode. Move away and escape when you feel the need to retreat. Silently negotiate if you are both in the same mode, possibly circling each other.

What Happens: The dynamics of the scene are clarified. It becomes clear who is on the attack and who retreats. The changes in the relationship are sharper. Some moves are strong enough to actually incorporate in the blocking.

Character Confidence

The next four exercises, in which each actor faces the audience as the character but without the script, can make you feel you own the role. If your preparation has been inadequate, they can also make you aware of how much more you need to dig in. Most actors, however, develop greater confidence the more they get to take the character before an audience, without the absolute necessity of the playwright's words. When the security of the words is then returned, a new surge of authority may enter them.

EXERCISE 6.37

CHARACTER HOT SEAT

A variation on the character interview but with somewhat greater intensity, more like a grilling by a district attorney. Audience gets to ask any questions they want of the character, but all should focus on forcing her to justify her behavior, much like a prosecutor might approach the defendant. A class member may be chosen to play head prosecutor. Any ethically questionable act by the character should receive particular attention.

What Happens: By this time, actors are secure enough to enjoy the confrontational challenge and take on all comers. The Magic If gets a genuine workout, since it is essential to become the character from a totally nonjudgmental perspective. You retain the character's own sense of conviction regarding the appropriateness of her acts.

EXERCISE 6.38

COMPARISONS

The character appears before the class and speaks about the actor.

1. What does the character think of this person presuming to play him?
2. What does the character feel the actor still needs to accomplish?
3. What does the character feel the two of them have most and least in common?
4. Would the character like to know the actor or would they probably not get along?

The character presents this basic information, then the audience is free to ask questions about the actor being described.

What Happens: The perspective is pleasurable and illuminating since the actor is being discussed as if he is not here. The actor tends to feel he has finally got the character down if he can actually discuss himself as the character. It is as if the immersion is finally complete.

EXERCISE 6.39

CHARACTER ENCOUNTER, PART II—THE SEQUEL

Unlike most sequels, this one can be as good as the original. Now that the actors have been together as the characters for some time, a more challenging encounter is possible and productive. With the same format as the partner and character encounters from chapters 4 and 5, complete the following sentences as the person you are playing. (If you're feeling adventurous, you and your partner might try doing this as yourselves.)

1. You tend to hurt me most often when you . . .
2. The single time you hurt me most was when . . .
3. What I love most about our relationship is . . .
4. The part of my life I prefer not to discuss with you is . . .
5. I cannot stand the way you . . .
6. I was proudest and most moved to know you (be your friend, related to you, married to you) when . . .
7. You and I are most similar in . . .
8. You and I are completely different in . . .
9. I envy the way you . . .
10. If I could wish and make something happen for you, it would be . . .

What Happens: The relationship is explored with greater depth and emotion than in the past, than indeed would have been appropriate before. The shared histories of the two people solidify and their relationship often emerges with more layers.

MEET ANOTHER CHARACTER

1. Either the teacher or groups of classmates should pick characters from different scenes and set up circumstances in which they might encounter each other.

2. A public place, where these two conceivably could run into each other, works best.

3. Keep your character's point of ignorance regarding the other person and respond without your audience knowledge of the scene you watched your classmates perform earlier.

What Happens: In addition to absolutely requiring character perspective and concentration, this lets different scenes benefit from each other more than in the simple act of observation. These characters you have seen in other contexts now provide enjoyable challenge to yours. Actors inevitably begin to think about how their characters would respond to all the others.

Scene study provides a great chance to take a small part of a script and come at it in so many different ways that both you and the script seem to grow. No matter what you discover, there is always another possibility.

> *Anger isn't just yelling. Anger has a thousand faces.*
> *That's what acting is. Which of those thousand*
> *faces? Often the least obvious is the*
> *most interesting.*[9]
> —STEVE MARTIN

Notes

1. Interview by David Jones, in Hal Burton, *Great Acting* (New York: Bonanza Books, 1967).
2. Michael Riedel, ''Great Scott,'' *Theatre Week,* October 14, 1991.
3. Kenneth Turan, ''Harrison Ford Wants to Be Alone,'' *Gentlemen's Quarterly,* October 1986.
4. Cynthia Robins, ''Final Curtain,'' *San Francisco Examiner (Image),* November 10, 1991.
5. Interview by Derek Hart, in Hal Burton, *Great Acting* (New York: Bonanza Books, 1967).

6. Curtis Bill Pepper, ''Still Mastroianni,'' *New York Times Magazine*, September 20, 1987.

7. Jack Kroll, ''William Hurt and the Curse of the Spider Man,'' *Esquire*, October 1986.

8. Pope Brock, ''Jeff Daniels Up in Michigan,'' *Gentlemen's Quarterly*, October 1987.

9. Elvis Mitchell, ''The King of Anti-Comedy,'' *Gentlemen's Quarterly*, July 1990.

PERFORMANCE PROCESS

Recognizing Standard Procedure and Appropriate Behavior From First Audition Through Closing Night

The director's job should be to open the actor up and, for God's sake, leave him alone![1]
—DUSTIN HOFFMAN

Acting is horrible, painful, and yet also intoxicating and emotionally liberating.[2]
—JODIE FOSTER

Childbirth is easy compared to giving birth to a role in a play.[3]
—HELEN HAYES

We in the theatre like to believe we have no rules. We're more tolerant of personal eccentricity, and more encouraging of emotional display, than most groups. We never require our members to all be the same. We're unusually loving and supportive of one another. Actors, who are forced to compete against one another for parts, nurture one another in every other way. But the process of putting together the performance of a play has definite rules of both procedure and personal behavior, most of them unspoken.

There have to be rules for any huge group or the group won't work as a unit. Look for the silent standards of any world you wish to join. Every rule in the theatre is made to be broken. But a rule needs to be learned before it can be broken. Only by mastering it do you earn the right to break it—when the time is right.

ACTING ETIQUETTE

Every year talented newcomers join the acting family. Full of potential, some get well cast, but then offend so many people that they are immediate history. Or it takes a long time for anyone to risk working with them again. Often the offending newcomer is no more than a victim of his own ignorance—unaware of what's happening next, much less how to handle it. I once heard a veteran actor, watching a recently fired young actor depart, refer to this phenomenon as "choking the baby on meat."

Some things you are better off not having too early. You don't play Lear when you're 17, and you don't want to play *anything* until you understand basic behavior in the theatre. This chapter deals especially with what makes onstage different from off.

Taking Time

If you have some theatre experience, use this chapter to review, brush up, and, most importantly, look for some gaps in your own acting etiquette or some factor you may not have considered before. If you are new to theatre, use it to study beforehand how to join the club.

The biggest surprise for most newcomers is, inevitably, the enormous time commitment. Although the process of putting together a production varies wildly, the following list will do as a model of traditional rehearsal patterns.

1. *Audition Notices*
   Posters and ads describing when, where, and how try-outs are to be conducted.

2. *Auditions*
   Basic try-outs, often spread over more than one day, usually held in the evenings.

3. *Call-backs*
   Smaller group narrowed down by director for another look, possibly a different set of audition activities. Often no one is actually "called" on the phone, but rather a list is posted. Know where and when it will appear.

4. *Cast List Posted*
   Notice of casting may involve initialing next to your name by way of acceptance.

5. *First Company Meeting*
Introductions of participants to each other, and sharing of director's production concept with the company.

6. *Show and Tell*
Costume and set designers (plus other possible specialty designers) demonstrate their renderings and explain visual concepts.

7. *Read-throughs*
Exploratory sessions, with players often sitting in a circle, just reading aloud, focusing on script, possibly stopping to cut some passages and discuss relationships.

8. *Blocking*
Physical staging, slow and laborious, may range all the way from director meticulously preplanning and simply instructing actors to director planning none of it, and weeks of exploration.

9. *Fittings*
Costume pieces tried on you and adjusted at various points in construction process.

10. *Character/Ensemble Development*
Rehearsals geared toward getting individuals into character and feeling like a group.

11. *Coaching*
Sessions devoted to individual acting problems, seldom involving more than director and one or two actors at a time.

12. *Intensives*
An "anything goes" period, usually working on very small portions of script over and over, in great detail, out of sequence.

13. *Polishing*
Work on flow while building for whole show; more and more running through an entire act or whole script without stopping.

14. *Promotion*
Taping media ads, doing interviews, taking scenes to special events, posing for publicity photos, selling the show.

15. *Tech-ins*
Adding lights, props, sound, set pieces, all technical elements; lengthy sessions requiring infinite patience from everyone.

16. *Dresses*
Rehearsals just before opening, done as close as possible to time of

actual performances, with all ingredients present; seldom more than three dress rehearsals, one of which is sometimes a preview.

17. *Opening*
Official first night, after months of prior work.

18. *Run*
Scheduled performances, usually with adjusted calls or times you are expected to arrive at the theatre.

19. *Brush-ups*
Rehearsals called, when considerable time exists between performances, to review lines and get it back in shape, often done without technical elements, unless cues are tricky and also need review.

20. *Closing and Striking*
Final performance, followed by taking down set, storing props and costumes, cleaning make-up and dressing rooms, taking down lights, and so on; process involves both actors and technicians.

Usually, audition notices go out two to three weeks before try-outs; the audition process takes less than a week; rehearsals occupy at least four weeks; and the show itself rarely runs longer than three weeks, if it is a college or community theatre production. (Commercial productions, however, may close after a single performance—or run for years. In fact, all time frames vary widely in commercial theatre.) So the entire process takes, on the average, a few months, but this time may expand greatly if the show is large and complex. Big musicals and Shakespearean productions often rehearse a good twelve weeks, because of all the extra training involved to develop the dancing, singing, fighting, and other special skills needed in those styles of performance. Most shows rehearse at least five evenings a week for three to four hours, and in the final stretch may rehearse daily, weekends included, with tech and dress rehearsals going into the wee hours.

A popular ratio for computing minimum play rehearsal time is one hour of rehearsal for every minute of the play's running time. So a small cast, working with a single set on a contemporary, realistic play which runs two hours (120 minutes) plus intermission, would rehearse a bare minimum of 120 hours. This figure could easily quadruple for plays with large casts and difficult scripts. Obviously, you need to determine if you have the *time* to do all this before you ever attend auditions.

Checklist: From Pre-Audition to Pre-Rehearsal

What follows are some basic questions to consider at each stage of the performance process.

Audition Preparation

Are scripts available to check out and read beforehand? Find out where and for how long. Why go in blank?

Is there a definite production concept that might affect how you could be used? Is there something about yourself that you can punch up? Ask around.

Are any roles precast and not worth your shooting for? Ask only people who *know*. There are always false rumors on this one.

Will there be cold readings, or are you to prepare material? If you need to present something memorized, need it be from script? Even if it is a cold reading, there's nothing stopping you from practicing and making your reading at least lukewarm. Does ''prepared'' mean to the director a polished reading or a fully staged, memorized, finished presentation?

Can someone who knows your work and the play advise you on where your best casting potential is in this show?

Does this director regularly use certain audition methods, ask certain questions, show definite preferences? What kinds of actors does this director seem to admire? What kinds of procedures are known to be standard when this person is in charge? You can research the director, not just the script.

Can you get into the space beforehand, to get comfortable and maybe have a friend help you check your projection?

What to wear? Something that will not interfere with the director's imagination in visualizing you in the final production. Full costume and makeup are too much, but try not to look all wrong for the play. If it's an elegant drawing-room comedy, your sweats and sneakers are a bad choice. Pick the closest thing in your closet to the *spirit* of the play.

Have you thought of all your potential time conflicts over the next few months, so that you can list them? Have you thought of responses to questions that might be on the forms?

Audition Behavior

Which night(s) are you going to attend? Most people suggest going the first night, especially if you're new. Directors go home with actors in their minds after the first night, no matter how hard they try to wait to cast.

How early should you get there? Right at the beginning, which is often when a series of instructions is given and questions are answered.

Is there someone in charge here besides the director? A stage manager or assistant or some trouble–shooter? This is the person to ask things.

Is the director the only one who can help you? Leave him alone until there is a break. Never, ever, talk to him while another actor is up there reading.

Are there instructions written down? Read anything handed out carefully so you don't need to request info that's already been given to you.

What if you're asked (on a form or in person) if you will accept any part? If you'll work on a crew? If you can miss work for some rehearsals? If you're willing to change your hair color? Lose some weight? Grow a beard? *Gain* some weight? These are fairly standard requests, and no one can tell you how to answer. But give yourself some time to think about it, so you're not so staggered by the question that you can no longer concentrate. It is always okay to say you will think it over and let them know by the end of the evening or the next day.

Are you tensing up? It is always all right to warm up. Are you getting too loud and chatty because you're nervous? Remind yourself to support every person who reads. Don't ever get so thrilled because some hot-shot actor you admire is talking with you that you distract someone else struggling onstage.

Are you studying the other actors? This session can turn into a master class if you observe closely. Watch not only those who do well but those who don't. You probably have hundreds of examples of what to do and what not to do right before your eyes.

Do you need to leave? Make sure it's all right. If you can't do that, tell at least one person who plans to stay that you're going and where you'll be. Do you know when you might hear something about the results? Where the list will be posted? Are you absolutely clear on all details for call-back time, place, procedure?

Audition Activities

Are you asked to do something weird? Think of it as a game and give yourself permission to have fun. Often your poise, imagination, and sense of adventure are being tested. It doesn't always have to make sense.

Do you get a chance to choose a partner to read with? Check out everyone for those you think look right with you—people who make you comfortable. This is a chance to use your insight instead of just grabbing someone.

Are you asked to change your reading? This is always a good sign. Respond positively. Directors at auditions rarely direct people who do not interest them.

Are you puzzled by the range of activity? Remember, anything that could happen in acting class can happen here in a highly condensed form. You study improv to release your spontaneity. If improv is used here it is probably to *test* your spontaneity.

Do you sometimes have to just stand there while the director studies you and others? She is looking at combinations: families, lovers, agés, and so forth. Relax. Try not to look like a hunted animal. You are being *considered*.

Is there a chance to volunteer to read? Take it. You've just been up there? Fine. They'll see you again. Within reason, actors are aggressive, and enthusiasm to be onstage now says you will carry this enthusiasm through rehearsal.

Are you rushing and not connecting when you read? Stop and ask yourself what you want, what's in the way, what your plan is, how much the person opposite means to you—the quick basics. Don't let yourself forget the way you always act most effectively. Take time to feel the words and see the person reading opposite you.

Call-backs

Is there something you need to prepare, check out, a person you are to work with in advance, information you still need to provide? Read the notice with incredible care, so your joy over making the list doesn't cloud your sense of detail.

Are you not on the list? You still need to check the cast list, because some
directors call back only those people they are undecided about, and do
cast some roles based on the initial reading.

Is there something the director would like to see from you that you have
not yet shown? Ask. If you make call-backs, you are a contender. A
mannerism she would like you to modify, a quality to punch up, some
alteration in your appearance? You have a golden opportunity to show
what kind of actor you will be if cast.

Any last-minute reservations? This is the time to get out. If you drop out
after the cast list is posted, you do serious, possibly irreparable, damage
to your reputation. You inconvenience many. And no matter how
thrilled the person who replaces you may be, he and everyone else will
always know he was not first choice. All because of you.

Preparation for First Rehearsal

Are you supposed to check out a script beforehand? Probably. This is a
good time to mark your lines with a highlighter or in some other way that
helps you focus.

Is there a callboard for this production? Start checking it daily. This is
where they'll tell you when they need to take your measurements for
costumes and each subsequent time you're needed for a fitting. This is
where you may get a deadline for a form that needs to be filled out so
that something can be sent to your hometown newspaper. This is where
last-minute messages of all kinds are posted.

Do you have your rehearsal supplies? You may need several pencils
(not pens—you may do a lot of erasing), a notebook or journal, basic
supplies (mouthwash, mints, whatever you need to feel good about
being close), script, and special clothing or shoes. It helps to keep all
this stuff together and ready.

Rehearsing Outside of Rehearsal

A common error made by new actors is to schedule yourself so tightly that
you can fit in rehearsal, but very little else each day. This is what you are
generally expected to do outside of rehearsal:

1. Analyze the character.
2. Memorize lines.

3. Research the role for background information to better understand the world of the play.

4. Apply the director's notes from each previous night's rehearsal.

5. Experiment with character approaches.

6. Develop the vocal life of the character.

7. Develop the physical life of the character.

8. Brush up on material that hasn't been worked in a week.

9. Attend costume fittings.

10. Participate in publicity photo sessions and interviews.

This list could expand if you need to work with a coach on a particular skill or if you and an acting partner need to explore some aspect of your characters' relationship.

To keep your bases covered, it's a good idea to plan on allotting yourself an hour of offstage rehearsal, usually by yourself, for every hour you spend onstage with the rest of the company. You may not need this much every day but sometimes you may need more. And few things are worse than having a director say to you, ''Your work was sluggish tonight. You've got to get more rest.'' Then, after she walks away, you look at your already-crammed schedule and ask yourself, ''When?''

Checklist: From Rehearsal Through Performance

Rehearsal Behavior

What is the scheduled starting time? Whatever it is, it means that you have already arrived, unpacked, gone to the john, warmed up as necessary, and taken care of chitchat by that time. It's not the time at which you breeze through the door out of breath. It isn't a bad idea to arrive a half-hour before the scheduled time, and take care of business during that interval.

How far ahead of rehearsal will you know when you are called? There is no guarantee. Some directors post each day what will be on that night, and never post ahead. That's an extreme, but even if you have what looks like a detailed schedule, check the callboard daily for last-minute changes. Someone may be sick, and your scene is now scheduled to be worked instead.

Some of your favorite lines are cut? Try not to gasp, moan, or collapse on the floor. Strive for grace. Should you try to get these words put back in? Only if you are *completely convinced* they are essential to your character. Not just because you like them. Think about this for a while.

Feeling inhibited by the reputations of some big guns in the cast? Get to know them as soon as possible. Work past the images to the real people. Feeling cautious generally? Don't let yourself start bottling up. No one expects a performance yet. Rehearsal is where you need to feel free to experiment before finalizing, where you dare to be foolish and vulnerable.

Conflicts between class demands and show demands? Can you expect theatre teachers to let you out of assignments or delay them because you are in a play? No. You can ask, but realize it is a big favor, and one due to your own failure to structure your time.

Missed a fitting? Beg the designer's forgiveness. Go volunteer to work in the shop. (Costumers can put pins places you would rather not feel them.) Need help in feeling like your character? Wear rehearsal clothing that's as close to the actual costume as you can get, whether you check it out from the costume shop or drag it from your own closet. If the character wears heels and fitted skirts, don't wait. Get into them the first week. The character is a cowboy? Get boots. Even throwing your coat over your shoulder in place of a cape that will eventually be there is better than nothing. Don't underestimate the power of clothes to transform you. Don't be embarrassed by adding these things. Some in the company may tease you, and secretly recognize you as a serious actor.

Blocking coming at you fast and furious? Write it in shorthand. There is standard code for common stage movements. In addition to using initials (DR for down right, UC for up center, and so on, for stage areas), actors often employ the shorthand shown in Figure 7–1.

EXERCISE 7.1

STAGE SHORTHAND

Write the following directions as quickly and economically as possible.

1. Cross down left to the table, pivot right and exit.
2. Cross to the door and face up right.

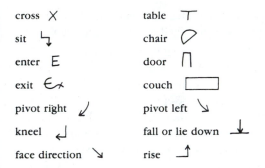

Figure 7-1 Stage Shorthand
Here are some common codes, but if you don't like them, invent your own.

3. Enter up center and sit on the couch.

4. Move from the table to the door to the chair, then exit left.

5. Enter down left, kneel at door, rise, cross down and sit.

Practice ways of getting lengthy directions down on paper with the least possible amount of writing.

Or make up your own shorthand. Confident that you'll remember the movements without writing them down? Don't be. There may be lots of time before this scene is called again, and you may be struggling with lines by that time, so your concentration will be divided. Write them down. And check them again before you sleep tonight to make sure you've got it.

Being asked to do things you don't understand? Unclear about the objectives of some rehearsals? Ask, right away. Unlike an audition, there should be no hidden agenda here. You have a right to know why and wherefore.

Are tech staff or crew members attending rehearsals? Are you encountering office and front-of-house staff? Treat every person on this show with maximum respect. Don't succumb for an instant to acting as if these people were your servants. They are fellow artists. And they don't get curtain calls.

Feel like you need a haircut? Like lightening your hair color? Like going on a crash diet? Clear any potential change in your appearance with the

director beforehand. Do you have any idea how many actors have fool-
ishly altered the very thing the director liked best about their looks?

What to eat and drink before rehearsal? Keep it light, so you don't get sluggish. Most actors choose long-term energy food instead of stuff that
gives you a surge that dies long before the end of rehearsal. No, don't
even consider arriving even mildly drunk or stoned (or stunk and
droned, a combination). Any role-related experimenting (like rehearsing
an alcoholic character by drinking heavily) is on your own time, or by
mutual agreement with the director and anyone else involved.

> *I had a lot of trouble working with my co-star, who*
> *was from "the Cocaine School of Acting."*[4]
> —SHIRLEY MacLAINE

Getting bored or tired waiting for your scene to come up or to be called
in to work? Bring other work (stop-and-start stuff) that can be done
while waiting. Write in your acting journal. See if the costume shop
needs someone to sew on buttons. Or work on your character in these
stretches. Keep yourself energized and occupied.

Likely Deadlines

The deadline for your character analysis work? Usually about two weeks
into the rehearsal period. To be handed in? No, not usually, but shared
with the group or just integrated into the rehearsal process by this time.
Be prepared to answer all the character questions asked in chapter 6.

For completing any outside research? It varies. Anything you don't know
about the historical period, country, art, music, or cultural styles of the
people in the play is worth a few trips to the library. Will others feel
disdain for you as an eager beaver? Only the motivationally impaired.
And the jealous.

For knowing your lines? Some directors want them memorized as soon
as possible; most expect it the second time a scene is called after it is
blocked. Commonly, everyone is off book at least two full weeks before
opening.

If you are a slow study, start scheduling daily line workouts from the first
day. Realize you tend to lose a lot of solid memorization once in front of
the other actors, so consider checking memorization with the other
people in your scenes before the actual deadline.

Running lines? Usually an assistant director will help you. Other actors will usually be glad to do so. Are you calling for lines? Stay in the scene. Try not to look at the prompter. Give yourself a beat for the line to come. Try not to break character or concentration. Lines will come much faster if you stay in the moment itself, even when the words are rough.

After Opening

Should you adjust your performance? Only in consultation with the director and anyone else influenced by being onstage with you.

Reviews? Look for trends, if reviewed by a number of publications. If reviewed only by one not-very-respected local critic, ignore it altogether. Never take a copy to the theatre, or quote it, or grumble about it, or in any way inflict the review on others, who may wish to rise above it.

Let down? It's inevitable after the rush of opening night. Don't succumb to second-night blahs. Consider yourself a source of energy and fresh air for everyone you work with. It is always opening night for the audience. Always. Renew that night every night. These people deserve nothing less than your miraculous best.

> *I want to come out of a theater feeling that someone*
> *has touched me. The whole point is to have a*
> *revelatory experience, to be carried to the heights.*[5]
> —KATHY BATES

Brush-ups? May be called if the show has been dark for a while. Lots of plays perform just on weekends, and so may go Sunday through Wednesday or Thursday dark, and need at least a run-through before going to an audience again. Give yourself the same charge as above.

Some performances better than others? Inevitably. But these things happen for a reason. Try to make sure *you* aren't the reason. Which performance is best? Ideally, closing night. You grow a little bit every time you go out. And on closing night, you look forward to the next time you'll get to work with this script or develop further this kind of character.

Time to strike? All actors become crew members until everything is put away. A tradition, and not one to be violated. This is not the moment to suddenly decide to have a fling with irresponsibility. See the experience through to the end.

WAR STORIES

Many of us learn theatre etiquette by messing up once or twice. This is a good time for the more experienced members of the class to share their experiences in failing to plan well or to show maximum consideration for others in the process. Describe the event, what you got out of it, and the particular vows you made to yourself about working on productions in the future.

ADAPTATIONS

Adapting Show Process to Class Process

What happens in a production can simply be scaled down for a course in acting. How? You just look at the time-frames, responsibilities, and deadlines, then modify them. It's alarming how many actors function brilliantly when someone else imposes the schedule, but collapse when they have to do some of this themselves.

Preparing a ten-minute scene? That means the bare minimum rehearsal period prior to the first time it's done in class is ten hours. Remember? The operative phrase here is "bare minimum." Full productions develop a cumulative effect. Scenes late in the play sometimes require less rehearsal because so much groundwork and layering has preceded them. Once you know these characters and have experienced them in previous situations, you somehow earn the right to discover quickly in the final stretches. A lone scene never has this advantage. So you only add rehearsal time. Also, your entire rehearsal period is more likely to be a few weeks, so you are condensing the performance process.

Shortcuts? You and your partner have discovered that you are soulmates—probably brother and sister separated at birth? You are so well cast that each line of dialogue sounds as if it rolled off your very own tongue? A shining light descended on a rehearsal, and every word uttered for the next five minutes was magic? There *are* no shortcuts. You can always afford to rehearse a few more times, and discover some more values.

Look at each stage of the traditional preparation of a play and make sure that, to some extent, you've done that preparation for your scene. Any chance to develop and share your work with an audience is a very big deal. Your scene is an important production in miniature.

Schedules and Objectives

As soon as you get a partner, sit down together and map out a rehearsal period. Reserve generous time-frames between now and the due-date. You can always cancel an unnecessary rehearsal more easily than you can squeeze in an impromptu one at the last minute. In class you often have a partner before you have a scene, so selecting a scene may be your first objective, with a definite deadline.

Many actors just sit and read through the script for lots of sessions without any progression. Then one day it becomes obvious that they've got to stand up and do some blocking, so they do that, and from then on in they just run through again and again, without progression. A certain amount of progress takes place in spite of this vapid approach. But not nearly as much as if you establish an objective for each session. One meeting might be solely to get to know each other better, another to work on vocal technique and line delivery, another to clarify subtext, another to develop the characters' shared history. There are so many tasks to be accomplished that the main problem is just which one today.

Stated objectives will also make you feel, when you leave, that you know why you were there. A great deal of acting is magical and mysterious. There is always plenty of that, no matter what. Some organization will actually free you to unlock the magic.

EXERCISE 7.3

SETTING A SCHEDULE

1. With your partner, copy a calendar and identify how many days you have until the "opening" of your scene, and, if it is to be presented twice, how many days between "opening" and "revival."

2. Identify a specific meeting-time, with never more than two days between rehearsals.

3. Identify specific goals for some of the rehearsals, leaving others for pure experimentation.

4. Overdo the time commitment, because it will be easier to cut back later than to cram in rehearsals not planned.

5. Consider working from a rehearsal schedule for a full production, crossing off irrelevant items like photo calls but keeping some version of everything else. Make sure you each have a copy, and that

you both understand not only the schedule itself but those times (such as memorization or analysis) when both of you agree to commit to considerable solo time outside of rehearsal as well.

Memorizing

Some actors are quick studies and others are painfully slow. There is a definite trend to ask for lines earlier and earlier in rehearsal. It used to be thought that if actors memorized too early they would lock the delivery of the line as well. So many exercises are now designed to liberate and vary delivery that the problem of locking is rare. If you have trouble getting lines down, here are some suggestions:

1. Work from your cues, not from the first word of each of *your* lines. Memorize at least the *last half* of your partner's speeches. Many actors are sent into paralysis because they weren't expecting their partner to stop talking.

2. Cue yourself off of motivating words (action cues) within your partner's speeches, the words that stimulate response, not off of the last word (line cue) of his speech. Responders always start gearing up on a certain word or phrase within the body of the other person's lines.

3. Work on lines for short periods only, ideally a single beat mastered at each session. Marathon sessions are rarely retained.

4. After you learn about half a page, go back and drill, then drill again. Never assume you've got it without backtracking.

5. Place a card over your lines, and reveal only as much to yourself as is absolutely necessary as you cue yourself and master each speech.

6. Try taping your partner's lines with spaces or, if your partner is feeling helpful, have *her* tape her lines, so you can run yours when she's not around, and still hear the right voice giving you cues. *Alternative:* Tape everything, both your parts. This allows you to listen to a complete text while doing other tasks (driving, shaving, getting dressed) so you can let the words act on you without having to stop other activities. It also allows you to walk through your blocking without having to speak, which can enhance your sense of subtext.

7. Some actors find flash cards helpful, with the other actor's lines on one side and their own on the other. Putting the cards together is time-consuming, but frequently the mere act of doing it gets you off book.

8. Always memorize according to what the character wants, rather than doing words by rote. Memorize thought-clusters and intention-clusters rather than word-clusters. You should be able to paraphrase in a pinch. Actors who forget lines are invariably those who have just placed the words in their heads, so that when the word is gone, so are they.

9. Remember Stanislavski's images, and use them to get a firm film-and/or still shot associated with each group of words. The visual image will tend to bring the lines with it as it pops back into your mind.

10. Every time you memorize, review everything *else* you've memorized in the past few days, too. Go back to the beginning for a brush-up, which serves as a warm-up to get you in the memorization mode.

Working with a Director, Coach, or Teacher

A director, a coach, and a teacher are all three guides to help you, but in different ways. It's important to separate their functions so you know what to expect. There are many exceptions to the following distinctions, but they hold true most of the time.

An acting teacher creates an environment (physical and emotional), and provides exercises, to help you explore and discover your potential. The teacher rarely inflicts his will or forces change. He aims to make you self-sufficient, and, particularly in beginning acting classes, is usually more concerned with your overall awareness and growth as a person than with technical precision.

An acting coach functions much like a coach in sports: working with you on specific problems, having you try a number of solutions, fine-tuning the same moment over and over, driving you a little further than you thought possible. You go into a coaching session with definite problems to be solved. If it's a good session, you leave with some solved, and more to work on because the coach has stimulated you to move ahead in specific areas. A coach's attention is in many ways the most direct or personal, and the efforts the most precise.

A director is the most likely of the three to impose his will on yours. He is the most likely to tell you (at some point sooner or later in the rehearsal process) exactly what he wants and (very late in the process) to lock much of what you do. This is because he has an opening night and a huge group of other company members to think about. In a show, you are part of a much larger package, one which will ultimately be in some way marketed.

One of my favorite directors said regularly to casts, ''You are all like hands on a clock, very important, but I'm standing out here, and I'm the only one who can tell what time it is.'' The director is ultimately concerned, to a larger degree than the coach and to a much larger degree than the teacher, with a finished product. The teacher is the one most concerned with process.

These distinctions are arbitrary and often contradictory. Sometimes, for example, a director mounts an experimental work that is highly process-centered, with no interest in slick surfaces. Some teachers act as gurus, and instead of making their actors self-sufficient they make the actors highly dependent emotionally on them. A director mounting shows involving styles or skills unfamiliar to his cast may move through all three roles. He may start by teaching, then evolve to coaching each performer, and only toward the end become a traditional director.

The distinctions among the three are useful, however, in terms of your own anticipation. Actors are sometimes naively disappointed because their work isn't polished in a class, failing to realize that surface is not the purpose. Others will go for a coaching session, expecting everything to be fixed, upset when they leave, aware of even more work that needs to be done. All three of these guides, if they are conscientious artists, are trying to help make you strong. Even the director will only fix things for you because he has an audience to think about. Work with all three with realistic expectations for long-term growth.

Working without a Director

For years I went around saying, ''What I really like is a strong director who knows exactly what he wants and will tell me.'' It took me quite a while to realize that I was really saying, ''I don't know what I'm doing so I want to be told.'' The ideal relationship with a director is collaborative, full of mutual strength and support. No one has summed up the ideal more vividly than Stanislavski, who said: ''A talented director may come along and drop just a word, the actor will catch fire and his role will glow with all the colors of his soul's prism.''[6] How's *that* for a good working relationship?

A director who tells and shows you everything, giving no encouragement to explore, is hardly treating you like a collaborator. Such directors are probably eagerly awaiting the time when robots get sophisticated enough to use them instead of you.

*Actors are basically pawns. If you want someone
else to design your life and take responsibility away
from you then it's great to be an actor.*[7]
—GOLDIE HAWN

At the other extreme, any actor should be prepared to survive the absence of a director's help. There are many productions where someone is listed in that capacity, but that person did precious little to provide vision and coordination. And remember, the director can leave the theatre, the town, the country. You are the one who has to go out in front of the audience.

So, if you're lucky enough to have help, grab it and relish it. But if you're on your own, you can do it. You can survive. The primary switch you need to make is in attitude. Every time you have to block yourself, or go to a friend for feedback on a speech, or make up a rehearsal objective without being told to do so by the resident authority figure, think of it as one more chance to grow self-sufficient. "I need a director" is too easy to say and impossible to survive.

Working with a Non-Director

Sometimes you simply get no feedback whatsoever from the person in charge. It doesn't usually work to go up to her and say, "Give me some feedback." You tend to get an answer like "You're doing fine." It doesn't usually work to stop her after rehearsal, and ask, "Got any notes for me?" You'll probably be told, "No, I'll let you know."

Now it's important to remember that, if everything is going smoothly, *no notes are good notes*. There are many directors who address only what is wrong, and you may indeed be doing well. But if you feel insecure and awkward, you have to devise a strategy. Your best bet is to ask questions that *must* be answered, like "Why do you think my character does this?" or "Which of the ways I tried that sequence has been working best?" or "Tonight, I'm going to try this. Tell me if you think it adds, or if we should go back to the other approach." Always, of course, keep it friendly and respectful. You need to be not only aggressive but a bit clever. If you are getting no help, you can take the initiative. But you must provide the framework for a reticent director to respond to you.

All directors find it easier to edit your work than to relentlessly feed you ideas, energy, and courage. Actors who bring a lot into the process allow a director to add shape and nuance, which is the director's ideal function. It is a good idea to bring a lot of choices to rehearsal.

> *I do not believe acting should be smaller than life.*
> *I just enjoy throwin' myself at stuff, risking*
> *being too much. I'd rather have someone say,*
> *"Tone it down, Hunter, WHOOAAH!" than*
> *not feel I'm giving enough.*[8]
> —HOLLY HUNTER

Working with Untrained Observers

Almost everyone observes human behavior. And most people are quite good at detecting when that behavior is dishonest, phony, stiff, or distracting. So you don't need to go to a supposed theatre expert to get feedback while working on a scene or monologue. Sometimes friends and family, though completely unconnected with the theatre, can give you some of the best information and a fresh perspective on your work.

Obviously, you shouldn't drown them in actor lingo or in any way make them feel less than expert. Just show them what you're working on and have them respond, human to human. Here are some questions that you can ask absolutely anyone about your scene:

EXERCISE 7.4

WHAT YOU SEE

Show your work to a friend who has no specific theatre background, and use the following questions as the basis for soliciting feedback:

1. As my character, what kind of a person do I seem to be?
2. How old am I? What kind of background do I have? What beliefs?
3. Where am I when this speech takes place?
4. What had happened to me just before the scene? Where did I come from? What had I been doing?
5. What do my movements and gestures say about me? When do my moves look unnatural?
6. How would you imagine me dressed and looking if the show were fully produced?
7. To whom am I talking? What is my relationship to her? Her reaction to me? Does she ever move or respond? When? How?

8. Which moments do you find hardest to understand? Most difficult to believe?

9. What do I seem to want in this scene? What does this person seem to want out of life?

10. What do you notice going on between my words? What am I deciding *not* to do or say?

11. What, if any, changes do I seem to go through? How do I modify my behavior?

12. Is there anything getting in the way between me and what I want? What is it?

13. What about this character is just like me? What is different?

14. Do I remind you of anyone else when I do the speech?

15. When do you find the whole thing least interesting?

16. How would you feel about being friends with this character?

17. What effect did my imaginary surroundings have on me? Any you could see?

18. Does this scene take place right now, in the present? If not, when? How can you tell?

19. What kinds of feelings did listening to and watching me create in you?

20. At what points did you think my concentration seemed to be more on myself, the actor, than on the needs and desires of the character?

Notice that all these questions are open-ended, the same kinds of questions needed with non-directors. None can be answered "yes," "no," or "maybe." The person you're talking to has *got* to give you information.

There are also almost no value judgments or implied requests for compliments in the above questions. Why? Most people want to tell you what you want to hear. So if you just do your speech and ask only, "What do you think?" your friend is likely to say, "Great." Their "appraisal" is likely to continue in that mode:

> You: Any suggestions?
> Friend: No. Boy, I could never do that.
> You: Was I believable?
> Friend: I guess so. Sure.
> You: The character is younger than I am. Was I young enough?
> Friend: Oh, absolutely.
> You: Could you sense the wind blowing?
> Friend: Wind? . . . Uh . . . Yeah, wind.

You can see that this goes nowhere. You are implying a desired answer. But if you instead just ask how old the character is, you get what the other person really thinks. If your friend says 53, and your character is a teen-ager, you know you have some work ahead of you in rehearsal.

Clearly, you will not want to ask everything on the list above of everyone you know. Expand or contract the list according to the needs of the scene and your personal respect for the opinions of your auditor on life in general. Substitute other questions based on your character analysis. An added benefit of sharing your work regularly with friends and family is that the unveiling in class will be less tense because you have already unveiled it in bits and pieces. Don't neglect this source. You may get a lot of the help you need right at home.

EXERCISE 7.5

A LITTLE HELP FROM MY FRIENDS

1. Pick three friends or family members who know nothing about theatre.

2. Identify what you particularly value about each in terms of their wisdom or understanding of human behavior. Where are they wise and compassionate?

3. Share your scene or monologue with them, using the questions above as a guide.

4. Think of your friends as experts on truth, and use that expertise to help you shape the scene.

Criticism: Give and Take

Criticism in acting class is a free gift that actors give to one another. It is especially important in assignments which will be repeated to give your classmates all your reactions, to help them go back into rehearsal armed. If theatrical terms aren't coming as quickly as you want, just revert to the kind of non-professional vocabulary and categories above. If you say to a fellow actor, "I wasn't always sure what you wanted from him," that's a valid expression, which may mean the actor's objectives weren't clear. It could also mean that you weren't looking very carefully, but at least you have *shared* it. What the actors choose to do with these free gifts is up to them.

Many beginning actors simply will not take part in critiquing a classmate's work, leaving it all up to others. It is one thing if you're simply drawing a blank, but if you're worried only about others thinking that you're cruel, opinionated, or out of line, you are sabotaging yourself and them. It's selfish to keep to yourself and not dare to risk disapproval. Remember, you have invested in these people and they in you. Shying away from generous confrontation is not generous at all.

I've worked hard as a person, and as an
actor, to fight my way through shyness. It's our
responsibility as human beings to share with others.
Being shy and withdrawn is selfish.[9]
—MICHAEL DOUGLAS

How do you take criticism that seems harsh? Remind yourself that nobody criticizes unless he cares; it takes too much energy. It beats not being noticed at all. And it goes with the territory. Drama critics have the right to print comments on actors which would get other writers sued for libel. The healthiest actor I know carries the following review with him in his make-up kit, and puts it up on the mirror in each new dressing room he occupies:

> Mr. _____ spends the entire evening onstage making a pitiful attempt to prove his masculinity. The attempt is not just pathetic; it's boring and he completely fails.

He manages to find humor and solace even in this old review. He's home free. No one will ever write anything worse about him.

Process vs. Product

Process does not stop one day in rehearsal as suddenly product replaces it. If the distinctions between these two are too sharp, the work changes radically—rarely for the better. People who do lousy, lazy shows will announce that they are concerned with process as a rationale for a complete lack of quality and polish on opening night. Others will refuse to tolerate experimentation and exploration because ''we have a product we need to get out here.'' So everyone involved in such a production is forced to set work at the earliest possible moment without any real chance to grow or discover.

In the rehearsal of a play or a scene, as opening night or class due-date draws near, a shift in energy often occurs among actors. A sort of panic sets in that undoes a great deal of earlier work, as if now were the time to get serious and lose all the delight and spontaneity of our past weeks together. Then there is the procrastinator-actor, who does absolutely nothing until a performance date looms on the horizon, then suddenly crams—a very bad idea. A performance is not a term paper, where you can write all night, then drop off the product and collapse. Remember, *you* are the product. Not only can you not do work worth watching if you're exhausted and stressed, but your performance will have had no chance to grow. You need to start working seriously early, then give yourself periods in which you let things work on your imagination, in which you allow the character to visit you. Actress Laurette Taylor, the original Amanda in *The Glass Menagerie,* used to compare this process to bread-dough rising. Making bread from scratch is an apt metaphor for preparing for a performance, because there are interludes during which you have to stop forcing the product and just let the process take its course for a while. If you always look for results, you fail to savor the moment.

> *Fame is fun for a minute, but it gets very boring.*
> *I think the real fun part is the actual work.*
> *There's not a feeling in the world like manipulating*
> *yourself into feeling something and knowing you*
> *were honest for that one moment.*[10]
> —Winona Ryder

If you expose your evolving performance in bits and pieces to your loved ones and some of your classmates, as suggested earlier, it will enhance the gradual nature of the performance process. Doing things at least twice in class helps. Previewing scenes and speeches from a production and having an invited audience or an entire preview performance also help. Process is a way of thinking. Opening night is like a rehearsal in which the new problem is adjusting to the change in acoustics and to playing the house. Each night of the run is a chance to set a personal, process-oriented objective, the way the director may have set process during rehearsal. Closing night as your best work is an ideal to shoot for. Looking *beyond* closing is an even better idea, so that you keep yourself in the future, looking ahead to the chance to repeat this role or to play another of this type again sometime. There should be no moment in the process when growth stops and fear or sentiment replaces it.

Kiss the Line Goodbye

There is a great temptation at the close of a play to get maudlin. You love these people, and this project has engaged you for a long time. A constant in your life is being eliminated. Actors sometimes go onstage and relish each moment (usually a good idea) to the point where their performance resembles a memorial service. "Goodbye, little line. Goodbye, little prop. I'll never use you again. Goodbye, little upstage turn."

Don't misunderstand. We all tend to do this. I have been one of the worst offenders in the world. If you have loved the experience, how can you let it go? At least without saying goodbye?

The answer is: The audience deserves better. They deserve nothing less than your opening-night best. What have they done to deserve attending a wake? The other answer is: Your memory deserves better, too. You want to remember this last performance as crisp, strong, and full of control—a work of art. Backstage, afterward, during strike, is where you've earned the right to get messy and mushy.

Offstage Process

You decide to join a club, a co-op, or a corporation. You seek membership in a fraternal order, a team, a party, a family, a secret society, the military, a monastery, or the Daughters of the American Revolution. How do you do it? Follow the exact process outlined in the preceding pages, because although each group has its particular quirks, all share universal questions to be answered. Those who don't do well, socially and professionally, don't research their target. So they don't know how to (pardon the expression) act. Because theatre has so many restrictions, so many freedoms, and so many peculiarities, if you can case it out, you can case out anything. These are topics covered in this chapter:

Handling interviews	Adapting procedures
Taking the initiative	Working well with others
Mastering etiquette	Editing
Managing time	Handling criticism
Working unsupervised	Maintaining perspective
Setting goals	Finding innovative ideas
Meeting deadlines	Gaining confidence

One of the largest employment agencies in the country has reported continuous success in placing students who have studied acting into other fields because these students have such highly developed skills in each of the areas above. The theatre teaches these topics by necessity. If you get involved in a play production, it can do more for you than take up a lot of time and provide lots of fun. It can teach you fundamental survival skills.

PROCESSING

1. Go back over the fourteen categories in the list above, and adapt them to a job or group familiar to you but outside the theatre.

2. Pick a new area you know nothing about. Use the list above and the material at the beginning of this chapter to help you investigate it.

Circular Experience

The theatre is a circle. Impulses generated from the stage go out into the house and circle back, as laughs, gasps, or moments of utter silence feed the actors to throw something out again. It goes on all evening. It is the reason the theatre (often called "the fabulous invalid" because of its supposedly feeble condition) will never die. Nothing else quite like this interplay exists (rock concerts are far more predictable, and ask a smaller emotional range of their listeners). This wild circle keeps whirling invisibly for the whole evening. The audience has the power to change the actors, and vice versa.

For the actor, life in the theatre is circular: Audition through rehearsal through performance through closing, and back to audition as the pattern begins again. If the actor auditions and is not called back or cast, the circle simply grows smaller. Whatever happens, the actor is perhaps the ultimate optimist. She anticipates the future, and keeps, sometimes only by sheer force of will, the circle flowing.

> *Acting provides the fulfillment of never being*
> *fulfilled. You're never as good as you'd like to be. So*
> *there's always something to hope for.*[11]
> —GLENDA JACKSON

> *Mostly what I like about acting is that it's*
> *almost impossible to achieve perfection in it. No*
> *matter how good you are, you can always be better.*
> *That's the challenge.*[12]
> —KELLY MCGILLIS

Notes

1. Douglas Brode, *The Films of Dustin Hoffman* (Secaucus, N.J.: Citadel Press, 1983).
2. "All Grown Up and Everywhere to Go," *People*, Spring 1991 (Special Issue).
3. Helen Hayes, *A Gift of Joy* (Philadelphia: J.B. Lippincott & Co., 1965).
4. J. Rovin, "Shirley!" *Ladies' Home Journal*, August 1985.
5. "A Misery-able Trip from Stage to Screen," *People*, Spring 1991 (Special Issue).
6. Constantin Stanislavski, *Building a Character* (New York: Theatre Arts Books, 1949).
7. "Flying High at Home and on the Set," *People*, Spring 1991 (Special Issue).
8. David Ansen, "Five Foot Two, How She Grew," *Newsweek*, December 28, 1989.
9. Ovid Demaris, "Finally He Can Play the Bad Guy," *Parade*, February 14, 1990.
10. Aljean Harmetz, "On Screen, Winona Ryder Comes of Age," *New York Times*, December 9, 1990.
11. Kenneth Staats, "Aspiring to Greatness," *Century*, November 1980.
12. Dan Yakir, "Surprise, Surprise," *Cabletime*, November 1987.

8 ACTING ANTICIPATED

Setting Goals for the Future
Which Allow Both Artistic Growth
and Personal Satisfaction

I found that the only way I could cope with life was
to remove myself from social mores and routine and
run my own track. So I became an actor.[1]
—JEREMY IRONS

I'd like to become a slightly older actor.[2]
—BEN KINGSLEY (responding to ''What do you want to
be doing a few years from now?'')

Looking to the Future

If you take a beginning acting class, you want two things:

1. An increased level of self-awareness and confidence: the capacity to take an actor's poise, command, and concentration into your own life, even if you never go near a theatre again.

2. An increased understanding of what needs to be done if you *do* decide to enter the theatre again, part- or full-time, casually or seriously: a sense of how you might be able to make onstage acting a part of your life.

Most onstage awareness can be taken offstage and used. And the theatre does wait patiently, ready to have you back when you're ready to return.

Is the Art for You? Are You for It?

A primary question about acting to consider right now is whether you want to stick around. Expressing yourself artistically somehow is essential to living fully. Those who don't see the performing arts as basic, like the 3 R's, fail to realize that it's fundamental to feed the spirit. There are many creatures walking around still breathing but with dead, starved spirits. You probably realize this, or you wouldn't have chosen to study acting, even briefly. But is this the right place for you to feed regularly?

Ask yourself if acting has rewarded you, and if you can *collaborate*. This art form has pressure, deadlines, and constant candid criticism. It's a communal art form in which the group has to be put above the individual. It's uneven. It's always starting and ending, as another play goes into production or closes. There is no slow, steady flame, but rather bursts and explosions of light and heat.

Are the bursts, the explosions, and the groups what you love? Or do you find yourself frustrated and stressed by them? The god of the theatre is Dionysus, who embodies the irrational, the powerfully emotional, who gave the world wine. The actor who puts on the mask may take on the power of the god himself, but he risks the mask overcoming him. Unable to take it off, he flirts with madness. Do you need something less frantic and more constant? When you think back on your time so far, were you unsettled during quite a bit of it? Lots of performers could be called acting addicts. They are so desperately unhappy that acting seems more like a needle in their arm than a source of strength. They are wrapped up in acting, but without joy.

Do you find the brotherhood a source of strength? Or do you have trouble being on time, not letting partners down, not flirting with irresponsibility? Was it a strain meeting obligations and deadlines involving all those partners? If you're a flake, get out of the theatre. You can always go write verses on the beach, strum a guitar, get out the easel and oils—none of these objects can be hurt by your irresponsibility.

There are lots of reasons to stay with acting. The two big reasons for leaving it are the recognition of how easy it is to hurt yourself and to hurt others. The biggest reason for staying is because it feels so right.

Acting was the first thing that made the work
and the commitment effortless.[3]
—MICHELLE PFEIFFER

*I found that acting was like a virus, growing
stronger and consuming me. My true calling came
out. And it came with great force.[4]*

—ANDY GARCIA

TRAINING OBJECTIVES

If you decide to stay, take the self-awareness you've recently developed and translate it into goals, including the following possible training routes:

1. Pursue a theatre degree where you are now, assuming that each course in the sequence will address your areas of concern.

2. Transfer to a school that is larger, smaller, more or less professionally focused, closer to an academy or to a scholarly university, to match your needs.

3. Take courses in dance, movement, singing, and voice to release and express your physical and vocal instruments.

4. Study privately, with a coach, on areas in which you particularly want to move quickly ahead.

5. Set up sessions with a specialist, counselor, or therapist trained to address tension or inhibition which is standing in the way of your exploration.

6. Pursue a tangential therapy which addresses your own special concern and also appeals to you: bioenergetics, functional integration, Gestalt therapy, yoga, Zen sports, reflexology, Rolfing, relaxation response, biofeedback, meditation, aikido, t'ai chi ch'uan, psychodrama, or visualization.

7. Turn acting into an avocation or serious hobby, with no more formal training but some involvement in your theatre community.

8. Spend some time as a newly aware audience member, studying the work of actors from a distance, determining how much you miss the activity itself.

9. Postpone any decision until you've had a chance to take another course or two and determine whether your infatuation survives a test of time and familiarity.

10. Learn everything you can about auditions, because they are the next hurdle if you stay involved. In fact, they are always the next hurdle to leap over (and over) throughout an actor's life.

Before you pack your bags, take a good look at where you are. If you are learning here, chances are you should stay. When you stop learning is the time to go. The most pathetic actors are those who keep transferring to smaller and less reputable departments so that their casting chances improve. Is it really worth it to be surrounded by mediocrity when your chances for growth may be much higher where you are?

Many actors never stop taking classes, even repeating the local version of Acting I, in different locations, just to stay in touch. Each acting class is a separate event because the people are so different. And acting is not like the measles, where you have it and then it's over. A veteran once explained to me his penchant for always taking classes as ''just like going to the gym to stay in shape. No one would ask why someone still does sit-ups.'' Acting class is where your emotional muscles and imagination muscles can always get a good workout.

Production-Proof Actors

Aspire, as you train, to become a production-proof actor. As an audience member you surely have identified a few performers who always seem to do good work, no matter what vehicle they're in. The film or play can seem like chicken-poop, but the actor always transcends and illuminates the material. This is a good goal for any novice performer. Far too many actors go down with the ship in an ill-conceived vehicle that bombs in a big way; far too many go down with the dinghy, in smaller, inept projects.

This means not only managing to work with or without any kind of director, but having enough security in all areas of production to survive everything that touches your performance. The more production tasks you learn, the better able you'll be to save yourself. You don't study props or costuming just to fulfill course requirements, you need to be able to communicate effectively with every member of the design team to get the best work possible from them. It's insulting to their artistry for you to fail to understand how they work. Keeping yourself ignorant increases the chances of your ending up in a dumpy frock, lit like a cadaver, holding the world's most pathetic prop while sound effects drown out what you are saying—and finding it very difficult to be transcendent.

Post–Audition Mortem

Why deal with auditions at the end of the book? Because the audition is always the next step. If you know you want to be a professional actor, you audition to move on. If you know you want to leave the theatre for a while, you audition to come back. In the previous chapter the process of performance went directly from auditions to beginning rehearsals. For many, there's a stop between these steps because they weren't cast. On a professional level, acting has the largest unemployment rate in the world, and even on an amateur level, there are many more people than parts. So there's a lot of auditioning going on that doesn't lead directly to the rehearsal hall. What then?

You audition for a show and give it your best shot. You're not called back. Or you're called back but not cast. What to do next? (For the moment we'll omit giving up because you can't stand the rejection. That's always an option.) In educational theatre, in order to learn from the experience and train for next time, the actor may naturally seek out the director for feedback. Asking is appropriate because these people are there to educate you. You don't need to feel that discussing your audition with a teacher/director is a terrible imposition. This is our job. But review the following guidelines, which should help the process.

1. Never talk to the director until after the show is cast. Her efforts are entirely focused on that task. She probably doesn't have time right now.

2. Wait a good two or three days until after the final cast list is posted to give yourself time to put the entire experience in perspective. Only time will give you some objectivity. Only time will help you minimize responses that are purely emotional.

3. Use this waiting period to put together your own list of reasons why you may not have been used. Move beyond "no talent" as an explanation to real, concrete events that occurred during try-outs and to the specific needs of the production. Review your own participation in the audition process, step by step. Try to determine when you were functioning most and least effectively. When you consider all the decisions you made, which were most and least appropriate?

4. Use this checklist against your own castability:

Culturally bound (conspicuously contemporary, regional, ethnic, or any other characteristic that makes it hard to imagine you outside your own culture and inside that of the play)

Wrong appearance for this show (shape, size, bone structure, capacity to look right in the costumes, to seem like a member of that family, to fit into the visual world of the play)

Company balance (Sometimes an actor is very good, but would throw off a sense of focus, would be distracting, or would alter the dynamics of the ensemble.)

Movement limitations (There are demands, like mastery of intricate dance routines, handling period costume pieces, or radically altering your physical bearing, that are outside your range right now.)

Voice limitations (There are specific skills, like handling verse rhythms, singing in a certain range, or speaking in a different register, that you haven't yet mastered.)

Inexperienced (You simply lack essential experience, both in training and in living, to possess the technical and spiritual capacity for certain roles.)

5. Extend the list above with your knowledge of this particular show. Separate those things you can't do anything about from those you can. Use the "can" list to set some of your training objectives.

6. You may find that you don't need to see the director after all, because you've answered your own questions. If you still need feedback, go in with your own list of conjectures regarding your audition and needs for growth. Ask the director to verify, clarify, or help alter your own perceptions, not to do all your thinking for you.

7. Focus your conversation on the future. Consider the difference between these two requests:

> "Why didn't you use me? What did I do wrong? What is it about me you don't like? Why did you pick *her* instead of me? What did I do to blow it?"

> "I'd like to work with you as a director sometime and I'd like to work in this play sometime. Can you offer me suggestions for how I need to train? What would you like to see from me in future auditions that you didn't see in this one? Where do you see me needing the most growth?"

The same information is being asked for, but the spirit and focus is entirely different. The show is cast and auditions are history. You want to move into the rest of your life with a sense of obtainable objectives. You want to leave this office with some idea about what to do next.

8. Don't expect the kind of detailed response you would get in an acting class or a coaching session where work is centered on how to improve a performance. Remember, a director has been doing eliminations, not pondering how to fix things. She has not been asking herself why various readings did not work; she has been looking at those that did. There are only so many categories possible to focus on at any moment. The director is not thinking about critiquing work presented.

9. As you prepare for next time, don't let the cloud of an unsuccessful audition hover over your efforts. There is no such thing as an unsuccessful audition if you learn from it. Far from going into the next round negatively predisposed toward you, those who might direct you will be thrilled if you show any progress or development from last time. The most common reaction to weak auditions, however, is that, with the exception of the actor, *nobody remembers them.*

I have been visited by actors apologizing for lousy auditions they gave a year or two ago. I draw blanks. I ask others who were present, and they don't remember, either. While casting, one is so clearly an editor that inept work simply fades away. You almost need to walk out, knock over a few pieces of scenery, mistakenly assume that Juliet is the boy's role (Julio, maybe?), and interrupt your reading with painful personal anecdotes explaining why you think these lines are poorly written (especially if they're Shakespeare's) in order to register in a powerfully negative way. Take comfort in this.

> *They ask you basically to make a fool*
> *of yourself, which I was very good at. I made*
> *enough of a fool of myself that they thought*
> *they could work with me.*[5]
> —MEL GIBSON (on auditioning)

Constant Reminders

For future auditions, you should develop a strategy based on your own responses to pressure. If needlepoint samplers were put together to frame and hang on the wall in regard to auditions, I would offer two contenders, shown here as Figures 8–1 and 8–2.

1. Life Is Unfair.
2. Theatre Is Less Fair Than Life.
3. Acting Is The Least Fair Part of Theatre.
4. Humans Submit Themselves to Nothing Less Fair Than the Audition.

Figure 8–1 Life

If your experience has not led you to believe that number 1 is true, it will. Regarding number 2, look at the number of times that superb writers, directors, and actors collaborate for months and still come up with a bomb. Look at the number of unquestionably superb, critically lauded works that are ignored by the public and die. Look at the crap that can rake in millions of dollars at your local cinemas.

You can set out to be a theatre designer, stage manager, box office manager, shop supervisor, publicist, technician, or historian, and find a reasonable path to follow for career development as well as actual employment potential. Superb actors run into career snags and unemployment for interminable stretches. Terrible actors who are good at marketing themselves work all the time. There's number 3.

And number 4? When you go out on opening night, at least you know you were chosen for the part. Even if you bomb, you were designated by someone as better than someone else. You own the role, even if it may be repossessed shortly. At an audition you are as vulnerable as at any moment in your life. You lay out your skills and sensitivity with no guarantee of anything beyond a curt ''thank you'' and the memory itself. You may prepare for weeks for an exposure which may not last minutes. Yes, Auschwitz and Hiroshima were worse than auditions, but the participants did not willingly submit themselves. Yet auditions are the best way anyone has found so far to cast, and while technology surges ahead so rapidly as to take your breath away, auditions have remained virtually unchanged for the past two hundred years.

As Figure 8–2 indicates, selling yourself without feeling crass or immoral is tough. It takes a firm belief in who you are and a capacity to separate essential marketing strategy from the artist within. The water of the art of acting and the oil of the business of acting don't mix painlessly. Consider this testimony from one of the more respected actors in the world, musing on both young and old actors:

> *Acting is the most minor of gifts and not a very high-class way to earn a living. After all, Shirley Temple could do it at the age of four.*[6]
> —KATHARINE HEPBURN

Making the Rounds of Auditions Is Like Being a Fuller Brush Man. Only You Are the Brush.

Figure 8–2 Rounds

*Being an actor is such a humiliating experience,
because you are selling yourself to the public, your
face, your personality, and that is humiliating.
As you get older, it becomes more humiliating
because you've got less to sell.*[7]

—KATHARINE HEPBURN

So what's your strategy? The audition is a separate entity from the performance. The world is full of brilliant actors who cannot audition and brilliant auditioners who cannot act. Theatre shares this irony with politics, business, and many public service professions. Many actors give in to their own worst tendencies in an audition. Things they got over long ago and blocks they surmounted early in Acting I loom again like giants as they go to try out for a show or interview for a summer job. The same self-sabotaging occurs in offstage application/interview encounters.

*Some of the greatest actors in the world just cannot
audition well. They get nervous and self-conscious,
so they act weird around people. Instead of thinking
"I hope I'm right for this role" I go in thinking
"Look, I'm right for this role." I'll pick up on the
vibes in the room and go with it. Some people who
aren't great actors are great auditioners. You
wonder why they're getting work when they're not
that exceptional, but it's a different talent.*[8]

—PENELOPE ANN MILLER

What do you do? You find warm-ups, ways to focus your energy, philosophical positions that get you back to the creative state you have achieved onstage. You personalize and adapt warm-ups to serve you in multiple circumstances. You develop a playful attitude toward the audition experience itself that allows you pleasure. You put this into perspective. You step out of the center of the universe. You decide to enjoy being there. Eventually you either get used to it or you get out. Or you become an inevitability:

*But if you survive, you become a legend. I'm a
legend. I'm revered, rather like an old building.*[9]

—KATHARINE HEPBURN

General Casting

Early in your training, almost every audition you go to is specific; you know the play being cast and often the parts for which you are being considered. If you decide to pursue acting further, the general audition is inevitable. The format and objectives are different because a much broader look is being taken. The preparation level on your part is expected to be quite a bit higher. The general audition is often used for:

1. Moving on in an acting program where there are large numbers of applicants
2. Transferring to another school
3. Gaining admission to an academy or professional school
4. Studying with a private instructor
5. Getting into a restricted seminar or master class
6. Being accepted for a Master of Fine Arts program
7. Gaining representation by an agency
8. Winning a scholarship or some other acting competition
9. Employment in summer stock
10. Seasonal contracts in regional repertory

You need to learn this format even if you're not yet sure how big a place acting will have in your life. Even if you're just a serious shopper, this audition is needed to get into most of the sales.

In general casting, instead of saying that you fit into one play or part perfectly, you're saying that you are interesting, versatile, disciplined, and gifted enough to be taken on by the auditor for some long-term venture. If the season has a variety of plays, you'll fit in them all. If the program takes a series of approaches to acting, you'll adapt well to each of them. If the agency deals with various media, you fit them all. In offstage terms, it's similar to being hired by a company to function in a wide range of tasks (trouble-shooter, Person Friday, fund raiser, spokesperson) instead of a narrowly defined desk job. When you looked for your very first job, the requirements for delivering papers, pumping gas, or frying burgers seemed quite specific. Becoming a public relations representative or cultural ambassador is general. You are demonstrating a wider scope.

Fortunately the format is almost identical for all of these auditions, so that once your basic presentation is in hand, you can use it repeatedly. Usually the conditions are:

1. You are given less than five minutes to present two memorized monologues, and time limits are enforced.

2. Strong contrast between the two pieces is encouraged so that your range can be examined.

3. One monologue should be quite close to you and your evident type, while the other has some surprise. Fairly often, one of them is requested to be classical and/or verse, to show technical mastery and a sense of style.

4. All choices should involve material for which you are well cast now. The versatility should not come by playing radically out of your age or from shock value.

5. Introductory and transitional material is to be kept at an absolute clean minimum.

Why should this concern you if you are still in Acting I? Because the search for the right material is endless. It is almost impossible to start the search too early.

There are two main exceptions to the format above:

1. Auditions for teachers and coaches sometimes will involve only one monologue. You may be worried about demonstrating your range, but trust the perceptions of the observer. Do the monologue that is closest to you. The feeling, shared by many teachers, is that if the person comes across as interesting, truthful, and focused, versatility and virtuosity can come later.

2. The Irene Ryan competition of the American College Theatre Festival requires that one of your two pieces be done with a partner. This is a rare opportunity and one to be relished. You normally spend so much of your effort trying to play to your imaginary partner in an audition that having a real partner there to support you can be wonderful.

EXERCISE 8.1

AUDITION OBSERVATION

The best way to quickly assimilate the general audition is to watch one. Ask around for local versions. Then watch in the following categories which tend to be employed to evaluate actors. Ask yourself which decisions you would make in the actor's place. A glance will show you that these same categories can be used to evaluate any presentation in almost any line of work. This exercise is worthy of consideration for any presentation of self, offstage or on.

1. Appearance/attire (care, attractiveness, appropriateness)
2. Selection of material (suitability, originality, scope)
3. Control of material (understanding, analysis, credibility)
4. Use of voice/speech (quality, clarity, variety)
5. Use of body/space (movement, staging, focus)
6. Dynamics (stage presence, energy, imagination, poise, attitude)
7. Flow (set-up, introduction, transitions, ending)

---

1. *Appearance/Attire*

   Does it look like the actor gave some thought and preparation to how he looks today?

   Does this look suit this person? Does it seem to fit who the person is?

   Is it the human being we're looking at or are we watching clothes and hair? Is hair out of eyes and the actor fully visible?

   Is the outfit in any way fighting with the actor for attention?

   On the other hand, is the look so bland that it is impossible to remember?

   Is there a balance between stiffly dressed up and being so casual that the performer does not seem to respect the occasion?

   Is the look versatile enough that it works for both character and the actor herself?

   Does the actor accomplish any changes in appearance during the audition?

   Were these changes creative or merely distracting?

2. *Selection of Material*

   Has the actor picked pieces that seem to reflect herself?

   Do either of the choices indicate a lack of self-awareness?

   Are either of these characters too familiar or done too often?

   Are the roles too strongly associated with famous actors to view without being too reminded of the great original performances?

   Is there a feeling of having searched and uncovered new material?

   Do the lines have a sense of the unexpected and the fresh?

Do the pieces provide the opportunity to share two entirely separate
  human beings?
Do the monologues satisfy? Do they seem complete, clear, and fully
  realized?

3. *Control of Material*
  Do you feel the actor fully comprehends his characters and that each
    word is under his control?
  Is it evident that homework and research have taken place?
  Do you ever question the thoroughness or accuracy of the analysis
    behind the presentation?
  Are either of these characters outside the actor's range at this point in
    his growth?
  Is the actor believable as these people?
  Are you watching real human beings in crisis or are you always aware
    that this is a performance?

4. *Use of Voice/Speech*
  Does the voice seem comfortable and pleasant to listen to?
  Do you ever have any trouble understanding?
  If so, is it because of volume, articulation, or any other cause you can
    identify?
  Does the voice change enough between roles for you to hear a new
    person?
  Is there any tendency to make predictable or regular choices that are
    tiresome?
  Is the sound varied enough within the body of each speech?
  What is your response to the actor's sense of timing?
  Are any vocal effects labored or forced?
  Does this actor possess a rich, expressive instrument? Does it serve
    fully?

5. *Use of Body/Space*
  Does the actor move with assurance and authority?
  Does the actor appear agile and coordinated?
  Is there enough use of the space so that you can tell if the actor knows
    how to move?
  Is the action so busy that you cannot tell whether she can be still?
  Does action ever make you tense or uneasy?
  Can you see the imaginary listener(s)?
  Is the focus consistent or do you ever lose track of listener rela-
    tionships?

Can you always see the actor's facial expressions? Does she focus down or offstage too frequently? Does she ever upstage herself or throw attention elsewhere?

Does the actor have any trouble staying in the light?

Does the actor appear at home in the acting space?

Did you ever feel the need for more or less physical activity?

6. *Dynamics*

Does this person compel you? Does he command your attention?

Do you want to watch him? Are you curious to know more about him?

Is the actor the primary source of energy in the room?

Is that energy contagious or pushed?

Do you feel you are in the presence of a lively, creative spirit?

Does the actor seem to like being here, being an actor?

Does the actor appear gracious and friendly to the observers?

Do you ever get a sense of defensiveness or tightness?

Is there any feeling of apology or self-deprecation?

Does the actor put you at ease with his effortless assurance?

7. *Flow*

Does the audition proceed with smooth efficiency?

Are there awkward adjustments of furniture, clothing, or lines? Any unfilled pauses?

Is the introduction brief, pointed, but conversational?

Does each person go through realizable changes?

Do you get to watch a metamorphosis between characters?

Are you ever confused in a way that is clearly not intentional?

Do vocal and physical changes appear in sync with each other?

Does the actor bring it to a definite, clear, close, so that the curtains can close in your own imagination?

Does the actor return to herself after the last character so that you get to see the real person again?

Does the actor leave the stage with a sense of completion and pride?

Does the audition last all the way offstage?

EXERCISE 8.2

CHOICES

1. Note at least two instances in each category where you feel an actor made vividly appropriate and inappropriate choices. Debate with friends. Justify your reactions through the explanation above.

Avoid simple rating words in favor of concrete information. Which auditions linger in your mind now and which rapidly fade away? Why? What separates outstanding from adequate work?

2. If you know any of the actors, ask if the person you know really appeared in the audition? Were there any essential qualities that you find appealing in the human being that were missing in the presentation? How can these be integrated?

Post-Application Mortem

Everything in the past section would have a direct parallel in those offstage situations where you have put yourself on the line for the scholarship, the grant, the job, the admission to a certain school or program, the fellowship, the contract, or the commission, and it doesn't come through. Don't retreat from a defeat. Force it to teach you.

Whether or not the person making crucial decisions is available to counsel you, a systematic review of your participation, objectivity gained from some passage of time, and careful development of positive objectives are still the secrets to recovery and growth and the way for setbacks to set you forward. Auditioning is what you're doing whenever you are in a situation that is now tentative or temporary, but may or may not become definite and permanent. Learning to audition is learning to open up the full range of your offstage life.

EXERCISE 8.3

OFFSTAGE AUDITIONS

Pick one of the following events and observe choices made in exactly the same categories employed for the last two exercises. After observing others, make decisions regarding your own habitual choices which will help you the next time this kind of event comes your way.

1. an important social occasion

2. a public hearing on a controversial issue

3. a committee meeting where varying proposals are considered

4. an instance where competing bids or designs are dependent on rehearsed presentations

5. an informal or private encounter where the stakes are high enough to involve careful preparation.

Interviews

Being questioned is standard procedure when you are applying to move ahead. Here are some of the most commonly asked questions for actors, which you should be able to adjust quickly for situations outside the theatre:

The Dreaded Thirteen

1. Tell me something about yourself.
2. Why do you want to be an actor?
3. What have you done?
4. Why should we use you?
5. What's special about you?
6. What can you do for us?
7. Can you be . . . (funny, sad, sexy, commanding, and so forth)?
8. Why do you think you're right for this . . . (part, company, agency, and so forth)?
9. How do you feel about . . . (subject which follows may be anything from impossibly vague to controversial or private)?
10. Would you be willing to . . . (change something about yourself, play a role that is demeaning to your heritage, sex, and so on)?
11. By next week, can you . . . (relocate, leave your family, learn to do some tricky skill, and so forth)?
12. What are your real strengths as an actor? As a person? What do you like best about yourself?
13. If you could change one thing about yourself, what would it be?

Oddly enough, the ones with the widest choice of answers (like questions 1 and 2) seem to unhinge people the most. The good news is that almost any interview comes down to the list above or some variation. Think about all the ways you might answer, and feel no need to always answer the same. Realize that what you say matters far less than how you respond to the questions. Interviews, from politicians stepping into press conferences to beauty contestants stepping out of soundproof booths, come down to attitude. No one expects Senator Foghorn or Miss Ohio to have a startling, illuminating, pungent response (and they usually don't). What is expected is that neither recipient will be rendered comatose by the question, that both will keep a sense of poise, humor, perspective, and a willingness to give it a go. Almost any answer is better than drawing blanks. Just give yourself permission to respond like a reasonable human being.

What if you want to be startling, illuminating, and pungent? Remember *l'esprit de l'escalier,* or the spirit of the stairs? The beauty of interviews is that they are so relentlessly predictable that you can start reading, borrowing, quoting, shaping, practicing now for an answer you may not be called on to give for years. I once attended an audition at which the director (who had a reputation for unsettling actors) stopped the woman who was reading and asked her what she had done. She answered that, and then he asked, "And what is your favorite sexual position?" There was an audible hush and sudden tension in the room. The rest of us were in a state of shock. She paused, smiled, and said, "Number twenty-three." Everyone laughed and the audition went on in a normal way.

Was the director really trying to get personal information from her? Maybe, but I doubt it. He was testing her poise, humor, and reaction. She managed to say to him (subtextually), "You can't unhinge me. My humor is in good shape. And I'm not telling you a thing." The question is only a variation on question 9 in the list above.

> *You pack your suitcase. You outline possibilities,*
> *lines you might use, turns and changes that may*
> *happen. People expect you to be on the button. You*
> *don't want to be caught saying, "Uhhhhh . . ."*
> *So you pack your suitcase, putting all your*
> *stuff where you can find it.*[10]
>
> —BILLY CRYSTAL

The spirit of adventure essential in an audition can be carried into countless moments of your life. If you approach a job interview with a sense of the person on the other side of the desk functioning like a casting director (Could you co-star comfortably at IBM?), a great deal of this process can be fun. You're always auditioning in life for further chances. A first date is in many ways an audition for a second. And when you go to visit the family of your current companion, you are, without doubt, auditioning for the role of son- or daughter-in-law. Even if you aren't sure if you want the part, you are auditioning. If what you have now is temporary or tentative, but could become more permanent and definite, you are auditioning, even if you are nowhere near a theatre.

If you are looking at an acting career, should you plan now for being famous? I'd recommend instead that you plan for being good. And remember, fame has its drawbacks.

One time I went to the movies with my mother in
Georgia and I was in the bathroom. All of a sudden
this voice says, "Excuse me? The girl in stall No. 1?
Were you in Mystic Pizza?*" I said yeah and she*
goes, "Can I have your autograph?" and slides a
piece of toilet paper under the stall. I just said
"I don't think right now is the time."[11]

—JULIA ROBERTS

PERSONAL OBJECTIVES

If you never again darken the door of the theatre, you should now have a sense of the kind of figure you cut in space, the sort of sounds you generate, the impressions (accurate or not) you leave on those you encounter. You may also recognize circumstances in which you are easy/exploratory contrasted with those in which you are inhibited/stiff. A basic knowledge of self and of what constitutes a character should clarify certain life choices.

Choosing Partners and Playmates

Most of us search for a life partner with whom we need to do a minimum of acting, someone who makes it easier to deal with what the world wants or who helps us not to care. Feeling comfortable in a relationship because everything is so predictable, however, is hardly the same as feeling comfortable because unqualified love and acceptance are present, so whatever comes will be all right. The ideal companion for the full journey of life is one with whom we don't need to act at all but who will also, when we get the impulse, be there as an enthusiastic audience or dynamic scene partner who will join the fun. So why do so many people pick the wrong mates, friends, even the wrong one-night stands? Many fail to recognize the difference between having a relationship and playing scenes. Many cast companions based on surface impressions and misread signals. Sure, some "professional actors" are the worst cases of multiple failed marriages and destructive relationships. But these victims are rarely students of acting, who should be better armed and needn't be anyone's victim.

Theatre has an inner connection with the human
condition. You learn things about yourself through
the plays. Your character's circumstances and
emotions cause you to examine what
is going on inside yourself.[12]

—NICK NOLTE

Your understanding of acting principles can help you choose better who you want to play with, to make informed selections regarding friends and lovers. You should be better able to recognize playful performance vs. destructive self-deception, and to distinguish between nurturing comfort and mere predictability. The more you know about acting the more you know how much you want it in your relationships.

Theatre in Your Life

There is plenty of opportunity for theatre in your offstage interactions.

> *The oldest form of theater is the dinner table. The same people every night with a new script.[13]*
> —MICHAEL J. FOX

You can always continue to train yourself to perform your life better:

1. Take what you have learned about your body, voice, and personality and set up goals to clean up what is misleading in your behavior.

2. Identify the suggestible conditions present when you've given your most memorable life performances so far. Aim to set up those conditions deliberately more often.

3. Seriously scrutinize any role models you've been using and ages you've been lingering in too long. Make edits and replacements. Start shooting to become someone's role model yourself.

4. Either accept and acknowledge your own dominant influences (of your private audience and cultural binding) or free yourself from them. Make peace with them in any case. Take the long-run dueling performances of your life and make a judgment in each, deciding which will win and thus freeing yourself from the tiresome pressure.

5. Examine those strategies and tactics which you overuse in your life and those you neglect. Freshen your strategic choices. Expand your own working repertoire. Stop playing tired, worn-out tapes that nobody listens to.

6. Warm up for potentially difficult encounters rather than just thinking about them.

7. Observe all the performances being given around you more intensely, both for enrichment and pleasure, and to avoid being taken for a ride.

8. Conquer space! Not necessarily in a space ship seeking unbridled intergalactic ambition. Start with just keeping cool in any medium-sized room. Any space you enter may become yours. You now understand what personal bubbles are and the various means people use to break or invade them. You know how movement, composition, and business all make an impression. You understand the varying powers of sustained, intense, varying, indirect, and darting eye contact. You can, if you will, stage yourself.

9. Conquer sound! Dare to use your voice to influence others' behavior. Let your voice be known to you, useful to you, no longer a stranger. Devote at least as much time to ''working out'' your voice as you do your body.

10. Confront the way life has typed you so far and the various parts that you've been cast in whether you wanted them or not. Cast yourself more assertively. Vow not to accept some roles.

Casting Yourself

Most actors probably would like to be viewed by the world as a romantic leading man or a leading lady. Those types, on the other hand, lament the fact that interesting, offbeat character roles aren't open to them. Why are they forced, role after role, to be commanding, attractive, romantic? Why will the public not allow them to scratch and itch? It's obvious that no one is completely delighted with what he or she's got. You can waste an enormous amount of time lamenting. Or you can separate ''can change'' from ''can't change'' from ''don't want to anyway,'' and get on with your life. And you can begin to savor what is extraordinary about you. Sometimes it takes a long time for others to recognize it, because you haven't really decided to see it yourself:

> *In Hollywood, they only gave me parts where I was*
> *an old maid or some lost soul with a clubfoot. When*
> *I inspect old photographs, I now think, what were*
> *they talking about? I was fine. But it was in my head*
> *that I wasn't pretty, so that's the way my career*
> *went. I was someone useful, not special.*[14]
> —JESSICA TANDY

> *I got my Equity card playing a duck.*[15]
> —KATHY BATES

There are roles that life has undeniably and sometimes cruelly cast you in. If you look and sound more like Woody Allen than Robert Redford, or vice versa, the world expects certain behavior from you. In case you haven't noticed, there are a number of people who look more like one of those two, but feel more like the other. Their lives are often chaotic. Certain genetic and cultural limitations are placed on each living creature. Motivational and spiritual limitations are more often placed on the creature by the creature. While genetic limitations are undeniable, your capacity to transform yourself is considerable. I don't mean plastic surgery or psychotherapy (sure, those are alternatives), but rather the way you think about yourself and elect to present yourself to the world.

> *Acting is something that most people think they're incapable of but they do it from morning to night.*[16]
> —MARLON BRANDO

Transsexuals are vivid examples of people to whom the genetic game has dealt a tough set of cards. Most people are lucky enough to be able to discover their true selves with measures less radical than surgery. Surely you have discovered something as simple (and at first glance superficial) as a hat, a pair of shoes, a hair style, a way of moving, a song, a new color that suddenly made you feel you had found a way of expressing who you actually are. These items can be far more than trite indulgences. Like the keys to a character, they help you find you, and help you feel much more as if you live inside your own body. With an actor's awareness you can be far more alert, not just to finding keys to unlock other characters, but also to finding keys to your own.

> *Now I'm managing to carry performing power into my personal life and taking some personal life things onstage. The lives are starting to feed each other.*[17]
> —ROBIN WILLIAMS

Here is one extraordinary story of an actor's transformation for the stage. Similar offstage metamorphoses are accomplished all the time.

> Paul Newman's Broadway debut was in *Picnic*. He did not play the commanding hunk leading man, Hal, who mesmerizes every woman in town. He played the well-meaning, ineffectual rich boy who loses the leading lady to a man of physical magnetism. The director (Joshua Logan,

one of the most respected and successful in Broadway's history) wouldn't even let him read for Hal. He said Newman had no sexual charisma or danger. "At that point I probably didn't. That sort of thing has a lot to do with *conviction*."

The director also told him to get in shape. "The way I translated that was six hours in the gym every day." He eventually won the role on the show's national tour after working diligently on both pectorals and presence. How? He studied acting and women. "You can measure a woman and find ways of being gallant, of listening, of crowding and pursuing."[18]

If Paul Newman could lose a role because he was insufficiently sexual and commanding and still become Paul Newman, what might others do? What might you do? We are all looking to cast ourselves in the world. But much casting is just thrust upon us. The groups you deal with daily may force you into Earth-Mother, Trusted Confidant, Charming if Bubbly Airhead, Somber Companion, Brick, or Jaded Sophisticate, depending on the needs of those around you. Now is the time to identify those roles that you have had long runs in and are ready to close. Now is a good time to promise yourself some overdue performances that you've wanted to give for a long time. Now may be the time to decide to star in your own life instead of doing only featured roles and cameos in the lives of others. Or if you've been phenomenally self-centered, now may be the time to do just the reverse. Now may even be the time to create an altogether new type: The _____ (fill in your own name) type.

Living Fully—Onstage and Off

Let your abilities and your limitations
shape your career. When you look in the mirror,
know who is looking back at you. When you know
your strengths and recognize your weaknesses,
then you can create art.[19]
—DEBBIE ALLEN

You can become a better actor by becoming a more
complete human being and you can become a more
complete human being by becoming a better actor.[20]
—TED DANSON

Acting can liberate you as easily as it can imprison you. It can give you a wide range of choices and the means of cleaning up distractions that are cluttering your communication. You can enjoy watching tactics being employed that you might not have recognized before, taking pleasure that you are seeing and hearing more around you. You can look across a room and savor the compositions, enjoy the body language which may now make more sense, catch bits and pieces of conversation and idly analyze how a point might have had a different effect with a drop in pitch or by twisting the final consonant. The small details accumulate into a wealth of perception and pleasure. Acting not only can help you play your own life better, it can also help you to more playfully observe others living theirs.

The tools are now at your disposal. There is no doubt that you will continue to act, offstage at least. How well you act and how long each performance lingers in the memory of those who observe it is largely up to you. How much you discover and how much you enjoy yourself is also up to you. If you are open and alert, acting will offer you the potential for profound insight and a phenomenally good time—not a bad combination.

> *Acting is simply my way of investigating human*
> *nature and having fun at the same time.*[21]
> —MERYL STREEP

> *It's never too late to have a happy childhood.*[22]
> —TOM ROBBINS

Notes

1. Interviewed by Barbara Walters, on CBS-TV, "Barbara Walters Special," originally broadcast March 24, 1991.
2. Christopher Connelly, "Ben Kingsley's Blessed Career," *Rolling Stone,* March 17, 1983.
3. David Ansen, "Fabulous Pfeiffer," *Newsweek,* November 6, 1989.
4. Stephanie Mansfield, "Andy Garcia Keeps His Shirt On," *Gentlemen's Quarterly,* December 1990.
5. Tim Cahill, "Mel Gibson—Back from the Edge," *Premiere,* December 1988.
6. "The 128 Best Things Anyone Ever Said in *People,*" *People,* March 6, 1989.
7. Anne Edwards, *A Remarkable Woman: A Biography of Katharine Hepburn* (New York: William Morrow & Co., 1985).

8. "No Longer an Armpiece, But Still a Chameleon," *People,* Spring 1991 (Special Issue).
9. Alvin H. Marill, *Katharine Hepburn* (New York: Galahad Books, 1973).
10. Tony Kornheiser, "The Head of a Comic," *Life,* March 1990.
11. Johanna Schneller, "Julia Roberts," *Gentlemen's Quarterly,* February 1991.
12. Ovid Demaris, "First Make Peace with Yourself," *Parade,* March 22, 1992.
13. Bruce Buschel, "The Rise and Rise of Michael J. Fox," *Gentlemen's Quarterly,* December 1986.
14. Cindy Adams, "Jessica Tandy: The Classiest Star," *Ladies' Home Journal,* April 1991.
15. "Outtakes," *Theatre Week,* August 12, 1991.
16. Brian Bates, *The Way of the Actor: A Path to Knowledge & Power* (Boston: Shambhala Publications, 1988).
17. Lisa Grunwald, "Robin Williams Has a Big Premise," *Esquire,* June 1989.
18. Maureen Dowd, "Testing Himself," *New York Times Magazine,* September 28, 1986.
19. Wallace Terry, "Don't Be Afraid to Fail," *Parade,* November 17, 1991.
20. Robert L. Benedetti, *The Actor at Work* (Englewood Cliffs, N.J.: Prentice Hall, 1986).
21. Elaine Dutka, "Talking with Meryl Streep," *Redbook,* September 1982.
22. Tom Robbins, *Still Life with Woodpecker* (New York: Bantam Books, 1981).

APPENDICES

Name _____

MY ACTING HISTORY

Ages Experienced, Ages Observed

Mewling infant _____

_____

_____

Whining schoolboy _____

_____

_____

Sighing lover _____

_____

_____

Reputation-seeking soldier _____

_____

_____

Saw-spouting justice _____

_____

_____

Lean and slipper'd pantaloon _____

_____

_____

Second childishness and mere oblivion _____

_____

_____

Quasi-Theatrical Events

Pageants _____

_____

_____

Disguises _____

_____

_____

Alter egos _____

_____

_____

Role models _____

_____

_____

Understudying _____

_____

_____

Suppression _____

_____

_____

Deception _____

_____

Acting Onstage

If you come to this book with some scene work experience, or roles in plays, video, or film, add it here: _____

_____

_____

_____

_____

278

Observer _____

Onstage, or off? _____

Actor, or main character _____

Setting, or title of play _____

Other actor(s) or character(s) _____

Situation _____

Character's (or person's) objective _____

Character's (or person's) strategy _____

Character's (or person's) tactics _____

_____   _____

_____   _____

Dialogue: Text and Subtext

Write out four lines of dialogue, putting the text (the actual spoken words) in CAPITAL LETTERS, and the subtext (their implied but unspoken meanings) in lower-case letters. Paraphrase or summarize the lines if you cannot remember the exact wording.

FIRST SPEAKER [   ]: _____

_____

SECOND SPEAKER [   ]: _____

_____

FIRST SPEAKER [   ]: _____

_____

SECOND SPEAKER [   ]: _____

_____

    279

Evaluation

Cue _____

_____

Rejected response #1: _____

_____

Rejected response #2: _____

_____

Rejected response #3: _____

_____

Rejected response #4: _____

_____

Chosen alternative (actually spoken): _____

_____

Beat Change

Describe one moment in which a beat ended and another began (for a reason other than the entrance or exit of another character).

_____

_____

_____

_____

_____

_____

_____

_____

280

Observer #1 _____

Observer #2 _____

Observee _____

APPENDIX C   PHYSICAL LIFE OBSERVATION

Habits (Still)

Standing _____

_____

Sitting _____

_____

Expression _____

_____

Habits (Active)

Tempo and rhythm _____

_____

Motion _____

_____

Gestures _____

_____

Adaptations

Groups _____

_____

Contact _____

_____

Mood _____

_____

Cultural Binding

Geography _____

_____

Family _____

_____

Conditioning _____

_____

Interests _____

_____

Age _____

Sex _____

Isolations

Head _____

_____

Torso _____

_____

Hands, arms, feet _____

_____

Observer #1 _____

Observer #2 _____

Observee _____

APPENDIX D   VOCAL LIFE OBSERVATION

Habits

Quality _____

_____

Tempo _____

_____

Rhythm _____

_____

Articulation _____

_____

Pronunciation _____

_____

Pitch _____

_____

Volume _____

_____

Word choice _____

_____

Nonverbals _____

_____

Adaptations

_____

_____

_____

_____

Cultural Binding

_____

_____

_____

_____

How does the observee's physical life influence his vocal life? _____

_____

_____

_____

_____

_____

Name _____

OPEN SCENE SCENARIO

Actors

_____ and _____

Names of Characters

_____ and _____

Tentative Title

_____

Conflict _____

_____

_____

_____

What happens? _____

_____

_____

_____

_____

_____

_____

_____

_____

_____

How is each character different at the end? _____

_____

_____

_____

_____

_____

_____

_____

_____

_____

Name _____

OPEN SCENE SCORE

Actors

_____ and _____

Characters

_____ and _____

Scene Title

_____

Setting _____

Time _____

Conditions _____

Activity	**Intention**
1. _____	*To:* _____
2. _____	*To:* _____
3. _____	*To:* _____
4. _____	*To:* _____
5. _____	*To:* _____
6. _____	*To:* _____
7. _____	*To:* _____
8. _____	*To:* _____
9. _____	*To:* _____
10. _____	*To:* _____
11. _____	*To:* _____
12. _____	*To:* _____
13. _____	*To:* _____
14. _____	*To:* _____
15. _____	*To:* _____

16. _____   *To:* _____

17. _____   *To:* _____

18. _____   *To:* _____

19. _____   *To:* _____

20. _____   *To:* _____

21. _____   *To:* _____

22. _____   *To:* _____

23. _____   *To:* _____

24. _____   *To:* _____

25. _____   *To:* _____

26. _____   *To:* _____

27. _____   *To:* _____

28. _____   *To:* _____

29. _____   *To:* _____

30. _____   *To:* _____

31. _____   *To:* _____

32. _____   *To:* _____

33. _____   *To:* _____

34. _____   *To:* _____

35. _____   *To:* _____

36. _____   *To:* _____

37. _____   *To:* _____

38. _____   *To:* _____

39. _____   *To:* _____

40. _____   *To:* _____

41. _____   *To:* _____

42. _____   *To:* _____

43. _____   *To:* _____

44. _____   *To:* _____

45. _____   *To:* _____

46. _____   *To:* _____

47. _____   *To:* _____

48. _____   *To:* _____

49. _____   *To:* _____

50. _____   *To:* _____

51. _____   *To:* _____

52. _____   *To:* _____

53. _____   *To:* _____

54. _____   *To:* _____

55. _____   *To:* _____

56. _____   *To:* _____

57. _____   *To:* _____

58. _____   *To:* _____

59. _____   *To:* _____

60. _____   *To:* _____

Name _____

Character _____

Event _____

Given Circumstances
What relevant facts and circumstances influence the character's behavior?

1. _____
2. _____
3. _____
4. _____
5. _____
6. _____
7. _____
8. _____
9. _____
10. _____

The Magic If

How would you respond given the character's life perspective? _____

_____

_____

_____

_____

Objectives

What is the character's super objective? _____

_____

_____

_____

What is the primary obstacle? _____

_____

_____

Give a hierarchy of the character's *other* objectives.

2. _____

3. _____

4. _____

5. _____

Grouping

How does this character group other people? _____

_____

_____

_____

_____

Rehearsed Futures

How does the character envision his best possible future? _____

_____

_____

_____

. . . worst possible future? _____

_____

_____

_____

. . . wildest dream come true? _____

_____

_____

_____

Conditioning Forces

Conditioning forces on first entrance _____

_____

_____

Changes in conditioning forces _____

_____

_____

Endowment

How can you endow other characters and inanimate objects (props or set pieces) in this situation?

Other characters

1. _____

2. _____

3. _____

Props or set pieces

1. _____

2. _____

3. _____

Name _____

SCRIPT ANALYSIS

Play Title and Author

_____

Characters   **Played By**

_____   _____

_____   _____

_____   _____

1 Classification

A phrase that describes the overall feeling of the text: _____

_____

2 Style

Degree of probability _____

Kinds of improbability _____

General style of thought (realist, romantic, melodramatic, satirical, absurd-

ist, farcical, and so forth) _____

_____

3 Structure

Script length _____

Number of acts/scenes _____

Length of scenes _____

Place your scene fits into the whole _____

_____

4 Theme

_____

_____

_____

5 Cultural Binding

Date play was written _____

Date of play's setting _____

Cultural influences in text _____

_____

_____

6 Production History

_____

_____

_____

_____

_____

_____

7 The World of the Play

See the questions suggested in chapter 6 covering these important aspects of the play.

Time _____

Space _____

Place _____

Values _____

Structure _____

Beauty _____

Sex _____

Recreation _____

Sight _____

Sound _____

APPENDIX I CHARACTER ANALYSIS

Character _____

Play and author _____

Character's Past

I come from _____

_____.

My childhood was _____

_____.

Family conditions were _____

_____.

Three experiences that made a profound and lasting impression on me were:

1. _____

_____.

2. _____

_____.

3. _____

_____.

The five most important given circumstances in my life are:

1. _____.

2. _____.

3. _____.

4. _____.

5. _____.

The five most powerful members of my private audience would be:

1. _____, because _____
_____.

2. _____, because _____
_____.

3. _____, because _____
_____.

4. _____, because _____
_____.

5. _____, because _____
_____.

Crucial events that occurred prior to this scene were _____
_____
_____.

Details of the moment just before my entrance include _____
_____
_____.

Character's Present

Immediate conditioning forces on me are _____
_____
_____.

Other characters (and/or the playwright) describe me as _____
_____
_____.

I describe others as _____
_____
_____.

296

In groups, I tend to _____
_____.

I would describe myself as basically _____
_____.

My physical life differs from that of the actor playing me in the following
way(s): _____
_____
_____
_____.

My vocal life differs from that of the actor playing me in the following
way(s): _____
_____
_____
_____.

The actor playing me most needs to use the Magic If in this regard: _____
_____
_____
_____.

My usual style of clothing and type of accessories include: _____
_____
_____.

My most distinguishing characteristics are my _____
_____
_____.

My favorite things are _____
_____
_____.

My temperament could be described as _____

_____

_____.

I am most interested in _____.

I am not interested in _____.

Three examples where endowment must be used in the scene are:

1. _____.

2. _____.

3. _____.

The cue for my most critical moment of evaluation in the scene is: _____

_____,

and my rejected alternative responses and final choice are:

Rejected response #1 _____

Rejected response #2 _____

Rejected response #3 _____

Rejected response #4 _____

Final choice (my answer or action taken in response): _____

_____.

My scene breaks down into the following beats (number and title each, using extra paper as needed):

1. _____.

2. _____.

3. _____.

4. _____.

5. _____.

6. _____.

7. _____.

8. _____.

298

9. _____ .

10. _____ .

11. _____ .

12. _____ .

13. _____ .

14. _____ .

15. _____ .

16. _____ .

17. _____ .

18. _____ .

19. _____ .

20. _____ .

I make the following discoveries in the scene: _____

_____

_____

_____ .

Character's Future

My super objective in the entire play is to _____

_____ .

My primary objective in this scene is to _____

_____ .

My other significant objectives, in order of importance, are:

1. _____ .

2. _____ .

3. _____ .

4. _____ .

5. _____ .

I face the following major obstacle(s): _____

_____

_____.

My strategy in this scene is _____

_____

_____.

Specific tactics I employ over two pages of the text include (mark the script, if you prefer to do so): _____

_____

_____

_____.

Three futures I have rehearsed include this, my best possible future: _____

_____

_____;

this, my worst possible future: _____

_____

_____;

and this, my wildest dream come true: _____

_____

_____.

Character Abstracts

Helpful images _____

_____

_____

Name _____

Auditions for: _____

Actors observed (or, if you prefer, identify them by number only, as in numbers 1 through 5 below): _____

_____

Try to identify and explain *why,* in your view, the actor's choice of attire, material, approach, technique, and so forth, either worked or failed, based on the impact it made as you watched.

Appearance and Attire

Appropriate Choices	Inappropriate Choices
1. _____	1. _____
2. _____	2. _____
3. _____	3. _____
4. _____	4. _____
5. _____	5. _____

Selection of Material

Appropriate Choices	Inappropriate Choices
1. _____	1. _____
2. _____	2. _____
3. _____	3. _____
4. _____	4. _____
5. _____	5. _____

Control of Material

Appropriate Choices	Inappropriate Choices
1. _____	1. _____
2. _____	2. _____
3. _____	3. _____

4. _____   4. _____

5. _____   5. _____

Speech and Use of Voice

Appropriate Choices	Inappropriate Choices
1. _____	1. _____
2. _____	2. _____
3. _____	3. _____
4. _____	4. _____
5. _____	5. _____

Use of Body and Space

Appropriate Choices	Inappropriate Choices
1. _____	1. _____
2. _____	2. _____
3. _____	3. _____
4. _____	4. _____
5. _____	5. _____

Dynamics

Appropriate Choices	Inappropriate Choices
1. _____	1. _____
2. _____	2. _____
3. _____	3. _____
4. _____	4. _____
5. _____	5. _____

Flow

Appropriate Choices	Inappropriate Choices
1. _____	1. _____
2. _____	2. _____
3. _____	3. _____
4. _____	4. _____
5. _____	5. _____

SAMPLE SCENE: *THE REHEARSAL*

(Two actors, FRED and ETHEL, enter the room tentatively.)

Fred: I can't believe there's no one in here.

Ethel: It's freezing in here.

Fred: You know what Katharine Hepburn insists on whenever she rehearses?

Ethel: No, what?

Fred: She insists that the temperature always be kept at sixty degrees.

Ethel: Really?

Fred: Yeah.

Ethel: Why didn't you ever tell me that before?

Fred: I just read it. She says it keeps actors from getting sluggish. She also brings sweaters for the people who need them. A box full of sweaters.

Ethel: Well, Fred, you're a good actor, but you're no Katharine Hepburn. At least not yet. And you didn't bring me a sweater either. It's really freezing.

Fred: Maybe we need to warm each other up.

Ethel: *(pauses)* What do you mean?

Fred: I mean that we both need to read this scene so well, so brilliantly, that we get our blood rushing. You know.

Ethel: Oh. Right. Well, let's read it and see.

(They begin reading the parts of Beatrice and Benedick from Shakespeare's Much Ado About Nothing, *act II, scene iii.)*

Fred: ". . . When I said I would die a bachelor, I did not think I should live till I were married.—Here comes Beatrice. By this day, she's a fair lady: I do spy some marks of love in her."

Ethel: "Against my will I am sent to bid you come in to dinner."

Fred: "You take pleasure, then, in the message?"

Ethel: "Yea, just so much as you may take upon a knife's point, and choke a daw withal.—You have no stomach, signoir; fare you well." *(Ethel/ Beatrice exits.)*

Fred: "Ha! Against my will I am sent to bid you come to dinner—there's a double meaning in that." *(To Ethel:)* Do you think I should give those first and last lines to the audience? Like I'm confiding in them?

Ethel: *(re-entering)* Sure. I would. Do you think she knows she loves him yet?

Fred: I think she loves him, but I don't think she knows it. She thinks she hates him.

Ethel: Yeah. That's what I think, too. Let's just take it from my entrance, okay?

Fred: Right. I'll cue you in. "I do spy some marks of love in her."

Ethel: "Against my will I am sent to—" Have you noticed what's going on in this assignment?

Fred: What do you mean?

Ethel: We're all working with our first partner from back in our first acting class. At least I'm pretty sure that's true.

Fred: My God, I think you're right. Karen and John, and Tim and Ralph, and—I think you're right.

Ethel: I wonder why.

Fred: It's probably supposed to give us some sense of perspective or something. *(He discovers a jacket someone has left in the room.)* Hey, look!

Ethel: What?

Fred: Who says there's no sweater here for you? *(He drapes it around her shoulders.)*

Ethel: Do you even remember our first open scene?

Fred: Sure. Best thing I ever did. *(She looks at him witheringly.)* Just kidding. But we did okay. How come we were never partners again? Until now?

Ethel: You mean, why didn't I ever ask you?

Fred: Yeah. I asked you the first time.

Ethel: Well, as I recall, you missed two rehearsals entirely, you were late more than a few times, and you didn't even get your lines until the day before it was due. How could I resist working with you again?

Fred: But I matured a lot after that term. You know that. I got much more disciplined. So how come we never worked together again?

Ethel: I don't know. We're together now. Or . . . I guess it was our names.

Fred: Our names?

Ethel: Fred and Ethel. I didn't like the idea of anyone thinking of us as the Mertzes.

Fred: The Mertzes?

Ethel: Lucy and Ricky's neighbors. You know—"I Love Lucy"?

Fred: Oh. Is that the real reason?

Ethel: I don't know. Let's get back to work. From my entrance again?

Fred: Right. "I do spy some marks of love in her."

Ethel: "Against my will I am sent to bid you come in to dinner." Did you know that Katharine Hepburn played Beatrice?

Fred: She did?

Ethel: At the Stratford Festival. I just thought I'd impress you with some Hepburn trivia of my own.

Fred: "You take pleasure, then, in the message?"

Ethel: Now I just can't stop thinking about all the rehearsal time I've spent in this place. And it's just about over. From open scenes to Shakespeare.

Fred: And next comes graduation. Then we have to deal with real life.

Ethel: All right. What the hell. The real reason I avoided working with you is . . . God, I can't believe I'm going to say this. I always thought you were attractive. I mean, I was attracted to you, and I just didn't want to get distracted, so . . . Well, you know.

Fred: Seriously? *(She nods.)* 'Cause I've never been exactly indifferent to you either, but I never thought . . . No kidding?

Ethel: "Against my will I am sent to bid you to come in to dinner."

Fred: "You take pleasure, then, in the message?" Don't you think we should talk about this?

Ethel: No. I think we should rehearse. "Yea, just so much as you may take upon a knife's point . . ." *(She is becoming agitated, skips lines.)* "If it had been painful I would not have come . . ." *(She can't go on.)* I'm sorry. I guess it's all this end-of-the-year stuff, and it's . . . *(She moves away from him to calm herself. A pause.)*

Fred: May I give you a hug? A very non-threatening, non-sexual, supportive friend-type hug?

Ethel: Please. *(They hug—at first tentatively, then relaxing into it.)* Listen, this room has more memories than I'm up to today. Do you think we could go somewhere else?

Fred: Sure. Let's find some place more Shakespearean. Then we can say we used sense-memory in rehearsal.

Ethel: And then, sometime soon, we'll talk.

Fred: Right. First we do a brilliant scene, then we work on . . . then we talk about . . . us. Okay?

Ethel: Good. Let's go. *(They exit. No sooner do they withdraw than she turns back, having remembered the jacket draped over her shoulders. She removes it, restores it to its place, starts to leave, pauses.)* Thanks for the sweater, Katharine. Uh, Kate. Umm, Miss Hepburn. God, it's freezing in here. *(Exits.)*

APPENDIX L | **BOOKS FOR FURTHER STUDY**

These books are suggested because they can be studied easily on your own, whether you are part of a class or not.

Benedetti, Jean. *Stanislavski: An Introduction*. New York: Theatre Arts Book, 1982. A direct and interesting guide to Stanislavski's works, providing background and perspective on the System. A good book to scrutinize before reading Stanislavski's own works.

Berry, Cecily. *Voice and the Actor*. New York: Macmillan, 1973. A compact, useful collection of voice exercises and insights. One of the few books which economically covers everything from simple relaxation through diction drills.

Cohen, Robert. *Acting Power*. Palo Alto, Calif.: Mayfield, 1978. A stimulating discussion, on theoretical level, of acting. Full of striking and original insights, connecting actor training with other areas of study, from computers to the behavioral sciences.

Gawain, Shakti. *Creative Visualization*. San Rafael, Calif.: Whatever, 1978. Effective, accessible images for mental warm-ups and focus. A basic introduction to visualization, and a help for actors in adding imaging to basic warm-up exercises.

Hagen, Uta. *Respect for Acting*. New York: Macmillan, 1973. A highly entertaining and personal approach to performance, with memorable examples from the author's own distinguished acting and teaching careers.

Hobbs, Robert. *Teach Yourself Transatlantic*. Palo Alto, Calif: Mayfield, 1978. A guide to eliminating distracting regional or nonstandard pronunciations, for those wishing to perform in classical or high-style plays requiring a more elevated level of speech than that of standard conversation.

King, Nancy. *A Movement Approach to Acting*. Englewood Cliffs, N.J.: Prentice Hall, 1981. A straightforward program for developing physical awareness, movement skills, and the capacity for transformation.

Markus, Tom. *The Professional Actor*. New York: Drama Books, 1979. Solid advice on achieving and maintaining high standards of civilized behavior in each phase of rehearsal and performance.

Moore, Sonia. *The Stanislavski System*. New York: Viking Press, 1965. A simple, clear discussion of basic ingredients of the System, written by one who was actually there, studying with the Moscow Art Theatre in the early 1920s.

Shurtleff, Michael. *Audition*. New York: Walker, 1978. The soundest advice available on the audition process, presented candidly and lucidly. It deals specifically with mental preparation and instant text analysis as well as procedures.

Silver, Fred. *Auditioning for the Musical Theatre*. New York: Newmarket Press, 1985. Gives the actor significant help in overcoming his fears not just of singing but of a wide range of high-pressure situations. Great help in acting a song.

INDEX